Greenhill Books

BRITISH MILITARY FIREARMS,
1650–1850

BRITISH MILITARY FIREARMS, 1650–1850

HOWARD L. BLACKMORE

Greenhill Books, London
Stackpole Books, Pennsylvania

This edition of *British Military Firearms, 1650–1850*
first published in 1994 by
Greenhill Books, Lionel Leventhal Limited,
Park House, 1 Russell Gardens, London NW11 9NN
and
Stackpole Books
5067 Ritter Road, Mechanicsburg, PA 17055, USA

British Library Cataloguing in Publication Data
Blackmore, Howard L.
British Military Firearms, 1650–1850.
New ed.
I. Title
623.440941

ISBN 1–85367–172–X

Library of Congress Cataloging-in-Publication Data available

Publishing History
British Military Firearms was first published in 1961 (Herbert Jenkins),
then reprinted with corrections in 1962, 1967 and 1969.

Printed and bound in Great Britain

PREFACE TO THE NEW EDITION

This book was first published in 1961, at a time when little factual information had been written on the subject of British military firearms. Previous authors like W.W. Greener, H.B.C. Pollard, Charles ffoulkes, J.N. George and R. Scurfield had worked on a combination of astute observation, keen perusal of printed works, and intuition. Their conclusions were often very near to the truth, but in some cases had been misleading. It seems strange now that the Board of Ordnance's enormous archive had never been consulted to any extent: judging from the dust and dirt that arose from the documents I examined in the 1950s, few had ever been opened since their deposition. Based mainly on information extracted from those Ordnance records, *British Military Firearms* was to have a surprising effect. Neither I nor the publisher was prepared for the enthusiastic reception it aroused. So many enquiries came from all over the world that the book had to be reprinted in 1962, 1967 and 1969.

Looking back, it is amusing to recall how difficult it was to convince some collectors—even a few historians—that statements which had previously appeared in print were not necessarily correct. It is hard to believe that before this book appeared, collectors were not sure of the exact dimensions of the various types of musket, carbine and pistol. Indeed, official names such as Short, Long and New Land muskets were not in use, and the more esoteric weaponry such as Burgoyne's Musketoon or the Prince de Bouillon's pistols were unknown. It gave me great pleasure, therefore, to be able to bring back the old, contemporary terms into modern usage. I also had the satisfaction of resurrecting the lives and achievements of many of the Ordnance officials whose work had long been forgotten. A particular case was that of George Lovell. Here was a man who, more than anyone, had been responsible for the design and manufacture of British service weapons at a crucial period in our history. Yet his very existence seemed to be in doubt. When I first came across his name in connection with the Enfield Small Arms Factory (for which he was mainly responsible) I wrote to the Superintendent for information. He replied: 'It is thought that George Lovell was employed here about 100 years ago, but we have no records concerning him.' *Sic transit gloria.*

One of the difficulties in writing *British Military Firearms* was the identification of specimens with the often meagre description appearing in the records. Military arms in the Armouries of the Tower of London, for so long regarded as the ugly ducklings of the arms and armour world, lay in unsorted heaps; few had even been catalogued. Now, decades later, they have been displayed in a special Board of Ordnance Gallery, the contents of the cases following the groupings in the chapters of this book. Appropriately, the gallery concerned was once used to store arms, the ancient wooden pillars still bearing the storekeepers' marks of BO and Broad Arrow. This first formal presentation of the development of British service arms, in book and museum exhibition, simultaneously solved and raised problems. It has certainly brought forth a flood of comment, argument and new discoveries.

In the last thirty years a number of books and countless articles have appeared dealing with British military firearms, both of a general and specialised nature. Professional researchers have been engaged to delve deep into the Ordnance records, and the published results have been of most impressive countenance and content. The most important of these books have been set forth in a new Bibliography. In comparison with all this new literature, *British Military Firearms* now seems a humble volume, but in reviewing its contents only a few changes have been deemed necessary. These are indicated by new footnotes. The book still retains its importance as the basis of future studies, and is now reprinted in the hope that it will serve as an encouragement to new generations of collectors and arms historians.

Finally, I should like to say how appropriate it is that Lionel Leventhal, who was in at the birth of the original edition of 1961, should be responsible for its resuscitation more than thirty years on.

Howard L. Blackmore

CONTENTS

LIST OF ILLUSTRATIONS

Except where otherwise stated, all firearms illustrated in this book are in the Armouries of the Tower of London. Photographs of these arms, which were specially taken for the author, are Crown copyright and are reproduced by permission of the Ministry of Works.

Drawings by the author.

ABBREVIATIONS

In a book which is based largely on manuscript sources, one of the main problems has been to adopt a system of references which, while satisfying the reader as to the authority of some statement, did not obscure the text or break up the continuity. However, most of the information in this book has been extracted from the Minute Books of the Ordnance in the Public Record Office, London (WO 47 series). These Minute Books are well indexed and from the date given in the text the reader will, I hope, have little difficulty in finding the original source. The same applies to the Bill Books of the Ordnance (WO 51 & 52 series). although there the search may have to be extended over several volumes. Where no reference is given, therefore, it may be assumed that the information comes from the Ordnance Minute Books or Bill Books.

Other sources of information are indicated by the abbreviations listed below. Where a Minute Book of one of the City Companies is involved, the date in the text has been considered sufficient, but in all other cases, wherever possible, the full reference has been given.

It should be noted that for the sake of convenience dates before 1752, when the end of the year was altered from 25th March to 31st December, have been altered to the modern calendar. Thus the year of the Gunmakers' Charter, contemporarily recorded as 1637, and more correctly written as $163\frac{7}{8}$ is given in this book as 1638.

ADD   Additional Manuscript. British Museum.
AFR   Register of Freemen & Apprentices of the Armourers' Company. Armourers' Hall, London.
AMB   Minute Books of the Armourers' Company. Armourers' Hall, London.
BAB   Account Books of the Blacksmiths' Company. Guildhall Library, London.
BMB   Minute Books of the Blacksmiths' Company. Guildhall Library, London.
CSP   Calendar of State Papers, Domestic. Printed.
CVP   Calendar of State Papers, Foreign; Venice. Printed.
EIC   Records of the East India Company. India Office Library, London.
GMB   Minute Books of the Gunmakers' Company. Guildhall Library, London.
GWA   Renter Warden Account Books of the Gunmakers' Company. Guildhall Library, London.
HARL   Harleian Manuscript. British Museum.
HO   Home Office Papers. Public Record Office, London.
JAAS   Journal of the Arms and Armour Society. Printed.
JAHR   Journal of the Society for Army Historical Research. Printed.
PRO   Ordnance Office Papers. Public Record Office.
SP   State Papers, Domestic. Public Record Office.
WO   War Office and Ordnance Office Papers. Public Record Office.

'BROWN BESS'

In the days of lace ruffles, perukes and brocade
    Brown Bess was a partner whom none could despise—
An out-spoken, flinty-lipped, brazen-faced jade
    With a habit of looking men straight in the eyes—
At Blenheim and Ramillies fops would confess
    They were pierced to the heart by the charms of Brown Bess.

Though her sight was not long and her weight was not small,
    Yet her actions were winning, her language was clear;
And everyone bowed as she opened the ball
    On the arm of some high-gaitered, grim grenadier.
Half Europe admitted the striking success
    Of the dances and routs that were given by Brown Bess.

When ruffles were turned into stiff leather stocks,
    And people wore pigtails instead of perukes,
Brown Bess never altered her iron-grey locks.
    She knew she was valued for more than her looks.
"Oh, powder and patches was always my dress,
    And I think I am killing enough," said Brown Bess.

So she followed her red-coats, whatever they did,
    From the heights of Quebec to the plains of Assaye,
From Gibraltar to Acre, Cape Town and Madrid,
    And nothing about her was changed on the way;
(But most of the Empire which now we possess
    Was won through those years by old-fashioned Brown Bess.)

In stubborn retreat or in stately advance,
    From the Portugal coast to the cork-woods of Spain,
She had puzzled some excellent Marshals of France
    Till none of them wanted to meet her again:
But later, near Brussels, Napoleon—no less—
    Arranged for a Waterloo ball with Brown Bess.

She had danced till the dawn of that terrible day—
    She danced till the dusk of more terrible night,
And before her linked squares his battalions gave way,
    And her long fierce quadrilles put his lancers to flight:
And when his gilt carriage drove off in the press,
    "I have danced my last dance for the world!" said Brown Bess.

If you go to Museums—there's one in Whitehall—
    Where old weapons are shown with their names writ beneath,
You will find her, upstanding, her back to the wall,
    As stiff as a ramrod, the flint in her teeth.
And if ever we English had reason to bless
    Any arm save our mothers', that arm is Brown Bess!

Rudyard Kipling

BRITISH MILITARY FIREARMS
1650–1850

CHAPTER I

MATCHLOCK AND SNAPHANCE

THE middle of the seventeenth century may be taken as a convenient period at which to commence the study of British military firearms, as only a few arms made before then have survived, and it is with the end of the Civil War and the coming of the Restoration that the regimental history of the British Army begins. Many of the firearms in use at that time were out-of-date weapons resurrected and renovated by the needs of a war which had seriously disrupted the normal manufacture of guns and had, to some extent, arrested their development. For a better appreciation of the position, therefore, it is necessary to return briefly to the beginning of the century.

In 1600 the Tower of London, the national arsenal and home of the Office of Ordnance, was filled with a motley collection of weapons illustrating the development of firearms from the original handguns through all the varieties of the arquebus (spelt as "hagbut, half-hagis, demy-hake, hagbutte of crok, hagbushe of irone upon trindelle, etc.") to the caliver and finally the musket. The musket, incidentally, had been used for the firing of arrows as well as lead balls, and the Armouries still carried a considerable stock of musket arrows and their leather tampions.

Although many of these old firearms were not only lying in store at the Tower but were on issue to many of the garrisons, castles and storehouses under the jurisdiction of the Ordnance Office, firearm development had reached a point where current issues and orders to contractors were confined to two main classes of shoulder arms; matchlock muskets with barrels four and a half feet long, and calivers, with three and a half feet barrels. The latter were supplied with matchlocks or snaphance locks and the matchlock muskets were in turn divided into two categories, those with "tricker" or trigger locks and those with sear locks.

A delivery of arms for the army in Ireland in 1601 reads thus:

"Corne powder xx lasts at xs. ye pound
Match xxx tie Tonns at xxs. ye hundreth weight
Leade to be provided at Westchester xx Tonns at ixli. the ton weighte
Musketts of iiij foote Dim in length furnished with restes & moulds only 200 whereof 100 wth Tricker locks at xvjs. ye peece and 100 with Seare at xvs. the peece.

Bandaleeres of double plate 200 at ijs. iiijd. ye peece

Calivers of iij foot Dim in length furnished with moulds only 500 where—of 300 with Tricker locks at xis. ye peece and 200 with Seeres at xs. ye peece.

Bandaleeres likewise of Double Plate 500 at ijs. ye peece

Snaphance peeces of the same length and Boare of ye calivers wth moulds 200 at xviijs. ye peece

Horne Flaskes and Touch boxes to the same 200 at ijs. vjd. the peece."

(WO 55/1752)

It will be noted that the matchlock muskets and calivers were fired by charges kept in bandoliers—broad leather belts from which hung from a dozen to a score of wood or horn cylinders, covered with leather, containing the correct amount of powder. The snaphance calivers were given more careful loading by the use of powder flasks, one containing powder for the barrel and a smaller one with priming powder. In both cases the lead balls were carried in a separate bag. The heavy weight of these early muskets necessitated the use of a rest. This was described by Gervase Markham in his *Souldiers Accidence*, 1625, as "of Ash wood or other tough wood, with iron Pikes in the neather end and halfe hoopes of Iron above to rest the musquet on, and double stringes fastned neare thereunto, to hang about the arme of the Souldier when at any time he shall have occasion to the traile the same". The chaos which could be caused by soldiers firing and loading these cumbersome guns in close formation led to the use of a complicated drill. The physical effort required to wield the different weapons was nicely indicated in the same book. "The strong tall and best persons to be pikes, the squarest and broadest will be fit to carry muskets and the least and nimblest may be turned to the Harquebush." For harquebush in this instance one can read caliver.

The two types of matchlocks were due to the older sear lock being gradually superseded by the trigger lock. In the former the match-holder or cock was connected to a lever projecting under the butt which, when pressed towards the stock, brought the match down into the pan, which had a simple pivoted cover. In the trigger lock, the lever was shortened to a convenient curve for the forefinger and made separate from the lock. This had several advantages: the lock could be easily removed; the trigger could be enclosed within a guard to prevent accidental firing; and an easier grip gave a better aim. The majority of these muskets have triangular or fish-tail-shaped butts with a high thin comb, and octagonal barrels which have a priming pan and a tubular backsight brazed on (Plate 1).

The early forms of pistol and carbine, the heavy and clumsy dags and the ungainly petronel were still in use and they are mentioned in military instruction books well into the seventeenth century. Both types, however, were now being superseded by the true pistol, and carbine, made with both wheellock and snaphance locks. Of the two locks, the latter was most popular in England and Scotland because, as Markham puts it, "the others are too curious and too soone distempered with an ignorant hand".

The wheellock worked roughly on the same principle as the modern cigarette lighter, the spark being produced by holding a piece of pyrites or flint against a revolving serrated wheel. A heavy V-shaped main spring provided the power and was attached to the spindle of the wheel by a small chain. When the wheel was wound up by a key, the

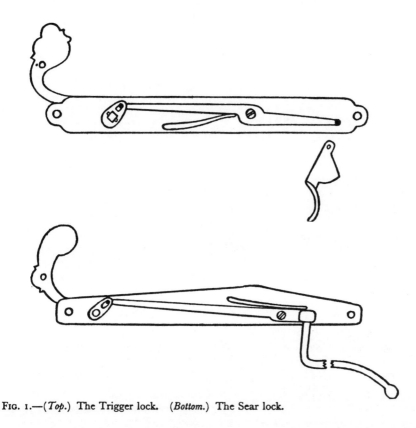

Fig. 1.—(*Top*.) The Trigger lock. (*Bottom*.) The Sear lock.

spring was compressed and held in this cocked position by a laterally acting sear which passed through the lock plate and engaged in a hole on the inside surface of the wheel. Part of the edge of the wheel intruded into the priming pan and the pyrites held in the jaws of the cock could be brought down on to it. A sliding pan cover was pushed to one side by a lever as the wheel started to revolve. It was a complicated mechanism and to be really effective the wheellock had to be well constructed. From the point of view of expense, therefore, the snaphance or flintlock was preferred.

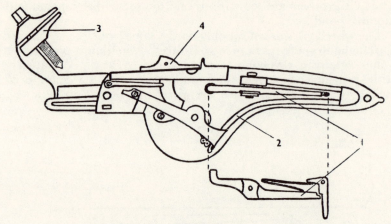

FIG. 2.—The Wheellock.   (1) Double sear.   (2) Mainspring.
(3) Cock.   (4) Pan cover.

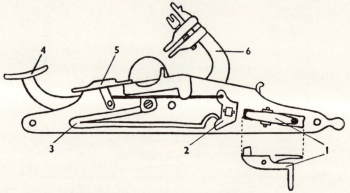

FIG. 3.—The Snaphance lock.   (1) Sear.   (2) Tumbler.   (3) Mainspring.
(4) Steel.   (5) Pan cover.   (6) Cock.

The word snaphance was used contemporarily to describe all types of flintlock, but the first snaphances—probably of German origin—were actually of the type with which we now associate that description —a lock where the steel* is separate from the pan cover. Although its ignition was achieved by the simple action of a flint striking a steel held over the pan so that the spark fell into the priming, its interior action had much of the complication of a wheellock. The sliding pan cover had to be worked by an inside lever attached to the tumbler, and the same type of lateral acting sear was used, with its effective end projecting through a hole in the lockplate to engage behind the tail of the cock; but the lock could be primed and cocked and be perfectly safe as long as the steel was pushed out of the way. Even so, some of these true

* This word has been used in preference to its contemporary "hammer" to avoid confusion. "Frizzen" is, of course, a modern incorrect term.

snaphance locks have a catch or dog at the rear of the plate, which can be hooked over the tail of the cock as an additional safety precaution.

Specimens of the snaphance with a separate steel are comparatively rare, for early in the seventeenth century an improved type of lock with the steel joined to the pan cover came into use.* The combined cover and steel pivoted on the lockplate, and the action of the flint striking the steel automatically threw up the cover. This simpler and more effective action unfortunately raised the problem of how to make the lock safe when it had been primed and cocked. The dog catch became a necessity, and it was supplemented by an interior safety or half-cock position, contrived by fitting a projection to the tumbler which could be held by a notched arm on the sear. Because of its popularity in this

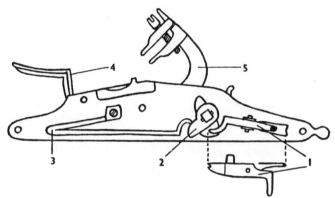

Fig. 4.—The English lock.   (1) Sear.   (2) Tumbler.
(3) Mainspring.   (4) Steel and Pan cover.   (5) Cock.

country, this type of flintlock has become known as the English lock. This is hardly a compliment to the English gunmakers for, to judge by existing specimens, very little workmanship went into their manufacture.

Nevertheless, even when crudely made, as were the military models, the lock had a reasonably sure action and was thus preferred to the wheellock. Several English writers drew attention to the peculiar disadvantage of the wheellock; if left spanned or primed for any length of time the lock would jam (John Vernon, *The Young Horseman*, 1644, p. 11).

On 6th November, 1613, the Doge and Senate of Venice wrote to their Ambassador in England: "We understand that the use of fusees [*fucili*] in arquebuses has taken the place of wheels in that kingdom as well as in Flanders and that the former are easier to use, quicker and of less hindrance to the user as well as being cheaper" (CVP). In this

---

* Many of the existing snaphance locks were converted to the new mechanism.

context, the Italian word *fucili*, from which is derived fusil, meant flintlocks.

The manufacture of military wheellocks in this country continued up to the middle of the century but was confined mainly to carbines and pistols. In 1631, rates laid down for gunmakers by a special Commission allowed £3 for a pair of wheellock pistols and £2 for a pair of snaphances. In 1640, sixteen London gunmakers, with Warner Pin taking a large share, supplied wheellock carbines and pistols described as:

"Pistolles with Fiere Lockes fournished with holsters.
worm scorer mould and keyes per pece at   £2   16   0
                                                        Holsters   6
Carrabines with Fier lockes furnished with Key worme
scorer mold Belt & swivell Rode Carthridges   £1   10   0
                                                     The Belt   1   0
                                              The Cartridges   1   0
                                              (SP 16/442/85)   "

The word firelock is one which bedevils the historian as it was used indiscriminately to describe both flintlock and wheellock, and to distinguish between the two, one has to rely on other evidence as, in this case, the key included in the accessories.

To return to the pistols, whatever the origin of the snaphance locks used, the majority of references describe the pistols as French. Edmund Nicholson, a merchant, offering complete sets of arms in 1600, includes a "French pistoll with case, mould and flask" in the equipment of the Light Horse and the Lance (SP 12/275/105). In 1607, the Ordnance accounts show payments to Thomas Laverocke the Younger (a freeman of the Armourers' Company) for "longe french pystolles with snaphance lockes furnished with cases flaskes and moldes" at "xxvjs the pece" (SP 14/39). An account of arms in the Tower in 1617 (SP 14/94) lists as the only type of pistol "French Pistolls 837, Flaskes for long pistolls 221, Cases of leather for pistolls 257": and it is not without significance that the French gunmaker Nicholas Masson, on becoming a brother of the Armourers' Company in 1594, brought in a "Snape hannce lok" as a proof piece (AFR).

The reader may, perhaps, wonder at the two references to members of the Armourers' Company and it is appropriate at this stage to say a few words about the London gunmakers. Very little information has been published about their activities before the grant of their charter in 1638, and this has led to the mistaken impression that the trade was virtually non-existent in the sixteenth century. In fact, there were numerous lockmakers, barrel forgers, stockmakers and inlayers, working mainly in the Minories and East Smithfield, near the Tower of London. Some were descendants of craftsmen from Holland, Germany and Italy, encouraged to settle in London by Henry VIII, and it may be noted in passing that this tradition was maintained throughout the seventeenth century. Arnold Rotsipen, the Dutch engineer, famous for his patent of 1635 for rifling gun barrels, was one of several aliens who were provided with workshops in the Minories for their experiments.

But the majority of gunmakers were native-born freemen of the various City Livery Companies, in particular the Armourers and the Blacksmiths. Each was subject to the laws of search and proof of his own Company, which often brought them unwillingly into opposition to each other. It was to avoid this that, in 1581, "a greate number of poore men that are Gunne makers" had petitioned Queen Elizabeth to set up a separate company to look after their specialized interests. In 1591, an order of the Privy Council was granted for the encouragement of the London gunmakers, and this was confirmed by Letters Patent in 1605. "Whereupon," as the Clerk of the Gunmakers' Company later wrote in his minutes, "they became united as a Brotherhood." This was an optimistic view of things but at least the Office of Ordnance now negotiated with the gunmakers as a separate body, and between 1627–33 gave them large orders for new work and repairs.

In 1628, the Council of War apparently approved of a new pattern bastard musket. Later in the year several of the London gunmakers, including John Norcott, John Eales, Thomas Addis and John Watson, received payment for "Musketts with tricker lockes of 4 foote in length furnished with moulds at 18s. 6d. a peece" (PRO 30/37). This reduction in the musket barrel from $4\frac{1}{2}$ to 4 feet may have taken place earlier for in the previous year Sir Thomas Kellie, in *Pallas Armata*, describng the weapons of a musketeer, gives the latter figure. In placing their orders for the new muskets the Ordnance Office rightly judged that the English gunmakers would not be able to supply sufficient numbers in time and sought supplies abroad. The gunmakers immediately issued a manifesto against the spending on foreign arms of "£20,000 assigned out of the citty moneyes and £10,000 more from the farmers of the Custom Howse" (SP 16/92). We may conclude that this had little effect, for, in 1630, the Ordnance Proof Master, Henry Rowland, and his six servants were employed for thirty days viewing and proving "sondrie Dutch Musketts brought from beyond the seas" (PRO 30/37).

There was some consolation in the fact that the imported arms were so inferior in construction that extensive repair contracts had to be placed with some thirty of the London gunmakers. This was opportune as they had for some years been negotiating, in conjunction with the Armourers' Company, for the right of inspection and repair of the common arms throughout England. In 1631, after much discussion and reference to the Attorney General, a Commission under Letters Patent for this purpose was granted to the Armourers and the Gunmakers, together with the Pikemakers and the Bandolier Makers. Although the Armourers' Company took the leading part in this, and their mark, the A crowned, was adopted as the official mark of the Commission, the gunmakers' status was now recognized. When the Commission fell into abeyance in 1633, they had sufficient power to gradually overcome the resistance of the two companies of Armourers and Blacksmiths, and finally obtain their Charter as a City Company in 1638.

While the gunmakers had been successfully organizing themselves, the authorities had been attempting to bring some semblance of order to the supply of arms. The country was full of arms of all sizes, shapes and makes, and there was an obvious need for some form of standardization. In 1630, the Council of War promulgated "Orders for the general uniformatie of all sortes of armes both for horse and foote" (SP 16/179/25). The following is a summary of the dimensions given.

	Barrel Length	Overall Length	Bore	
Pistol	18 in.	26 in.	24	Bullets
Arquebus	30 in.	45 in.	17	to the
Carbine or Petronel	30 in.	45 in.	24	pound
Musket	48 in.	62 in.	12	"rowleing
Caliver	39 in.	54 in.	17	in".

It was also stipulated that the pistol must be a firelock, which in this instance meant a wheellock as a key was included in the accessories. A duplicate of these orders (SP 16/458/93) also lists the accessories of an arquebus "a key to bend it wch may hould tutch-powder and iron worke called a swifle to it", which suggests that the arquebus also was a wheellock.

Towards the end of 1639 the Ordnance Officers started experimenting with barrel lengths and recorded that a pistol barrel of 16 in. was as accurate as one of 18 in. or 20 in. Nevertheless they agreed to allow the 18 in. length to remain as standard. But for muskets they recommended that the barrel should be reduced to 3½ ft. and the total weight brought to between 10¼ and 11 lb. Further, to lessen recoil, the charge should be only half the weight of the bullet instead of two-thirds.

The Council of War accepted these recommendations in part and gave an order to the gunmakers for 15,000 muskets, 5,000 with 4½ ft. barrels and 14 lb. in weight, and 10,000 with 3½ ft. barrels 12 lb. in weight. The price was to be 18s. each to be reduced eventually to 16s. 6d. This unfortunately conflicted with an offer by John Watson and others of the Gunmakers' Company to make 1,200 muskets, 200 carbines and 120 pairs of pistols per month at the following rates: Muskets 18s. 6d.; Wheellock carbines £1 16s.; Wheellock pistols £3 per pair; Snaphance carbines £1 2s.; and snaphance pistols £2 5s. per pair.

Immediately a dispute over prices began, accentuated by some of the minor gunmakers obtaining orders at lower prices behind the backs of the main contractors. Next the Ordnance endeavoured to buy arms in Flanders, sending one of their proofmasters, John Lanyon, with patterns of muskets, carbine and pistol. On learning that a musket with bandolier could be purchased in Antwerp for 2 dollars (10s.), the

Council of War reduced their order to the home manufacturers to 8,000 and placed the remaining 7,000 overseas. This roused the English makers to increase their production, more orders were given them and, in June, 1640, the Ordnance storekeepers reported that they had delivered 10,000 muskets, 505 carbines and 528 pairs of pistols (CSP). Having met with trouble over the foreign-made arms, the Ordnance were now disposed to look with favour on the London gunmakers. It was at this point, with the gun industry beginning to feel its feet, that the whole country was plunged into disorder by the Civil War.

At first confusion prevailed, as both sides endeavoured to seize military stores, purchase arms from abroad or make arrangements for their manufacture in this country. One of the results of this was to widen the field of supply. A book of deliveries to the Royalists at Oxford in 1642–3 (ADD 34325) lists local gunmakers, blacksmiths and armourers who supplied muskets. On the other side, the Parliamentarians were obtaining arms from the Birmingham district, marking the beginning of that town's association with the Ordnance. By 1645, however, bureaucracy was established and the Committee for the Army began giving contracts for new arms to the London gunmakers, headed by William Watson who was Master of the Gunmakers' Company and Master Gunmaker and Proofmaster of the Ordnance.

The majority of the arms supplied were cheap matchlock muskets accompanied by bandoliers on which strangely enough a stringent specification had been laid. An order for 1,500 to the bandolier makers Thomas Bostock, Henry Thrall and Richard Rumsey in June, 1646, reads:

> "The Boxes of ye said fifteene hundred Bandaleers to bee of wood with whole bottomes to bee turned within and not boared, ye heads to be of wood & to be laid in Oyle, (vist) three times on & to be coloured blew & white strings with strong thread twist & with good Belts at xxd. peece. . . ."
>
> (PRO 30/37)

The same book of contracts includes several orders for "paires of English Snaphance pistolls full bore and proofe with holsters of Calveskinns inside and outside, well sewed and liquored att xviijs p paire". Unfortunately no further details are given so that it is difficult to judge what type of flintlock was used.

By the middle of the century the flintlock had changed both in appearance and action. It was smaller; it had a flat wide cock, and the dog engaged in a notch cut in its rear edge. The sear, still with a lateral action, no longer worked through the lockplate but hooked on to the radial projections on the tumbler for full and half cock A pair of what may be termed officers' pistols, now in the Tower Armouries (Plate 2) by William Watson, who shared in the contract mentioned above, have these locks, with the additional refinement of enclosed steel springs. As William Watson died in 1652 and the barrels are stamped with Commonwealth proof marks (see Chapter XII) they can be dated between 1649 and 1652. A very similar pair of pistols in the Temple Newsam Museum, Leeds, according to tradition, belonged to Oliver Cromwell. In 1652, William Mansfield, a freeman of the Blacksmiths, presented for his proof piece a "halfe bent snaphance locke", and this type of lock is further described in Randle Holme's *The Academy of Armory*, 1688, as "an halfe bent lock, haveing the stay for to hold the halfe bent cock within the lock".

In 1647, 1,400 snaphance muskets were ordered for the Navy, but again no indication is given of their design. An unusual order in 1652 was for 500 fowling pieces with five-foot barrels for service in Scotland. These may have been similar to the "Smale Birding peeces called Barbary Gunns" which several London gunmakers were allowed to

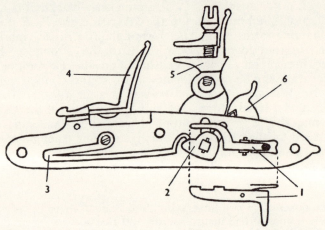

Fig. 5.—The Dog lock.   (1) Sear.   (2) Tumbler.   (3) Mainspring.
(4) Steel.   (5) Cock.   (6) Dog.

export to the Barbary Coast, on a certificate by Ordnance officers that they were "soe smale boared as wee conceive yem to bee noe way usefull for ye service of the State". On these Barbary guns the early form of snaphance lock was retained and it was copied faithfully by the native gunmakers until recent times. In 1701, a cargo of 2,000 of these locks was sent out to redeem English captives in Barbary on a basis of 100 locks for each prisoner.

At the end of the Civil War a considerable amount of repair work was, not unnaturally, available. The Gunmakers' Company, however, was growing fast; their craft was recognized as one of national concern and new work was necessary for the good of both master and apprentice. In 1653, therefore, an order for 5,000 matchlocks, 2,000 snaphance muskets and 1,500 pairs of pistols was carefully divided between 58 London gunmakers, and this was followed by several smaller orders. But with the Government discouraging the manufacture of private arms, this official work was not sufficient and, by 1657, the situation had deteriorated to the extent that many forgers and locksmiths were reported leaving the business. The situation was relieved by the demand for arms by the Navy under Admiral Blake, and one of the last tasks of the Committee for the Admiralty and Navy in 1658, after receiving several petitions from the gunmakers, was to arrange a three-years contract for the supply each year of 1,000 Matchlock muskets at 11s. each, 1,000 snaphance muskets at 12s. each and 500 pairs of snaphance pistols at 11s. 6d. per pair.

An interesting development of this was the introduction of Armourers—the word here meaning a gun repairer—for the "State's Ships", chosen from the members of the Gunmakers' Company, and vouched for by the Master and Warden to "bee of honest conversation and found to bee able and Sufficient Workeman". The Commonwealth, in other words, based its faith in a man first on his politics and then on his ability. Apart from the poorly paid Government work the gun-maker had few opportunities to augment his income by the sale of fine-quality weapons and there was little incentive to experiment. A gloomy picture indeed.

CHAPTER II

THE DEVELOPMENT OF THE FLINTLOCK

WITH the Restoration, in 1660, the gunmakers' trade was transformed. The King brought back with his Court some of the finest gunmakers in Europe. All the traditional Household appointments, the Gunmakers in Ordinary, the Keepers of the Handguns, the Furbisher of the Rich Weapons, the Yeoman of the Bows, etc., and even the Office of the Crossbow Maker (Lionel Emps) were restored. Most of these posts were given to those who had followed the King or had suffered in his cause. The great Dutch gunmaker, Harman Barnes (or Barnee), who had been imprisoned and plundered under the Commonwealth, became one of the Royal Gunmakers. All the colours of pageantry returned. Once more we read in the Ordnance accounts of rich gilt halberts and partisans, and the comment was made: "The King's restoration has brought back amongst other good things the old custom of weapon showing" (CSP 8.9.1666).

In the Tower of London, while the workmen were cutting off the Harps and Crosses of the Commonwealth from the lines of cannon, the storekeepers were preparing a new set of equipment for the Battle Axe Guard of Ireland; 64 gilt battleaxes at £4 each made by the Ordnance Pikemaker, William Edwards, and 64 "Snaphance Musketts of 3 foot one inch long of the Barrell being extraordinary with hardened locks, wormes, scowrers & swivell" at 25s. each, made by George Fisher.

The pleasant custom of "presents" was revived and in 1667 the King's gunmaker, Jonadab Holloway, was paid £93 for several fine pairs of pistols and "birding peeces" made to the order of the Lieutenant General of the Ordnance for this purpose. As an example of what a London gunmaker could produce, the pair of pistols, included in this order, made as a gift for Sir Phillip Warwick may be quoted:

"For a paire of Turn'd of pistolls Screwed, with Silver Capps and peirced & guilt Caps under them, the Stocks inlay'd with Silver plates and guilt plates under them and ye barrels damasked   £25 0 0"

Not of such fine quality but no less interesting to the collector was the pair of pistols presented to Capt. Thomas Story:

"More for a pre of Horsemans pistolls to turne of upon a Swivell ye barrels screwed and damasked ye stocks inlayed and ye worke Guilt. £12 0 0"

There was little discrimination against the London gunmakers—
the King's advisers soon recognized the need for encouraging them—
and the familiar names of the old contractors soon reappear in the
Ordnance records. The arms they were now called on to make were,
however, of new design. There was first of all a change in the design of
the stock. A hundred muskets made as a present for the King of Bantam
in 1663 were described as "well wrought with French Stocks". In a
survey of the Tower taken in the same year, matchlock and snaphance
muskets and the carbines are divided into those with French stocks and

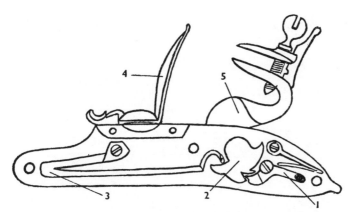

Fig. 6.—The French lock. (1) Sear. (2) Tumbler. (3) Mainspring.
(4) Steel. (5) Cock.

those with club stocks. All the old calivers and arquebuses receive the
latter description, which must refer to the fish-tail type. French stocks
are presumably those which have a butt with a straight upper edge and
a deep convex curve underneath.

The French influence was also apparent in the lock. Although the
new snaphance muskets, carbines and pistols were described as fitted
with "back ketches", this accessory was really superfluous as the interior action of the lock had been simplified and included a reasonably
safe half-cock position. The sear had a vertical action and the tumbler
was, in effect, a circular plate with a large notch in one edge to take the
hook of the mainspring, and two smaller notches in the opposite edge in
which the sear engaged for half and full cock as the tumbler rotated.
On 10th March, 1662, Ellen, widow of William Evetts the gunmaker,
was paid for "Carbynes extraord with French locks at 23s/-", presumably a reference to this type of lock, the true flintlock, which is
thought to be of French origin.

A more startling change and apparently a retrograde step, was
the preference for a new form of matchlock. Early in 1664 the gunmakers were informed that the snaphances on order were to be altered

"to ye new patterne of Matchlock Musqt with a Drawing pan lid". Another description was "wth ye pann cover to draw wth ye tricker". The old type of matchlock had the priming pan attached to the barrel and the lockplate was a straight ruler-like piece of metal. The later type of matchlock had a lockplate similar to the flintlock with a pan and cover attached to it. Those still in the Tower have an upright shield to the rear of the pan, and the pan cover can be swivelled to one side, but there is no connection with the trigger. In the special matchlocks referred to above, the interior mechanism was so arranged that pressure on the trigger not only operated the cock but caused the pan cover to slide out of the way. Curiously enough, the only example of this form of matchlock in the Tower is fitted as a replacement of the original wheellock on the so-called Henry VIII's gun (XII–1).

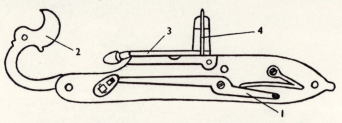

FIG. 7.—The late type of matchlock.   (1) Sear.   (2) Cock.
(3) Pan cover.   (4) Shield.

Along with the new weapons came two new pieces of equipment: the cartridge and the bayonet. The bandolier used for the matchlock had several disadvantages: they were clumsy to wear and rattled in the wind; loading with them and a ball carried in a separate bag was a tedious affair; and they were prone to accidental discharge. The cartridge, which was a charge of powder wrapped in suitable paper with the lead ball tied in one end, could be easily carried in a pouch with a considerable saving in weight. It was introduced on the continent in the first quarter of the seventeenth century and was then brought to this country*. The bills for the equipment of the Battle Axe Guard of 1662, previously mentioned, include the item:

"Tyn Cartouch boxes covered wth Leather of Calves Skins for Musketts wth Formers, prymeing boxes and neate leather girdles wth white buckles
64 @ 3 6d."

At least one English writer, however, mentions their use before this. John Vernon in *The Young Horseman*, 1644, p. 10, gives the following instructions:

"Now if you use Cartrages, you shall finde in your Crattreg case a turned wooden pin which you must take, having cut lengths of white

* This refers to military arms. Elaborately decorated patrons or cartridge boxes were made *en suite* with fine sporting guns in the sixteenth century.

paper something broader then the pin is in length, and rowle the paper on the pin, then twist one end of the paper, and file it almost full of powder, then put the bullet on top of the powder, twisting that end also, then put it into your Cartreg case, now when you come to lade your carbine or Pistols with these Cartreges, you must bite off that end of the paper where the powder is, powring it into your Carbine or Pistol, then put in that bullet and some of that paper will serve for a wad after it and Ram home. . . ."

The change-over was, of course, gradual and, five years later, bandoliers were still being made, the Duke of Albemarle's Regiment receiving 650 collars "covered with black leather and green strings". Their issue continued until the beginning of the eighteenth century.

Bayonets also appear to have been used on the continent before their introduction to this country. In March, 1663, 500 "short swords or Byonetts that lately were recd from Dunkirk" were cleaned and repaired by the cutlers Joseph Awdley, Samuel Law and Robert Steadman. The military writers were soon recommending their use. Sir James Turner in his *Pallas Armata* of 1670, wrote: "Knives, whose blades are one foot long made both for cutting and thrusting (the haft being made to fill the bore of the musquet) will do more execution than the sword or the butt of the musquet". The earliest manufacture of them for the Ordnance occurred in June, 1672, when the following arms were issued to Prince Rupert's Regiment of Dragoons:

"Matchlock Musquetts fitted for Dragoons 900
Byonetts 900
Bandaleeres 900
Pistols fitted for Dragoons 198 pairs."
(PRO 30/37)

All these bayonets were made by the Ordnance Sword Cutler, Joseph Awdley. In 1678 the sum of eight guineas was paid to Phillip Russell for the invention of a new sort of bayonet. This was probably some modification of the plug bayonet rather than the introduction of the socket bayonet, as that does not seem to have occurred in this country until nearly 1700. The plug bayonet appeared in several sizes of handle and blade. In 1685 there is mention of the issue of "Extraordinary Byonetts" in exchange for "ye like number of others of smaller handles". After 1690 in some cases the blade was so lengthened as to warrant the description sword bayonet. (Plate 6.) The military plug bayonet was normally made with a plain varnished wood handle and brass quillons and ferrule. The blade often bore the stamp of a London Cutler with the dagger mark of his Company. Fine-quality bayonets were also made privately and the blades were sometimes engraved with the date and a loyal slogan—one in my possession is inscribed "God save the Prince of Orange. 1688". The mounts were of brass or silver gilt cast with a cherub or female head and the handles turned out of ivory or horn, sometimes decorated with piqué work.

From 1670 onwards, the bulk of arms issued was divided roughly between matchlock and snaphance muskets. No definite proportion seems to have been established but the matchlocks predominated at first. The allocation of arms to an expedition to Virginia in 1676 included 300 matchlocks and 200 snaphances, whilst in another to Tangier in 1680, the ratio was 1,000 to 700. There were also small issues of snaphance dragoons, carbines, blunderbusses and musketoons. Blunderbusses or musketoons—it is difficult to distinguish between them—with heavy iron, or brass, flared barrels, were usually issued to the Navy or for some special service or guard duty. In this respect it is interesting to note the scale of small arms laid down for the Navy in 1684 in "An Account of Allowance of Ordnance, etc. to H.M. Shipps" (MSS in possession of Mark Dineley, Esq.).

RATES	1	2	3	3	4	4	5	5	6
GUNS	100	90	80	70	60	50	40	32	24
Snaphance Musqts.	150	120	80	80	60	60	40	40	30
Musquetoons	10	8	8	8	8	8	7	6	5
Musquet Rods	48	40	30	30	24	20	12	12	10
Blunderbusses	10	8	5	5	—	—	—	—	—
Pistols	40	30	16	16	10	10	8	6	6
Bandoliers	30	30	30	30	25	20	15	15	10
Cartouch Boxes	150	120	80	80	60	60	40	30	30
Flints	4,000	4,000	3,000	3,000	2,000	1,000	500	400	400

The word musquetoon was often applied to the dragoon or dragon, and the carbine. Markham described the dragons as "short peeces of 16 inches the Barrell, and full musquet bore with firelockes or snaphaunces". Measurements given in printed books of this period must, however, always be accepted with reserve. Official records give no help, but they at least confirm that the dragon was a different weapon to the "musquet for dragoons", as they are placed in different categories in inventories. The carbines were longer and smaller in bore. In 1668, Jonadab Holloway made fifty carbines for the Yeomen of the Guard with 2 ft. 9 in. barrels, "whole plated at ye butt ends, with a double ring naile and swivell". As an example of the contemporary nomenclature, these carbines are variously referred to as "short guns", "bastard carbines", "short bastard snaphannce musquetts", "extraordinary bastard musquetts", or just "musquetoons".

Another complication was the use of the word "fuzee" or "fusee", meaning either the fuse used with a grenade, or the fusil, which, with the flintlock in common use, now signified a light form of musket or carbine. A contract for "fuzees or long carbines" at 28s each was made with eight London gunmakers in 1680. In the previous year, new arms had been issued to Prince Rupert's Dragoons, the 80 men in each troop

1. *Top:* Matchlock musket with sear lock and tubular back-sight, *c.* 1600.
Middle: Matchlock musket with trigger lock. English, probably by John
Watson, *c.* 1630. *Bottom:* Musket with the English lock and London proof
marks, *c.* 1640.

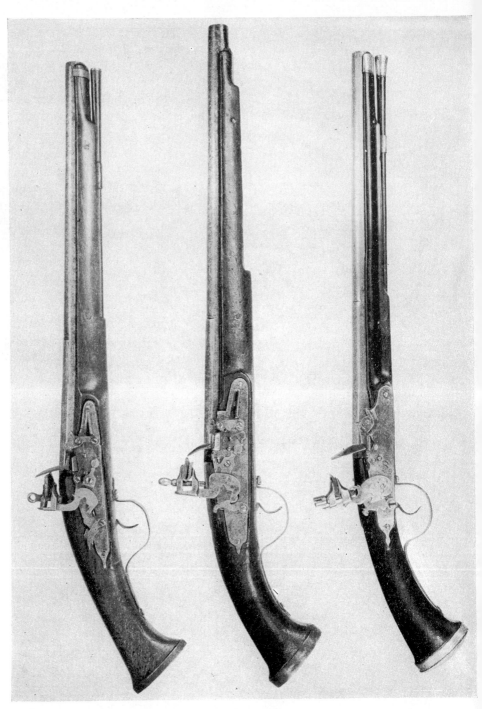

2. *Left to right :* (1) English-lock pistol. (2) A similar pistol. Both have plain iron mounts and early London proof marks, *c.* 1640. (3) Dog-lock pistol by William Watson, *c.* 1650.

sharing "12 Fuzees and 68 musquets with slings", all with cartridge boxes and bayonets The newly formed Grenadier companies were entirely armed with them. The company added to Sir Charles Wheeler's Regt. of Foot in 1679 had "103 Fuzes with slings, 103 cartridge boxes with girdles, 103 Granadoe pouches, 103 Bionettes and 103 Hatchets with girdles".

In "Regulations for Musters" dated 21st February, 1687, quoted by Walton in his *History of the British Standing Army*, 1894, p. 799, the carbines to be issued to Grenadiers and Miners were described as having barrels three feet two inches long. The Regiment of Fusiliers, so named because they were armed only with flintlocks, received however, "Snaphance Musquets, strapped, with bright barrels of three foot eight inches long", which were also carried by the Foot Guards and Dragoons.

The many references to grenades in the records of this period were due to the revival of interest in the firework as a weapon of war. The Ordnance Bills detail at great length the many ingredients used in the preparation of fire shot, arrows, pikes and grenades. Several casualties were caused during the experiments which took place, and John Brown, the Firemaster, lost his life "by the Breaking of a Hand Granadoe". Hand grenades were, of course, normally thrown by hand, but there were several engines invented for their projection.* Thomas Swain was paid £30 in January, 1681, for his Engine, which, however, "did not answer expectations".

In 1681, John Tinker, an Ordnance fireworker, was awarded a special pension of £5 per quarter for his invention of "a new way of shooting Handgranadoes out of small Morterpeeces". A bill dated 1685, for 50 "Hand Morterpeices of Tinkers invencon" with rests at £5 10s. each, suggests that these were the intriguing guns of which two are still in the Tower Armouries. The butt of these guns is formed as a hollow receptacle shaped to take a grenade and the flintlock is ingeniously adapted to fire either a charge in the base of this chamber or the charge in the barrel. A tube running along the inside of the lock connects the priming pan to the grenade cup. This can be filled with priming powder through a lid behind the cock and is controlled by a shutter in the rear of the pan which can be raised when the grenade is to be fired. A folding rest is hinged to the gun and the rammer is placed at the side. The butt only of one of these guns is illustrated by Francis Grose in *Military Antiquities*, London, 1812. He describes it (p. 360) as "an uncommon engine, supposed to be a tinker's mortar, which being fixed on a stick was used for throwing grenades".

There was probably more than one design, and another minute refers to the gunmakers Collins Groome, John Hartwell and James Peddell, stocking and locking brass hand mortar pieces made by the Ordnance Brass Founder William Wightman at Moorfields. The same contractors supplied the East India Company (EIC Marines Misc. 27/1). Most likely these were the normal type of grenade musket with a

* A late example of a grenade throwing machine was that designed in 1795 by M. de Loyauté, and made for the Ordnance by Matthew Boulton of Soho, Birmingham for the sum of £109 14s. 5d. See also *Gills Technical Repository*.

C

cup at the end of the barrel. Some of these, of a later date, are shown on Plate 16.

In the last quarter of the century, carbines, apart from special issues like those of the Yeomen of the Guard, had barrels of two standard lengths, 2 ft. 7 in. and 3 ft. Large numbers of the shorter models were ordered by Lord Dartmouth, the Master General, in 1685; "all made full Carbine Bore ye full length of 2 ft. 7 ins. every Barrll and Coloured Blue wth a Brydle Lock". One of these carbines is illustrated. (Plate 7.) It is a well constructed firearm with a brass buttplate with a narrow tang, two fluted brass rammer pipes and a brass escutcheon plate. The lock is held with three screws, the middle one also taking one end of the side bar. It has a pleasingly rounded shape with a cock of graceful swan-neck pattern. Inside, a vertical sear is fitted and the tumbler is supported with a bridle—a metal bridge which provides a bearing for the otherwise unsupported end of the tumbler axle.

In the same year an order was given for "400 New Extraordinary Carbines with Double Brydle Locks according to ye pattern at 35/- a pce". In these locks a second bridle was fitted to the screw axle of the steel on the outside of the lock. This order relates to an early example of the double bridle lock, as it was not brought into universal use until the second quarter of the eighteenth century.

The carbine with the 3 ft. barrel was a much plainer affair (Plate 7). The same type of stepped barrel with an octagonal breech end is used but it is held to the stock by two bands, the lower one being connected to the side bar. The lock is undecorated and has no bridle, inside or out. Only the minimum of furniture is fitted, a single rammer pipe and the plainest of trigger guards, with no buttplate or escutcheon. The hammer or steel of the lock does, however, have an unusual feature: a lip protrudes from the base and protects the touchhole in the closed position. Carbines of this pattern have been noted with the cyphers of William III and Anne.

With the accession of James II, the rounded form of lock was also introduced to the pistol (Plate 8). The latter was fitted with a plain brass butt cap, one fluted rammer pipe and a plain iron guard. The trigger was a curious dumpy design, set to one side—a type also found on some carbines—and the barrel with an octagonal breech was 14 in. long.

The older style of flat lock was, however, retained on some of the muskets. In June, 1685, the Board of Ordnance ordered "That ye 2300 Musquet Barrels last proved be forthwith stockt & lockt, that is all that are 3 foot or longer to be stockt with Wallnuttree Stocks & ye locks to be Double Springes French Locks with Kings Cypher engraven as the arms for ye Guards were. All ye Barrels yt are shorter than 3 feet to be stockt with Beech—to have good Locks of ye old fashion." Towards the end of the year the Master General of the Ordnance called for a specimen of all the different types of arms then in production.

The arms in use at this period were summarized in "A Generall State of all the Ordnance etc." from 1687–91 (HARL 7458–63). These lists of arms include armour, artillery and historic weapons, but the main categories of military firearms were given as follows:

"Matchlock Musquetts   Ordnary
                          With Draw Pan Covers
                          For Dragoons strapt
Snaphance Musquetts   Ordnary
                          Extrordnary (for sea service)
                          With Wallnutt Tree Stocks
                          For Dragoons.
Snaphance Dragoons
Carbines   Ordnary
           of 2 foot 7 inches   Ordnary
                                 Extrordnary
           Long
           of 3 foot   Ordnary
                       Extrordnary
Pistolls   Ordnary
           with Brasse Capps
Blunderbusses
Musquettoones"

The end of the seventeenth century also saw the rise of the Birmingham trade. In 1689, Sir Richard Newdigate, a member of Parliament for Warwickshire, obtained the first orders for snaphance muskets on behalf of the Birmingham gunmakers; two pattern guns and a proof bullet being sent to him by the Ordnance. First payments were made in 1690 and, from 1692, annual contracts called for the delivery of 200 muskets a month at 17s. each. One of these contracts gives this specification for the musket:

"[the barrel] to be 3 feet 10 inches long with walnutt tree and ash stocks and that one half of the said musquetts shall have flatte locks engraven, and the other half round locks and that all of them shall have brass pipes cast and brass heel plates and all the stocks varnished and to have six good thrids in the breech screws and that all the said gun stocks shall be well made and substantiall and none of them glewed."

(Clive Harris, *History of the Birmingham Gun-Barrel Proof House*, Birmingham, 1946, p. 10.)

This description is particularly interesting as it discloses that what was to become the standard length of a musket barrel for many years, 46 in., had been adopted.

This account of the seventeenth century can be closed with two items taken from the Bill Books of the Ordnance that need no comment. While the Storekeeper of the Ordnance, William Meester, in 1697, was arranging payment for arms bought in Holland and desperately needed for the army in Flanders—2,136 muskets, 441 carbines and 4,381 pistols for the sum of 23,337 Gilders (£2,593)—the furbisher John Harris was transporting hundreds of carbines, pistols and bayonets in barges up the Thames for the decoration of the walls of Hampton Court Palace and Windsor Castle.

The reign of Queen Anne saw the final withdrawal of matchlocks from the line regiments of the British Army. Bandoliers were converted into musket slings and orders for match were reduced to a minimum. It must be added, however, that in 1707 some Dutch matchlock muskets were made ready for sea service. It is a striking feature of the issue of arms throughout the period covered by this book that obsolete or inferior quality arms were always being issued to the Navy without eliciting any real protest from the Senior Service.* Not so the Army. The withdrawal of pikes and their replacement by snaphance muskets— the word flintlock was not yet in use—seems to have determined every regiment to arm itself with the latest muskets. Unfortunately for them the Ordnance was inundated with requests for arms. Many of the coastal towns in England and the colonies of North America were at this time expecting attacks from the sea and were demanding equipment for their forts and forces.

Col. Nicholson, Governor of Virginia, reported that all his store of arms had been destroyed by fire. The Ordnance obviously considered this and other requests an opportunity to dispose of their remaining store of matchlocks and old snaphance muskets; but the recipients exhibited little signs of appreciation. The Governor of the Leeward Islands protested that the matchlocks issued to him were "dangerous in marches through a Country full of Sugar Canes," and as a result, in 1706, 500 new pattern flintlock muskets were sent out to St. Nevis and St. Christopher. The Lieutenant Governor of Jamaica complained to the Lords Commissioners of Trade and Plantations that "he had received about 200 pieces of Iron that had been Firelocks but never can be made so again" (WO 55/343). As more and more demands for new arms came in from regiments, the Ordnance were finally obliged to acquaint the Earl of Nottingham, Secretary of State, in 1703, that they had "no objection to supplying Firelocks which have undergone Tower proof and are very serviceable, But as for Firelocks after the new Pattern wee shall find it difficult to gett the Quantity already demanded for the envoy of Portugall". This referred to the terms of a treaty with Portugal under which England was to supply her ally with 6,500 stand of arms.

In 1705, the Ordnance had just placed their orders for muskets with the London gunmakers, when they were faced with a request for 10,000 muskets, 600 fusils, 600 carbines and 600 pairs of pistols from the authorities in Ireland. This was accompanied by a list of rates at which the arms could be made in Ireland, a suggestion that was resisted on the grounds that "it was in King Charles the 2nd. time not thought fit for ye service to have any Stores made there". A further request for

* See p. 49. The Navy did not worry about the appearance of their small arms, as long as they were strong and serviceable. The plain, solid furniture of the early muskets remained in naval use long after the army had replaced it.

these arms from the Duke of Ormond was referred by the Ordnance to Her Majesty's Council, so that they should know "how much her Magazines are exhausted by the late vast issues". The Queen herself expressed the wish that the Government of Ireland should buy its arms in England rather than in Holland, so the orders to the gunmakers were increased to 2,000 guns per month and regiments were told that once armed they were expected to effect any replacement at their own expense (WO 55/344). However, by the end of the year it was obvious that the manufacturing resources of the country could not meet the demand. On 16 May, 1706, the Ordnance contracted for the purchase of 10,000 arms from John van Bylaart a Rotterdam gunsmith, Major Wybault being sent to Holland with a pattern musket and appropriate tools and powder for their view and proof. Payment of £11,690 for these muskets was authorized by an Order in Council of 8 July, 1706.*

The first efforts were now made to establish what may be called the Ordnance system of manufacture. Up to now, with few exceptions, complete arms had been bought from the contractors, leaving them to arrange the details of the manufacture. The Ordnance had made one attempt to obtain arms from the workmen gunmakers—the various outworkers who normally supplied the contractors—but they had been obliged to pay for them in cash, a disadvantage to a government department which never seemed to have enough money. One of the requisites of a successful contractor was the ability to wait for his money. Having given bond for security, he was faced with a financial system of warrant and debenture which seemed reluctant to finalize itself in actual payment. The idea now was to break up the manufacture of a gun into its main processes, to place contracts for these only and thus to be able to control the various stages of manufacture. The Ordnance hoped also to reduce some of the contractors' profit, and by building up stores of parts, to prevent the frequent breakdown in production that always occurred when a rush of orders was received.

From the beginning of the eighteenth century the Birmingham district was always capable of producing more barrels and locks than London, and it was to the Midlands, therefore, that the bulk of the orders for these parts was given. The London gunmakers, on the other hand, could not be surpassed for the quality of their woodwork, and the stocking of guns became their traditional responsibility. Briefly, the barrels and locks (though the latter were sometimes made in London) were made in Birmingham, where an Ordnance Viewer was available to view them. They were then sent to be proved and stored in the Tower. When necessary these "materials" could be distributed amongst the gunmakers in the vicinity of the Tower to be set up into complete firearms.

There were two other sets of materials, brass and iron, necessary to complete the job. As the musket settled down to a standard pattern the mounts, known as the furniture—the buttplate, trigger guard, rammer pipes, sideplate and escutcheon—were made of cast brass and these

---

* John van Bylaart of Rotterdam, as he usually appears in English documents, was described in Dutch records as 'Jan van Bijlaert' or 'Bijlaerd'. Ten thousand Dutch muskets were also sent to the Tower of London for English use.

were purchased at so much per pound weight, depending on whether old or new brass was used. At the beginning of 1715, Matthew Bagley and William Bargill were contracted "to cast Brass Work for Small Arms according to patterns delivered. . . . each Furniture to weigh 1⅛ lb. at 14½d. per lb." Bagley's work was shortlived. His brass foundry at Windmill Hill to the north of the city, used mainly for the casting of cannon, was the scene of a disastrous explosion in 1716, in which Bagley, his son and many officials, including Mercator, the Ordnance Clerk and Proof master, were killed.

The iron materials, the trigger, screws, loops, sights, etc. were usually supplied by a Birmingham forger. In 1707–8 the Birmingham gunmakers started sending in plain locks "with ketches" at 3s. 9d. each, bridle locks at 6s. and musquet barrels at 6s 6d each. A few years later their London rivals were reported rough stocking and setting up

> "Musquet Barrels & Locks of His Maj. for Land Service according to the Pattern, the Brass Work for the Heelplates, Trigger Guards & side Plates to be delivered them out of Store, at 8/9d. a peice."

There were small supplementary charges for filing the barrels and making off the stocks. Sometimes the stocker supplied his own walnut, but normally government rough stocks were issued, the prices being adjusted accordingly.

The locks were engraved separately in London, Edward Cooke being the engraver at this period, at a price of 4d. per lock. Another 4d. was allowed for hardening the lock afterwards. Perhaps the most famous lock engraver of all was the type founder William Caslon, whose font is still renowned. In April, 1719, a rival offered to do the engraving cheaper and the Board of Ordnance warned that "if Caslon do not do them well that Mr. Woolridge look out for another who will stay the course of the office". *

The system really got under way in 1715. In that year the London gunmakers, having received contracts for Land Service muskets at 22s. each and pistols at 27s. per pair, were forced to confess to the Surveyor General their failure to obtain barrels and locks, and were obliged to ask for a supply. By the middle of the century a fairly standard procedure had been established and prices for the various parts and processes remained fairly constant for another fifty years. I have made an analysis of these prices in Appendix B. The years 1775–85 were chosen because the Bill Books for that decade appear to be complete and it is the most interesting part of the century.

The men mainly responsible for controlling this work were officials of the Ordnance Office working in the Tower of London under the Principal Storekeeper. One of the divisions of his department at the Tower was the Small Gun Office, a group of armourers, gunsmiths, furbishers and labourers under a Master Furbisher. Their activities were normally confined to the care and repair of arms and at times their

---

* The lock of a musketoon in the Royal Armouries (No. XII.279), engraved on the outside WOLLDRIDGE [17]15, is stamped inside CASLON.

assembly, but the Master Furbisher was often called on to produce some suggested modification of an arm and in many cases was allowed to put forward an idea of his own. His technical advice was sought by the Board and the Master General in all their dealings with gunmakers and inventors, and often influenced the subsequent design of a new firearm.

At the time of the Restoration Robert Stedman or Steadman, a cutler, held the office of Furbisher, but his position is hard to define. Any responsibility he had for firearms was overshadowed by the Master Gunmaker to the Ordnance and the various gunmakers to the King, all of whom, while enjoying official remunerations, were still able to carry on their own businesses. At the beginning of the eighteenth century, Henry Crips, a gunmaker, is mentioned as the Furbisher. He was a Freeman of the Gunmakers' Company who shared in Government contracts from 1680 onwards. In 1703, however, his duties as an Officer of the Ordnance took precedence. His bills from then on are mainly for the supply of gunsmith's tools and travelling expenses in viewing arms. When he died, his widow, in 1715, was given a pension of 10s. a week as compensation for the house and sheds built by her husband near the west end of the chapel in the Tower.

Crips was succeeded by another gunmaker, Richard Wooldridge or Wolldridge, who is first referred to as Master Furbisher in 1718. Before that date, although obviously in the employment of the Ordnance, his duties are not clear. His name does not appear in any of the gunmakers' contracts and he was not a member of the Gunmakers' Company. His name, however, appears on a musket in the Tower dated 1704; the Minute Books record that he was granted 10 days sick leave in 1705 and in the following year he made a pattern musket which was sent to Major Wybault in Holland "for his better regulating the Survey of the Arms to be made there".

At the beginning of 1715, when he apparently took charge of the Small Gun Office, he was instructed to deliver to the Duke of Marlborough "two Land Service Musquetts ye one of ye Former Pattern, ye other as now proposed wth Bands instead of pinns that his Grace's opinion & directions may be had therein". In June of that year, he was paid £20 5s. 8d. for several brass pattern stocks for muskets, and a year later he was in Birmingham arranging for the manufacture of iron materials and "shewing to ye workmen ye way to fitt locks to the mould". Members of the Gunmakers' Company were also concerned in firearm design at this time. Andrew Dolep, many of whose magnificent weapons grace our museums, was paid 30s. in 1711, "for making up Three Pattern Guns for ye Board of Ordnance" (GWA), and ten years later William Brazier was reprimanded by his Company for selling "Two Pattern Guns to Mr. Farmer of B'ham to ye great prejudice of the Trade in Generall" (GMB).

Having described some of the men responsible for the design and production of firearms, we can now turn to an examination of the arms made in the first quarter of the eighteenth century. Fortunately for our purpose there are several muskets of this period in the Tower Armouries all conveniently dated, the last two numbers of the year being engraved on the tail of the lockplate.

The first in this series is the one made by Wooldridge dated 1704 (Plate 5). Basically it is little different from the William III musket with the flat doglock, except that the lock has a square instead of a pointed steel; but it has several refinements and it has a better finish throughout. The brass buttplate is thicker and the iron trigger guard is properly filed and shaped, although the breech screw passing up through the guard to the barrel tang—a seventeenth-century characteristic—is retained. The three side screws are supported by a sideplate of a double-S pattern. The most important alteration is that the stock has been cut away from under the muzzle, a brass nose-band fitted and a bayonet stud *cum* sight brazed on. It is therefore one of the first muskets made for socket bayonets.

It is almost impossible to decide when these new bayonets were introduced. There is an apparently earlier musket in the Tower which is adapted for a socket, bearing the WR and Crown on its lockplate, but so many muskets must have been converted at a later date that one has to be careful in accepting muskets before 1700. The obvious disadvantage of the plug bayonet was that the gun could not be fired when its bayonet was fixed, although there is the statement of Thomas Elliott, a cutler, in 1676, which makes one wonder. He reported receiving an order for knives with cross pieces "such as Prince Rupert shot out of his guns" (CSP). Some of the earlier type of socket bayonets are shown in Plate 14. The one looking like a plug bayonet has a socket attached to the brass quillons and a grip of maple wood, often used on English pistols in the last quarter of the century. The standard socket bayonet with its zig-zag slot and reinforced rim came in much later. It must be added, however, that socket bayonets are mentioned but not described in the Ordnance records (WO 55 series) as early as the 1680's.

Interesting light is thrown on the bayonet situation by the arguments of the Ordnance against the issue of bayonets to Lord Mark Kerr's Regiment in 1706. They had, first of all, observed that bayonets could only be issued officially to Grenadiers. This had been countered by the regiment, who pointed out that as firearms were being issued in lieu of pikes an equal number of bayonets would have to be supplied. The Ordnance closed this dispute with the reply that "all Regiments raised since the disuse of pikes have provided Byonets as they do Swords and belts at their own Charge. . . . Few of the Officers agree on the sort of Byonets fit to be used or in the manner of fitting them to the Musquets as may appear by the various sorts that there are of them in ye Army."

However, to return to the dated series of muskets. We have seen how, in 1692, the contract to Birmingham gunmakers was divided equally into muskets with flat locks and those with rounded locks. This division of design continued throughout the first quarter of the eighteenth century, and there are two separate lines of development. Plate 10 illustrates that of the flat lock which appears to have been discontinued in the middle of the century. The lock of the top musket, although made by Wooldridge in 1715, is exactly like the one he made in 1704 with a square steel. It is interesting mainly because it is the musket mentioned in the Ordnance Minute as having the barrel held by bands instead of pins—there are two brass bands farther up the barrel just out of the photograph—and it is one of the first guns with the breech screw going downwards through the tang to the guard.

The middle musket shows the next step. Originally assembled in 1710, it has been altered at a later date. The dog catch has been taken off and its screw-hole filled in, and the notch filed off the back of the cock. It will be noted that this musket has been fitted with one of the old barrels with an octagonal breech. The order for the change from this type to the completely round barrel appears to have been made in 1707, when a new contract was concluded with the gunmakers, and some consternation caused by the Board's refusal to take barrels "with Square Breeches". It also specified that the heel or buttplate was to be an inch longer, the rammer pipes were to be plain, and there were to be "sockets on the ends of the Rodds instead of Nailes".

The lower musket, dated 1720, shows the flat lock in its final stage with a proper chamfered-off cock. The square steel has been retained and no bridle has been fitted to hold its screw. The breech screw is now screwed downward through the barrel tang. These muskets with flat locks generally have heavy flat brass buttplates and trigger guards and were probably intended for Sea Service, thus according with the Ordnance policy of using up old materials for naval arms. In 1719, Elias Cole, who had previously been allowed to send in out-of-date barrels, also supplied musket locks which, although not answering the Land Pattern, were accepted for Sea Service.

The three muskets shown on Plate 11 have the rounded lock with swan-neck cock and pointed steel almost unchanged from those of the James II and William III period. It was this type of lock which was to become the accepted Army or Land Pattern. The top musket, dated 1718, is, in fact, a true forerunner of the Brown Bess, made by William Wilson. The flat brass buttplate is replaced by one with a hollow cast heel* much better adapted to fit the shoulder. An escutcheon is fitted for the first time. The rounded side plate with the tail has been adapted for two screws—up to then three screws had always been found necessary to hold the lock—and the rammer is given the benefit of a tail pipe where it enters the stock. All these mounts are of what was to become the Brown Bess pattern, but are made of iron. Several references are made in the Ordnance Minute Books in 1717–18 to muskets being set up with iron furniture.

All the muskets in this pre-Brown Bess series so far have the standard

* In March, 1716, William Burgin supplied brass patterns for "Bumpheel plates for musquets" (WO 53/403).

Land Service barrel of 46 in. length, but the middle musket on Plate 11, also with iron mounts, made by Wooldridge in 1722, has a barrel of only 42 in. It may be the musket mentioned in the minute of 28th July, 1722, when 2,000 arms were ordered "according to the Pattern, His Lordship delivered to the Surveyor General which was approved by his Majesty and by Mr. Wooldridge produced to the Board". In the same year, Lewis Barber, the London gunmaker, was paid £3 for "Two new Iron work Short Musqts with Bayonets". The Wooldridge musket is also an example of a curious period in the development of the British military firearm. Having seen in the years 1718–20 the establishment of a plain graceful musket, the forerunner of the Brown Bess, the authorities for a short period encouraged a series in which the Dutch influence is marked. Stocks with curious swellings—no apology is offered for the title of Plate 12—long fluted trigger guards and elaborate buttplates of the kind shown in Plate 13 become fashionable.

Much of the resultant profusion of firearms was caused by many regiments buying their own arms. Three regiments of Foot Guards were allowed to return a supplementary issue of arms in 1716, so that they could be allowed their value and buy muskets of their own particular pattern. Maj.-Gen. Sabine, Colonel of the 23rd Regt. (later the Royal Welsh Fusiliers) had been previously granted this privilege, his arms being of an "extra pattern". A musket of this period made by James Freeman with the regiment's name, ROYAL WELSH, and the device of the Prince of Wales engraved on the barrel—it may well have been one of Sabine's arms—was certainly proved by the Ordnance, but the steel mounts have their own flamboyant character. (Note the curious escutcheon shown on Plate 13.) Another London gunmaker, Joseph Clarkson, made the musket shown on Plate 12 for the regiment of Gen. Sir Richard Kane, Colonel of the 9th Regt. of Foot from 1725–30. Engraved on the escutcheon, KANE A No. 1, it has another style of mount and an unusual stock shaped apparently to give a better grip for bayonet fighting.

All these regimental fancies were gradually discouraged and the minute of 28th July, 1722, quoted above also decreed that "all Collonells [sic] who have any new Arms made shall be obliged to make them according to the said Pattern and proved and viewed by the Proper Officers of the Ordnance". Very slowly, then, a standard pattern Army musket was evolved. It was identical to the 1718 model already described except that the mounts were made of brass instead of iron. As we shall see it was made in two basic models with barrel lengths of 46 in and 42 in. Described officially as the Long Land and Short Land muskets, they are known today, somewhat erroneously, as the first and second models Brown Bess.

CHAPTER III

THE origin of the name Brown Bess is obscure and I will leave etymologists to argue whether Bess is a corruption of the German word Büchse (Gun) and whether Brown refers to the colour of the stock or the barrel. Although it was never used in the contemporary records—the earliest printed reference is in 1785—it is now commonly applied to the flintlock musket which formed the main weapon of the British Army from the 1730's to the 1830's. Yet during that period the flintlock firearm underwent several important changes. From 1730 to 1780 it remained the same distinctive pattern. In the 1780's an attempt was made to introduce a revolutionary type of arm, but under the stress of the Napoleonic Wars this was replaced by the cheap so-called India Pattern, and was finally succeeded by a plain, but well made, series known as the New Land Pattern It is with the first category that this chapter deals, the graceful musket and associated carbines and pistols made between 1730–80, which many collectors will acknowledge as the only group worthy of that affectionate phrase the Brown Bess and her Family.

During the first twenty years of this period very little information is available, there being a large gap in the Ordnance Minute Books. Fortunately the custom of engraving the lock of the gun with the name of the contractor and the date was continued, and the Ordnance Bill Books contain much which is of interest. Dated specimens of the Brown Bess commence between 1725–30; the musket in the Tower Armouries often quoted as 1717 is really 1747. The trigger guards of these early models have a slightly different shape to the accepted Brown Bess pattern, the part of the loop behind the trigger being solid instead of having an open spur. The first model Brown Bess, or the Long Land Musket to give it its proper name, had a 46 in. barrel with a wooden rammer, retained by three pipes of equal size and a tail pipe where it enters the stock. At this point the stock swells out and, generally speaking, the bigger the swell the older the gun. One sling swivel is fastened to the front of the trigger guard bow and the other is screwed through the muzzle end of the stock between the first and second pipes. The lock of the Brown Bess was very like the William III rounded pattern, about seven inches long and with a drooping tail. This bend

45

gets less pronounced in the later models until, towards the end of the century, the bottom edge of the lock is practically straight. At first the steel bridle is omitted and it is described as a single bridle lock. The bayonet which went with the musket had a socket about four inches long and a triangular blade seventeen inches long.

Thus was the Brown Bess in her original form, but it would be wrong to assume that, once it was in production, it was the only pattern made. Although the Ordnance was always prepared to buy complete arms, the main production line was the supply of parts by Birmingham, the storage in the Tower and the assembly in London. It was only when the stock of some pattern part became low that they were sold off by

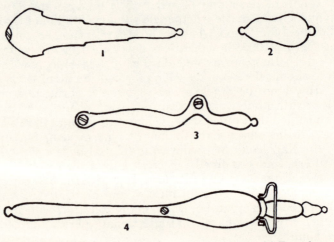

FIG. 8.—Brown Bess pattern furniture.   (1) Butt tang.   (2) Escutcheon.
(3) Side plate.   (4) Trigger guard.

auction in the Tower; otherwise they were issued irrespective of their date of manufacture. Iron furniture was still being issued for setting up into muskets in 1736, although, in 1730, the use of brass furniture was well established for the new pattern musket "as approved by the King".

Another pattern of which there is increasing mention from 1740 onwards is the Short Land musket, with the same style of stock, lock and furniture as the long model but with the 42 in. barrel originally tried in 1722. There were soon two standard pattern muskets in production, the Long Land with steel rammers and the Short Land with wood rammers, a curious distinction between the two being that only the short pattern had a brass nose cap. By the middle of the century, however, an improved pattern noseband or cap was fitted to both types of muskets

Steel rammers were in use as early as 1724. On 4th August, Richard

Wooldridge gave his opinion that they could be fitted to muskets made in Ireland "after the same manner practized here in the Tower upon the new Pattern Firelocks which were made for Wooden Rammers and afterwards fitted with steel Rammers". The conversion was effected by "a Spring put in the Taile Pipe" and "a Ferrell Braiz'd within the upper end of the Fore Pipe to keep the Rammer from shakeing too much" (ADD 23636). It should be noted that Fortescue's assertion (*History of the British Army*, Vol. II, p. 51) that steel rammers were introduced in 1726, on orders from the King, is incorrect. The reference quoted by him (SP 44/180) is merely a royal warrant for the issue of muskets with bayonets and steel rammers to Ireland.

The number of contractors engaged in London and Birmingham in the second quarter of the century was unusually small. Whether this was due to a slump in the trade or the orders being monopolized by a few of the wealthier gunmakers is not clear. Whatever the reason, the Ordnance had once more to seek supplies abroad. In 1741, a series of bills were passed for imported arms. One for 16,000 muskets and bayonets and 8,000 musket barrels, including duty, commission and brokerage, amounted to £16,526 19s. 11d. The price of the complete musket was given as 9 Florin 10 Stivers and the barrel 3 Florin 2 Stivers (11 Florins—£1). This importation of barrels is most unusual and the Bill Books indicate they were all set up in London. Thomas Hollier supplied brass pipes at 4½d. per set and furniture at 1s. 4d. per lb. The rough stocking was done by Richard Waller and the setting up divided between Lewis Barbar and Charles Pickfatt. To add to the foreign mixture, the Board, in 1745, purchased from the merchants Philip Protheroe & Company 2,500 Spanish muskets complete at 16s. each.

So far mention has been made only of muskets. Information concerning the other arms is admittedly slight. The evidence suggests only a small manufacture of pistols and carbines. The pistol appears to have been made in both carbine (17) and pistol (24) bore until 1742, when it was decided to confine their calibre to pistol bore (WO 47/IND 8236). In the following year Richard Wooldridge supplied 330 "Pistols, Pistol Bore complete with long ear'd Caps & Brass furniture, Barrels 10 inch" at 35s. per pair. Plate 18 shows a pistol dated 1738 with a 12 in. barrel of 17 or carbine bore. Although made before the order quoted it has the same long projections or ears running up the grip of the pistols. The lock with its drooping tail and the style of the brass furniture are copied from the Brown Bess. Pistols made for sea service are similar but have a flatlock and a belt hook or rib attached to the side plate.

Examples of carbines of this period are rare but, judging from their descriptions in inventories, they were mainly of the kind for use without a bayonet. Two most unusual carbines in the Tower are illustrated on Plate 17. Both have the same overall length of 43 in. with 27 in. barrels of enormous bore, one of 4 and the other of 5 balls to the lb.

Despite this size they were both designed for bayonets, one of which has been preserved. It fits the carbine which has no rammer and has a triangular blade 32 in. long. The signature on one of the locks is that of John Probin, the Birmingham gunmaker. Carbines with long bayonets always exerted a fascination and, as we shall see, were resurrected from time to time for some special purpose.

Wall pieces or swivel guns were also prominent during the first half of the century. They were supplied in the usual way in parts for later setting up, but at least one maker, James Farmer of Birmingham, supplied them complete at £4 8s. in 1747. As their name suggests, they were used in fortified places where their long barrels and considerable range could be utilized to advantage. A number of them survive in the Tower, all exactly alike but with dates ranging from 1729–44. For their size they are surprisingly well made, with engraved mounts of the

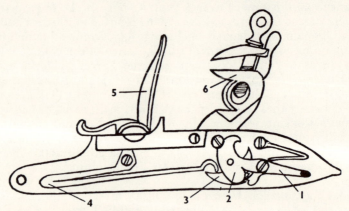

FIG. 9.—Double bridle flintlock. (1) Sear. (2) Bridle. (3) Tumbler. (4) Mainspring. (5) Steel. (6) Cock. The second bridle is on the reverse supporting the Steel screw.

Brown Bess pattern. Their barrels are 4 ft. 6 in. long with a bore of nearly one inch, fully stocked and mounted on a swivel. The diameter of the ball they fired is given by R. Adye in *The Bombardier and Pocket Gunner*, London, 1802, as ·89 in. or 6¾ to the lb. The design of the gun appears to have been unchanged up to the end of the century and there are several wall pieces in the Tower Armouries—identical to the above, except that they do not have escutcheons—made for the East India Company in 1793.

The state of small arms in the Tower at the middle of the century is given by detailed lists in the Ordnance Minute Books. They present a confused picture. What we now call the Brown Bess came under the heading of "Land Musquets to the King's Pattern with Double Bridle Locks". The latest long pattern with steel rammers had begun to come in from the gunmakers, but the bulk of the stock was still of the old pattern without nosebands, with wood rammers. The older muskets with single bridle locks were relegated to what may be called the oddment department. This included various marine muskets, the remnants of the Spanish importation, and a stock of Dutch muskets remaining from those imported in 1741. The last were soon disposed of. In 1754, Arthur Dobbs, the Governor of North Carolina, appealed for arms from the Tower "that are not of an Assortment proper for his Majesty's Forces here", for a regiment which was to be raised to march to the assistance of Virginia against the French and Indian attacks. On 1st July a warrant was issued for the supply to the colony of "3,000 Musquets and Bayonets of Dutch Fabrick" with tanned leather slings, cartridge boxes and sea service swords. A further 500 Dutch muskets were sent to Georgia in 1756 (WO 55/412).

As always, the store of sea service muskets was a hotchpotch of old and new muskets, rightly described as "of sorts". For normal purposes these were divided into two classes, those with black barrels and those with polished or bright barrels. In 1752, the Admiralty directed that in future all sea muskets should have bayonets. After some difficulty in getting the bayonets to fit, the Ordnance agreed to supply each ship with equal numbers of bright and black barrels. Plate 22 shows a representative group of these naval arms, the long muskets with roughly 3 ft. barrels and the short one with a barrel of 2 ft. 2 in. The top musket was made by Farmer in 1745 and has the early flat lock and buttplate with a wooden rammer. The next one has a rounded lock and a steel rammer, has been converted to a bayonet, and has sling swivels fitted. The third one dates from the last quarter of the century but still retains an early solid trigger guard. The bottom short musket is an odd mixture, with a late lock and form of stock but with early pipes and wooden rammer and an old flat buttplate which has been rounded off to fit the different shape of the butt.

The manufacture of all these arms was under the control of two groups of men, the independent gunmakers of Birmingham and London and the staff of the Small Gun Office in the Tower. Since their early days the latter had considerably expanded. A group of workshops and houses had been built in the Tower and on the Tower wharf which reached the proportions of a small factory. At times there were in the region of 100 gunmakers employed in the cleaning, repairing and assembly of arms. Many apprentices of the Gunmakers' Company left their masters after their seven year's apprenticeship and joined the Ordnance staff. Often a son was apprenticed to his father at the Tower and was never registered with any of the city companies.

There were two main classes of employment: Piecemen and Daymen. As the first name suggests, the gunmaker was paid according to his production. The Daymen, paid by the day, were the permanent staff, with more privileges, sick pay, medical treatment and the prospect of a pension. Owing to the shape of the bench at which they worked, they became known as the Round Table Men. This famous table was destroyed in the fire of 1841. In 1750, a list of Daymen included 4 viewers and foremen, 2 prime smiths, 1 prime gunmaker, 37 common men and a lad. Working with the piecemen, sometimes, were the employees of the contractors, and a sharp watch was kept on any gunmaker trying to recruit staff. When Thomas Jordan was given an order for musket barrels in 1756, he was at the same time "enjoined faithfully to keep his Promise not to entice or employ any Person now employed as a Dayman or Pieceman in the Tower of London or any Person at B'ham working for the Board". As a further incentive to their men the Board were forced to raise the Daymen's wages by 6d. per day, "in order to animate & encourage them in this time of hurry".

One of the attractions of working in the Tower, apart from an exemption from the Press Gang, was the possibility of a job as an armourer on board ship or at one of the overseas depots of the Ordnance at Boston, New York, Annapolis, Jamaica, Gibraltar, etc. There were obviously recognized perquisites to these jobs. When John Stevens, Master Armourer at Minorca, was dismissed in 1753, the Ordnance Officers there complained that as "they have had more trouble with the Master Armourers than with all the rest of the Artificers, they entreated the Board would be pleased to send a Man of good character who may not expect to keep a private shop of his own which is a great Temptation to Dishonesty nor to bring any Tools with him but what are for the Kings Use". Stern measures were now adopted against such incidents. Another gunmaker applying for the post of ship's armourer was thoroughly investigated and reported to be "an ingenious workman but dishonest". He was refused the job and his name solemnly entered in a Black Book.

The Ordnance also began to tighten its control over the gunmakers, and to insist on higher standards of manufacture. After complaints, in 1752, that with the bullet of 14-bore the cartridge could not be forced down the barrel after a few shots, it was decided to alter the official size to $14\frac{1}{2}$ to the lb. All moulds were changed and existing stores of shot recast accordingly. The Ordnance Proofmaster, comparing British and Hanoverian arms, later reported that the British musket calibre was 76/100 inch and the carbine 66/100 inch. It was no small feat that the measurements were now discussed in terms of a hundredth of an inch. In December, 1755, the lockmaker Richard Davis was sent to Birmingham "to give the Workmen proper directions and to see that their Tumbler Tools, Screw Plates and Taps are all made to the same Gauge". At the beginning of 1756, the pattern of the locks was said to be "improved, better filed and all the parts made to particular Gauges". In spite of this, complaints were received from the Army and Militia of frequent breakages. In December, 1759, therefore, the Ordnance insisted that the locks should in future be made of the best Swedish Iron, and sent George Markby their viewer round the workshops to see that this was done.

The contract work had now assumed the semblance of a closed

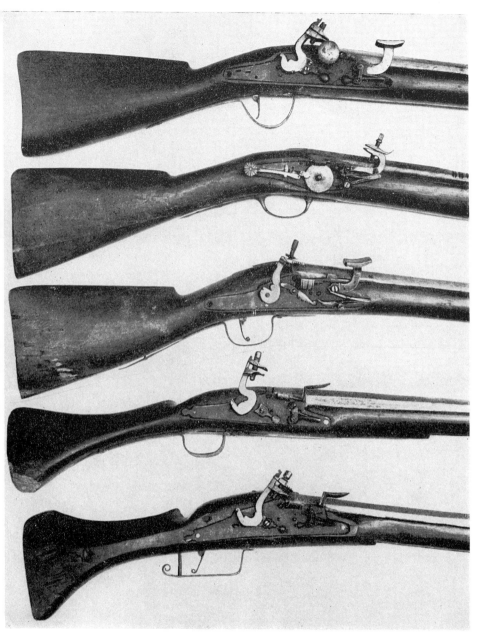

3. English military muskets from Apethorpe, Northamptonshire, believed to have been used in the Civil War. Two with snaphance locks, two with English locks and one with a curious wheellock. All have been badly repaired and only the bottom two retain their original stocks.

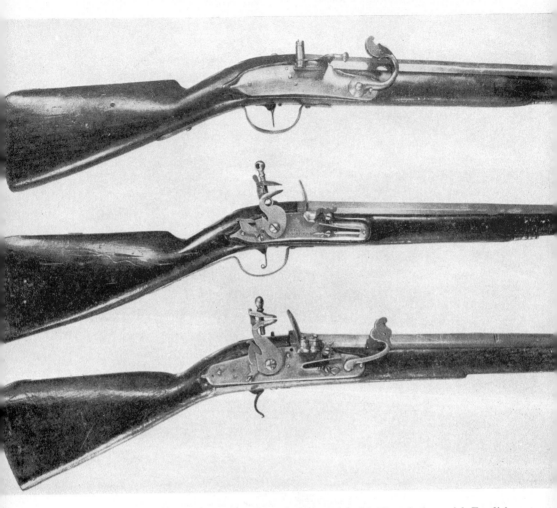

4. *Top:* Late type of matchlock musket, probably Dutch, but with English proof marks, *c.* 1660. *Middle:* A similar musket fitted with a doglock. *Bottom:* An experimental combined flintlock and matchlock. An English version of the so-called Vauban lock.

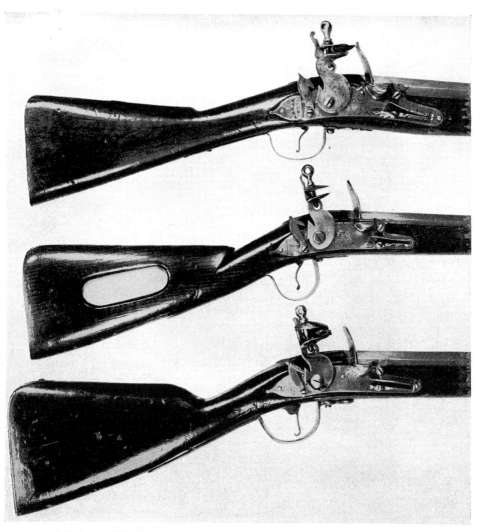

5. Muskets with dog-locks. *Top:* James II. *Middle:* William III. Note the butt, shaped for a better grip for bayonet fighting. *Bottom:* Queen Anne. Lock signed by Richard Wooldridge and dated 1704.

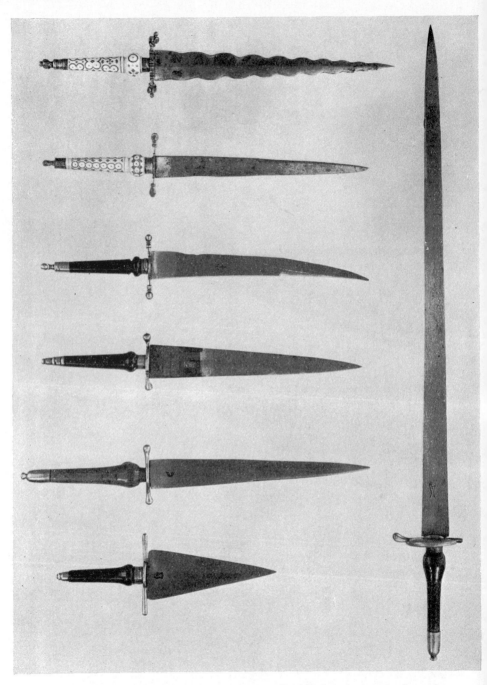

6. A selection of English plug bayonets, all with London cutlers' marks, except for the sword bayonet on right which has a German blade with the "running wolf" mark.

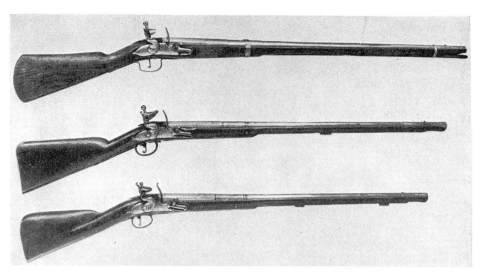

7. Seventeenth-century cavalry carbines. *Top:* William III carbine with 3 ft. barrel. *Middle:* Privately made carbine by John Dafte, *c.* 1680. *Bottom:* James II carbine with 2 ft. 7 in. barrel by Humphrey Pickfatt.

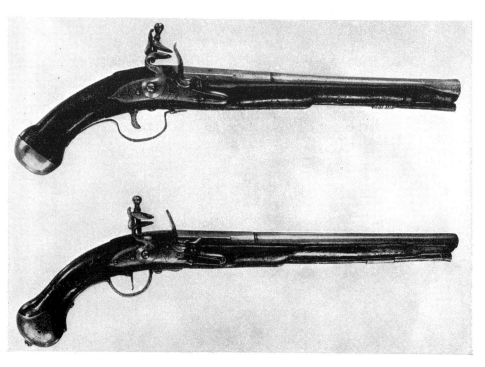

8. *Top:* James II pistol by Robert Brooke. *Bottom:* Queen Anne pistol by Thomas Fort dated 1710. Both pistols have 14 in. barrels.

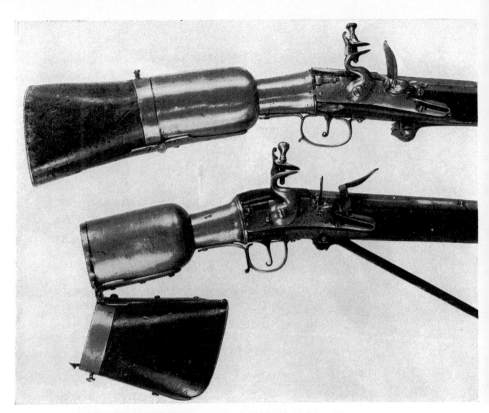

9. Tinker's mortar carbine. *Top:* With butt closed. *Bottom:* With butt open and stand lowered. Note the priming hole behind the cock, and the shutter of the pan raised to allow the flash to enter the connecting channel.

shop. In Birmingham, the manufacture of barrels and locks was under the control of a few families of gunmakers such as the Farmers, Galtons, Whatelys and Grices; often inter-marrying and forming partnerships. In London, the work of rough stocking and setting up was almost exclusively in the hands of two men: Richard Waller (joined by his son James in 1755) and John Hirst. Waller had, in 1740, undertaken to work only for the Ordnance and had gradually built up a team of some forty craftsmen engaged in the carving of the rough walnut stocks. The more exacting task of fitting the barrel, lock and other parts into these stocks was performed by Hirst who once reported that he had a staff of thirty-four. One man's work depended on the other and the two often received identical orders (as far as numbers were concerned). Their capabilities may be judged by the orders given to them during the Seven Years War (1756–63). Reaching a peak of 60,000 per year in 1759 and 1760, Hirst's orders for this period amounted to approximately 298,720. These figures have been compiled from the Minute Books and do not necessarily agree with actual production. However, they are substantiated by Waller's statement in 1777 that he had, in the same seven year period, supplied 263,000 new stocks and repaired 18,000 others.

The other London gunmakers did not lack for work. Coincident with the Ordnance's task of supplying the British Army was that of the East India Company with the commitments of a large private army in India. The history of arms production by this distinguished Company runs parallel with that of the Government. The gunmakers who worked for the Ordnance normally accepted orders from the Company. When the Ordnance introduced a new weapon, the Company cautiously followed suit and, as we shall see in a later chapter, the two could act in amicable partnership. Most of the Company's arms were made in similar fashion to the Government's except that, once set up, they were stored in a warehouse adjacent to the Gunmakers' Company Proof House in Whitechapel, where they were proved.

In 1766–76 the East India Company withdrew its proof from the Gunmakers' and sent their guns to the Ordnance Proof House on Tower wharf. The Proofmaster made periodical reports of the numbers of barrels proved and from these we learn that in the two years 1768–69, 95,558 barrels of all kinds were proved for the India Company. These figures compare with the orders for 44,100 barrels given by the Ordnance in 1766–67 (figures for the same two years are not available in the records). This manufacture of private arms rivalling and sometimes exceeding that of the Government was the main reason for the Ordnance's frequent failure to obtain arms in this country. For this the gunmakers can hardly be blamed as the Company's specifications in design and proof were not so strict, and their method of payment was better.

What were these arms that were produced in such large quantities at this time? We can best start with the year 1757. The British forces

D

had suffered a succession of defeats and the loss of Minorca had shocked the people. A wave of new energy swept through the administration and, as Fortescue comments: "The nation was stirred by such military ardour as it had not felt since the Civil War." Two Highland regiments, Fraser's and Montgomery's, were formed, the Royal Artillery and Marines were augmented, and a Militia Bill was passed to raise men from every county. All these precautions were to have their effect on the kind of small arm required. In September the Board of Ordnance decided that the following state of arms was to be maintained in the Tower:

"Long Land Musquets with Steel Rammers and Long Fore pipes

			50,000
Short Land Musquets with wood Rammers for Dragoons			10,000
Short Musquets of the New Pattern for Marines or Militia			30,000
Carbines with Bayonets for Artillery and Highlanders			5,000
Carbines without Bayonets for Horse			2,000
Land Service pistols		pairs	12,000
Sea Service Musquets with Bayonets { Bright			10,000
Black			10,000
Musquetoons			2,000
Sea Service Pistols		pairs	10,000 "

It will be noted that the Long Land Musket had been further modified, the rammer pipe nearest to the muzzle being extended to a trumpet-like shape to facilitate the entry of the long thin steel rammer. Most of this work was done by the Piecemen in the Tower who were paid 4d. per gun. The Short Land musket with the 42 in. barrel, used by Heavy Dragoons, still had a wooden rammer, although by this time there was an increased conversion of all muskets from wood to steel rammers, and, in October, 1756, the Daymen in the Tower were permitted to work until eight o'clock in the evening by candlelight with an allowance of 1¼d. per day for this purpose.

The Marine or Militia musket was designed to meet the demand for a large number of muskets for the new recruits. The Viewer at Birmingham reported in April, 1758, that few barrels were being delivered to him, the gunmakers being occupied with large and more favourable orders from the East India Company and the Irish Government. The Board were advised that "if a second sort of Barrel for Marines or Militia were to be admitted, the Board would be supplied with Double the Number and 6d. per Barrel cheaper and they would undergo the same proof and be equally serviceable but not Filed to the exactness which have been required of late and that the difference of Filing will not be perceived by an Indifferent Person." This was agreed to, and the viewers' reports of barrels inspected soon include the category "Short 2nd sort for marines". A warrant for arms for the Dorsetshire Regt. of Militia, in 1758, describes them as "Musquets

new patt. 3 ft. 6 in. in the barel complete with wood rammers"
(WO 55 /412). An example of this Short Land musket in the Tower,
dated 1762, is marked MILITIA NEW PATTERN on the barrel
(Plate 15).

This musket has what is often termed the second model Brown Bess
type of furniture. The tang of the buttplate is shortened, the escutcheon
discarded and the sideplate, although of the same shape, is flat instead
of being rounded. This pattern of furniture was apparently put into
universal use in July, 1775, when the order was made for "the Brasswork for Land & Militia & Marines to be of one pattern".

New names in the list of arms were the carbines for Artillery and
Highlanders. The rise in prominence of the carbine was due to the
change in the type of warfare now experienced by the British forces.
On the open, flat plains of Flanders fighting had been conducted by
masses at close quarters, where discipline and drill were the main
consideration. Despite its later detractors the British musket was the
ideal weapon for this purpose, simple, strong and easy to load. An
accuracy of 50 yards was enough and the quick deadly volleys of the
British infantry never failed to win in the end.

The French and Indian wars presented a different problem. The
troops had to force their way through thickly wooded and often moun-
tainous country where parade-ground tactics were of no avail against
a hidden enemy. The disastrous defeat of Gen. Braddock at Monon-
gahela in 1755 brought matters to a head. The tactics of Braddock and
his mentor, the Duke of Cumberland, based on the fanatical Prussian
drill books were discarded. Men like Howe, Forbes, Washington and
Bouquet entered the field determined to "learn the art of war from the
Indians". The emphasis was on mobility. Light Infantry, Light
Dragoons and light arms were steadily introduced. Carbines were
carried by artillerymen, highlanders, light infantry, officers and
certain cavalry.

The difficulty is to decide what these carbines were. The description
in the first place meant the dimension of the bore rather than the length
of the barrel, which varied from 42 in. to 28 in. In the Tower Armouries
there is a bewildering variety of eighteenth century carbines and any
attempt to sort them out must be described as tentative. To begin
with, the cavalry arms can be distinguished by their side bars, some
with bayonets and others, usually with wood rammers, without.

In 1756, warrants were issued for the establishment of eleven troops
of Light Dragoons, and, on 14th April, "Regulations for the Cloathing,
Appointment, etc." of these troops gave this description of their
firearms: "a Carbine with ring and Bar Four Feet three Inches
long with a Bayonet of Seventeen Inshes in length, One Pistol of Ten
Inches in the Barrell, and of Carbine bore" (WO 26 /23). This can be
reasonably identified with the carbine, dated 1761 (Plate 19), which
has this overall length and a 36 in. barrel fitted for a bayonet. A
straight 9 in.-long side rib is fastened to the sideplate and a large

trumpet pipe has been fitted to the fore end of the stock to take the wooden rammer. Dated a year later, is a carbine (Plate 19), almost identical in design, which has no provision for a bayonet and whose wooden rammer is retained by two plain pipes; presumably the "carbine without Bayonet for Horse" of the 1757 list.

Carbines for artillery and highlanders are so often mentioned together in the gunmakers' orders as to suggest that one arm sufficed for both services. Yet there is no obvious candidate for this dual-purpose carbine. There is a carbine in the Tower with a 37 in. barrel engraved ROYAL ARTILLERY, but this is of a later date with a steel rammer. The first model artillery carbines evidently had wood rammers for, in 1772, the Board called in one of their best workmen to decide on the best method of converting them to the steel pattern (it was to cost 2s. 3d. per carbine).

There are several examples in the Tower of a carbine which is simply a lighter edition of the Short Land musket with a 42 in. barrel of carbine bore (Plate 15). The brass mounts differ slightly from the Brown Bess pattern, the tang of the buttplate being smaller, the trigger guard flatter and wider, and the escutcheon of a different shape. Three plain pipes retain the wooden rammer. The stocks being much lighter are also less sturdy, and the majority of the surviving specimens are damaged. All the locks are engraved with the names of the lock contractors (Grice, Edge, Galton, and Vernon & Haskins) and are dated from 1757–62. The finish of the carbines is poor and one hesitates to classify them either as highlander or artillery carbines. It is more likely that they are muskets made for light infantry or colonial corps. In October, 1780, for instance, 1,000 stand of "Light Musquets which carry a Ball of one Ounce with Bayonets" were sent to Antigua for the use of the local militia.

It will be noted that so far in this chapter nearly all the examples of firearms quoted have been dated and, allowing for the time taken in manufacture, the dates on the guns agree with the dates of the orders in the records. This was not always so and, as I have said earlier, small arm parts could lie in store for years before they were set up into complete weapons. On 29th June, 1764, the Clerk of the Small Gun Office reported to the Board:

"that in the late war many Gentlemen of the Army objected to such Guns as were sett up or repaired with Locks of a late date, which they imagined to be old Guns, though the same perhaps have never been in service, he therefore proposed that all new Locks (instead of the Makers Name and date of the Year) should be engraved with the word Tower only, and that all the Old Locks, now in the hands of Mr. Grice to be repaired should be altered in the same manner and likewise all the Small Arms which are sett up or repaired at the Small Gun Office."

This suggestion was carried into effect and the dating of gun locks was not revived until the beginning of the nineteenth century.

The next important date in the development of firearms occurs in 1768. For some time the opinion had been growing that the Long Land musket barrel was too long. In 1769, Maj.-Gen. John La Fausille, after making some experiments in which he had reduced musket barrels to 20 in. in length without effecting their range, wrote; "Judge then of the absurdity of their being so long in the barrel, which prevents our men from taking sure aim, but also, by their length in the stock which makes them so difficult and troublesome to be presented by the low-sized men we are obliged to take at present". ('The Charlton House Papers', *Sussex Archaeological Collections*, Vol. X (1858), p. 46). In 1765, muskets in store with 46 in. barrels, which had worn thin at the muzzle, were cut down to 42 in. Finally, at the beginning of 1768 Maj.-Gen. Hervey began a series of experiments on different kinds of musket barrels which ended on 11th June, with the issue of a Royal Warrant, on which the Ordnance made the following comments:

"that it having been represented that the Long Land Service Musquets now made use of by the several Regiments of Foot are too long and heavy and that Musqts of another Sort would be more convenient, a Pattern of which had been approved, and directing that for the future all the Musquets for the several Regiments of Foot be made agreeable to the said Pattern, vizt 3 Feet 6 Inches long in the barrel and weighing ten pounds and half at a Medium and that the numbers to be kept in Store be made up to 100,000 and that the said Number be esteemed the proper State to be kept in the Magazines; and further directing that none of the said New Pattern Arms be issued till after all those of the Pattern now in use have been delivered out of the Magazines."

Briefly it was an adoption of the Short Land musket as the standard weapon, and it continued as such until it was superseded by the New Land Series. It by no means meant the end of the Long Land or 46 in. barrel pattern of which both materials and complete arms were still in store. In February, 1773, rough stocks were made for over 3,000 Long Land musket barrels and, in July, 1775, the Board discovered that it still had some Long Land muskets with wood rammers which were hastily converted to steel. It was not until March, 1790 that Jonathan Hennem, working the Armoury Mills at Lewisham, was told to stop making Long Land musket barrels, as the Regiments of Foot were in future to be provided with Short Land muskets only.

However, the decision of June, 1768 soon had its effect and from September to November of the same year the return of barrels viewed by John Stewart at Birmingham refers exclusively to the new Short Land barrels (out of 14,928 barrels viewed, 3,452 were rejected). The new pattern muskets were set up in 1769, and two were sent to Gen. Hervey in Ireland as patterns for the arms to be made there. In April, there was another innovation: Sergeants of Grenadiers were ordered to carry fusils or carbines instead of halberts. Again it would appear 'that this new arm was made to a pattern presented by Gen.

Hervey and, on 12th March, 1770, the Commander-in-Chief issued the following orders:

> "The King has fixed on a particular Pattern for the Fuzils which are to be furnished in Great Britain for the Sgts of Grenadiers as also on a New Pattern for the Firelocks of the Infantry & Carbines of the Dragoons (excepting those of the Light Regts.) and orders are given to the Ordnance accordingly.
>
> H.M. has also ordered that the Arms which for the future may be made in Ireland are to be exactly conformable."

The use of the carbine spread steadily. On 31 July, 1770, an order was made for Officers of Fusilier Regts. to carry fusils (WO 3/25), and, in 1777, a warrant for arms to John Mackensie's Highland Regt. shows that sergeants of highland regiments were also carrying them (WO 55/371).

The Commander-in-Chief's order of 1770 refers also to a new pattern carbine for Heavy Dragoons. Up to then the Short Land musket with a wood rammer had been issued. The new carbine had the same barrel length of 42 in. but it was of carbine bore with a bayonet, a pattern originally made for the Horse Grenadier Guards (Plate 15). It is a delicate, beautifully made carbine with something of the quality of a fine sporting gun, although in dimensions it is identical with the light infantry carbine. The traditional pattern of furniture is incorporated, but on a smaller scale, and the side bar, instead of being straight, has its front end bent under the stock and fastened to the other side. A long fore pipe is fitted for the steel rammer.

The new measures had barely been introduced when the War of American Independence threw the military into confusion and drained the stores of weapons. Once more the Ordnance viewers went to the Low Countries and arms came pouring in from Liège, Rotterdam and Solingen, with the merchant firms of Thomas Fitzherbert and George Crawford acting as agents. As every conceivable form of firearm was brought into use, and many old patterns were converted, there was little time for experiment. However, many of the gunmakers were able to sell the Ordnance arms made for other customers, which included modifications which were later incorporated in the official pattern. John Pratt, the London gunmaker, provided two of these when, in 1777, his Short Land musket was approved. On this musket the second rammer pipe was bell-mouthed to help the path of the rammer, and a brass stop was let into the stock to prevent it from damaging the woodwork and getting stuck in wet weather. In the next year, James Hirst undertook to supply from 400 to 500 muskets a month of a pattern which the Master Furbisher reported only differed from the Land pattern in the shape of the long flat side-piece.

The arm which perhaps underwent most development was the cavalry carbine. Officers and men with practical experience of the guns began to take a hand in the design. Eliott's carbine was named after

Gen. George Augustus Eliott, commanding the crack 15th or King's Own Royal Light Dragoons. The carbine as first designed by him was probably that still in the Tower, which has "GEN. ELIOTT'S DRAGOONS" engraved on the 28 in. barrel and is the shortest of the whole series. Unfortunately some parts of it are missing and the side bar has been removed. It originally had provision for a sling, there being a special fitting moulded into the rear end of the trigger guard. The carbine is fully stocked, with a long trumpet pipe near the muzzle.

The later versions of this carbine, still with a 28 in. barrel, have been adapted for a bayonet and they have an ingenious rammer fitting. The rammer has a swell or bulge at the muzzle end, around which has been cut a groove or cannelure. Into this fits a notch which protrudes from the nose-cap, thus forming a simple but effective catch to hold the rammer in place (Plate 19). This model of the carbine was approved by the King in June 1773 and is often referred to as the carbine "with the catch to the nose cap". As usual, a pattern was sent to Gen. Hervey in Ireland and some appear to have been made there for the 21st Light Dragoons. There are several in existence bearing that regiment's markings on the barrel and DUBLIN CASTLE on the lock. An unusual feature of the Irish-made arm is that the barrel is held to the stock by slots and keys instead of the normal pin-and-loop method. In 1776, Eliott suggested that the nose-caps should be made of iron instead of brass, presumably because they were showing signs of wear, but this proposal was turned down on the advice of William King, the Master Furbisher.

Another general who gave his name to a carbine was Gen. William Harcourt, Colonel of the 16th Light Dragoons. As that regiment was also known as the Queen's Light Dragoons, Harcourt's carbine was presumably the one illustrated on page 123 (No. 1). Henry Nock supplied 500 of them, in 1794, at a cost of 50s. each. Special carbines with barrels of 3 ft. 1 in.—the only dimension given in the records—were also made for the Blues or Royal Horse Guards and were fitted with flat, better-quality locks. These were also fitted to the regiment's pistols, which were further distinguished by their masked butt-caps (Plate 18).

Little has been said of pistols so far because it is difficult to identify them from the records. As we progress into the last quarter of the eighteenth century the main difference is that the butt-caps lose their long side pieces. In the main, Heavy Dragoons carried a 12 in. barrel pistol and Light Dragoons the smallest pattern with a 9 in. barrel. In between were the 10 in. group originally intended for the Light Dragoons of 1756, but now given to some of the special mounted troops. Thus, in 1776, a new pattern pistol of carbine bore, with a 10 in. barrel and an overall length of 16 in. was introduced for the Horse Grenadier Guards. Their old pattern pistol with a 12 in. barrel of pistol bore is illustrated (Plate 18). The new design was stated to be the same as that of the Royal Foresters. The Life Guards' and Royal Horse Guards' pistols also had 10 in. barrels. The situation was summed up in a "Specification of Arms" issued by the Ordnance in April, 1794 (HO 50/371). This gives the dimensions and valuation of all the pistols as well as the other arms:

"	Barrel Length ft. in.	Bore	Valuation £ s. d.		
Short Land Musquet	3 6	Musquet	1	16	10½
Serjeants Carbine	3 3	Carbine	1	12	10
Heavy Dragoon & Life Guard Carbine	3 6	Carbine	1	13	5
Blues Carbine	3 1	Carbine	1	11	7¾
Light Dragoon Carbine	2 4	Carbine	1	18	10½
Heavy Dragoon Pistol	1 0	Carbine	1	17	10¾
Heavy Dragoon Pistol	1 0	Pistol	1	17	4¾
Life Guard Pistol	10	Carbine	2	0	11
Blues Pistol	10	Pistol	2	0	11¼
Light Dragoon Pistol	9	Carbine	1	15	8¾ "

The last arm in the list, the Light Dragoon pistol with a 9 in. barrel, was apparently introduced in 1759, when the success of the light troops of Dragoons led to the establishment of proper regiments of Light Dragoons. The first regiment to be raised was that of Colonel Eliott and it is more than likely that that enthusiastic officer, whose carbine has already been mentioned, was also responsible for the new light pistol. It was a simple weapon, with a flat side-plate, a butt cap without wings, a small lock and a wooden rammer with a heavy brass head, held in a single pipe. These characteristics were maintained in later models (see Plate 43), although the locks varied according to the reigning fashion. An even smaller pistol with a 7in. *brass* barrel, not mentioned in the above list, was designed in 1796 for Philip d'Auvergne, Prince of Bouillon*. A Captain of the Royal Navy, stationed in the Channel Islands, he was responsible for communications between the British Government and the French Royalists. Two hundred pairs of the pistols were made by Durs Egg and Henry Nock at 48s. per pair, but it is not clear whether they were intended for the Royalists (a list of arms sent to Bouillon for their use includes 200 pistols) or whether they were for Bouillon's small naval force (WO 6/1). Whatever their purpose, the Tower has a number of them showing little sign of use.

Brief mention can be made of two other carbines. The Cadets' carbine was made originally for the Artillery cadets at Woolwich, the corps being founded in 1744. Their arms were renewed in 1760 and 1773, but no indication of their size is given except that the bayonet length was not to exceed 9 in. Small though they must have been, they were not as small as the intriguing set of arms made by John Hirst, in 1773, for the Prince of Wales and Prince Frederick, described as "Small Fuzees with steel Rammers & Bayonets made very neat & in proportion to Musquets".

In 1781 the gunmaker John Waters took out a patent for guns with folding bayonets. It was a very old idea—Deschamps published his in

* See H. Kirke, *From the Gun Room to the Throne; being the life of Philip d'Auvergne, Duke of Bouillon*, 1904.

1718 (see *Machines et Inventions Approuvées par l'Académie Royale des Sciences*)
—but it seems to have led to a revival of interest in the gadgets and, in
1783, 100 carbines with a joint or folding bayonet were purchased for
the Norfolk Volunteers under Lord Townshend, at a cost of 75s. each.
The carbine must have been similar to that shown on Plate 17. Eight
carbines "with spring bayonets" were also issued for a secret mission
in September, 1794 (WO 46/24).

Finally, in our survey of the Brown Bess musket and its associated
weapons, we come to the oddest of them all—Burgoyne's musketoon.
The 23rd Light Dragoon Regt. was formed in 1781 with Sir John
Burgoyne as Colonel. The main armament was to consist of Elliott's
carbines, but Burgoyne asked for special pistols and 60 blunderbusses
or musketoons. The Ordnance refused to make a pistol to the pattern
he suggested, but rather surprisingly agreed to make 100 of the musketoons, estimated to cost £1 13s. 4d. each. The barrels were to be made
by Samuel Galton and the setting up was to be done by James Hirst
and Alex Davidson. The Bill Books refer to them as "Musquetoons with
oval noses" and I believe that the charming little blunderbuss in the
Tower (Class XII—284) is one of them (Plate 20). Its barrel is only
16 in. long and is belled out to an elliptical muzzle, 1 in. × 1½ in. It has
Elliott's swelled ramrod and nosecap catch, and a flat triangular
sideplate which had, at one time, a side bar attached.

Deane, in his *Manual of Firearms*, 1858, p. 54, wrote: "The Austrians,
in 1760, armed the front rank of their Cuirassiers with the so-called
trombones (blunderbusses), a somewhat short firearm, the barrel of
which increased considerably in width towards the muzzle, and threw
a charge of twelve bullets." An officer of Burgoyne's regiment referred
to the same country of origin in 1781: "Our swords are making at
Solingen—our Carbines & long Pistols in the Tower & a hundred of
these Austrian Blunderbusses with oval & horizontal muzzles, for the
flankers." (*Pembroke Papers*, London, 1950, p. 166.)

One other weapon merits inclusion in this chapter, a pistol which,
while having no affiliation in shape or style with the Brown Bess, was
closely associated with it. When the Highlander, either as an individual
or in company, was employed in the role of light infantryman or
skirmisher, he was suitably armed with a carbine or in some cases with
a rifle. But in 1757, two new Highland Battalions of Foot under
Colonels Archibald Montgomery and Simon Fraser received another
and more traditional weapon, the Scottish pistol. A warrant allowed
each battalion the following arms:

1,040	Muskets with wood rammers
1,080	Side pistols & straps
1,040	Cartouch boxes & straps
40	Halberts

(WO 55/412)

In May, 1757, the Board of Ordnance agreed to allow Montgomery
the Office price of pistols as he had provided them at his own expense.

A similar concession was granted Fraser and Lord John Murray in August, 1758. However, the Board began to be a little wary of these requests for money, and in 1761 demanded proof that the pistols had been provided before paying Col. Campbell of the 88th Regt. In 1762, they expressed the gravest of suspicions and told the agents of Col. Murray Keith that, although they had been granting the Colonels £1 15s. 7d. per pair, they had discovered that "the Pistols for the Scotch Regiments have been made at Birmingham and are of a very bad sort for which no more than 18s. per pair is paid at that place". They proposed, therefore, to issue them from the Tower. It is doubtful whether they did, in fact, endeavour to make the Scottish pistols for, in December, 1775, the agents for the 42nd or Royal Highland Regt. were obliged to ask for money in lieu of pistols, "as there are none in Store at the Tower fit for the service". The Ordnance Bill Books confirm that both Murray, commanding the 42nd, and John Campbell, with a newly raised regiment, were given an allowance of 16s. 6d. a pistol.

There are two known patterns of this Scottish military pistol. The first is based on the seventeenth century style pistol of all metal construction with a ramshorn or scroll type butt and a button trigger (Plate 21). The locks are signed BISSELL (Isaac Bissell of Birmingham) and the 8 in. barrel is usually engraved with the initials R.H.R. (Royal Highland Regt.). There is a 5 in. long belt hook. The other type is a plainer weapon of similar dimensions but with a gunmetal stock ending in a kidney-shaped grip. The barrels of this type normally bear the stamp of John Waters. It was to the second type of pistol that the Colonels of the 74th and 75th Regts. referred in April, 1788, when, asking for a supply of pistols, they inquired if they could be stocked in wood. The Master Furbisher, Ambrose Pardoe, gave his opinion that a wood stock would easily break, and quoted comparative prices per pair as: all-metal (it was called copper)—£1 2s.; Land Service pattern—£1 12s.; and Sea Service pattern—£1 5s. 7d. The matter was settled in rather curious fashion, the pistols being purchased at 10s. 6d. per pair from Mr. Drury, a silversmith, in the Strand.

This Scottish type of pistol was not held in any high esteem south of the Border and, when a certain John Murdoch applied for the job of gunsmith with the Ordnance in 1781, he was turned down on the grounds that he had only been used to making Highland pistols. In February, 1795, the Board were informed that the regiments were no longer wearing the pistols. The Sobieski Stuart Brothers wrote their epitaph:

> "The pistols, unlike the finely formed productions of Campbell, Murdoch, Christie, Mackay, MacNab and Stuart, which united in an eminent degree elegance and strength, were coarse pop-guns, resembling more the tin toys of a bazaar than the weapons of an army."
>
> (*Costume of the Clans*, Edinburgh, 1845, p. 125)

CHAPTER IV

EARLY RIFLES AND BREECHLOADERS

IN 1634, Arnold Rotsipen, working under official patronage in the Minories, obtained Letters Patent which included an invention "to rifle, cutt out, or screwe barrells as wyde or as close or as deepe or as shallowe as shalbe required, and with greate ease". All this he covenanted to teach to an English apprentice. However, no great interest was shown by Englishmen in rifles, and no attempt appears to have been made to introduce them into the British service until the middle of the eighteenth century.

They are first mentioned in "An Abstract of Small Arms in Store at the Tower" for the year ending 31st December, 1750, which appears in the Ordnance Minute Books on 8th January, 1751. This includes "60 Bullet Guns", and a later account refers to them as "rifled bullet guns of sorts". The latter description suggests that they were of different kinds, probably foreign-made arms brought back from the Continent. At least I can find no record of them being made in this country.

Shortly after this the French and Indian wars commenced, and, in 1754, Sir John St. Clair, Quarter Master General of the expedition about to embark for America, applied to the Ordnance for a "Dozen of Rifled Barrel Carbines". These were issued from the stock in the Tower together with moulds, four barrels of powder, half a hundred-weight of lead, and six dozen signal rockets. Three sets of armour, Cromwellian backs and breast plates with helmets, were also sent for "the Engineers, who in that Woody Country may be obliged to reconoiter within Musquet Shot".

The experiences of the British troops in the fighting which followed led to the introduction of light infantry, rangers and skirmishers, who were mainly armed with carbines and light muskets. Until these arms, ordered by the Ordnance in 1756, became available, the army seems to have made use of local supplies, mainly of French make. When these were withdrawn by Gen. Amherst in 1759, they were replaced by carbines without bayonets. Regiments concerned were the Royal Highlanders, the Royal Americans, the Light Armed Foot, and the light infantry companies of the Royals, the Inniskillings and Abercrombie's and Murray's regiments (WO 34/70).

While there is no evidence to suggest that there was any large-scale issue of rifles to regular troops, many of the provincial or colonial regiments carried them. The papers of Col. Henry Bouquet of the Royal American Regiment contain many references to them. In June, 1758, he wrote to Gen. Forbes:

"A large part of the provincials are armed with grooved rifles and have their molds. Lead in bars will suit them better than bullets—likewise the Indians—but they also need fine powder FF.

I have noticed a great inconvenience in the use of cartridges for them. They do not know how to make cartridges or rather they take too much time. In the woods they seldom have time or places suitable to make them. These cartridge boxes hold only 9 charges, some 12, which is not sufficient. I think that their powder horns and pouches for carrying bullets would be much more useful, keeping the cartridge box however, to use in case of a sudden or night attack. The difficulty is in providing them. I do not know if that is possible at Philadelphia. Col. Washington undertook to collect as many as he could for the Virginians and to make sacks of Raven duck for the bullets instead of leather."   (ADD 21652)

Forbes gave every encouragement to Bouquet and in the same month signified his approval to what was, after all, a startling innovation for the British Army: "I have been long in your Opinion of equiping Numbers of our men like the Savages and I fancy Col. Byrd of Virginia has most of his best people equipt in that manner. . . ." (ADD 21640). It was probably for such a detachment of bush fighters that Bouquet indented for 16 rifles from the Ordnance Store in New York in May, 1758 (Fig. 10). Francis Stephens who signed this indenture was the Ordnance Storekeeper and Paymaster in New York. He made a return of the small arms under his charge in April, 1762, but it contains no mention of rifles (WO 34/70).

The backwoods must have been the scene of many a strange encounter between Indians and British and American troops dressed like them. As a means of identification the soldiers were advised to wear "a yellow band around the forehead and a stream-like band of the same colour around the arm". Some of the Indian tribes were friendly and, in May, 1756, 700 Indian Guns, 20 cwt. of bullets and 20 cwt. of lead in bars were shipped to Lord Loudoun as a present to the Indians in the British interest. The gun was the Indian's most precious possession and in 1759, a treaty with some of the Indian tribes ratified the following rates of exchange,

1 gun	16 Deerskins
1 measure or pound of gunpowder	1 Deerskin
30 bullets	1 Deerskin
10 flints	1 Deerskin

(WO 34/40)

The conclusion of the war left the military strangely apathetic towards rifles and, in January, 1764, 35 "rifled bullet guns" of different patterns in the Tower were sold off by auction. With the commencement of the American War of Independence, however, a different outlook prevailed. The American backwoodsmen now turned their long rifles against the British soldiers who had not long previously come to their rescue. With local supplies restricted by the activities of the rebels, the military appealed to the Ordnance in London. Their reaction was

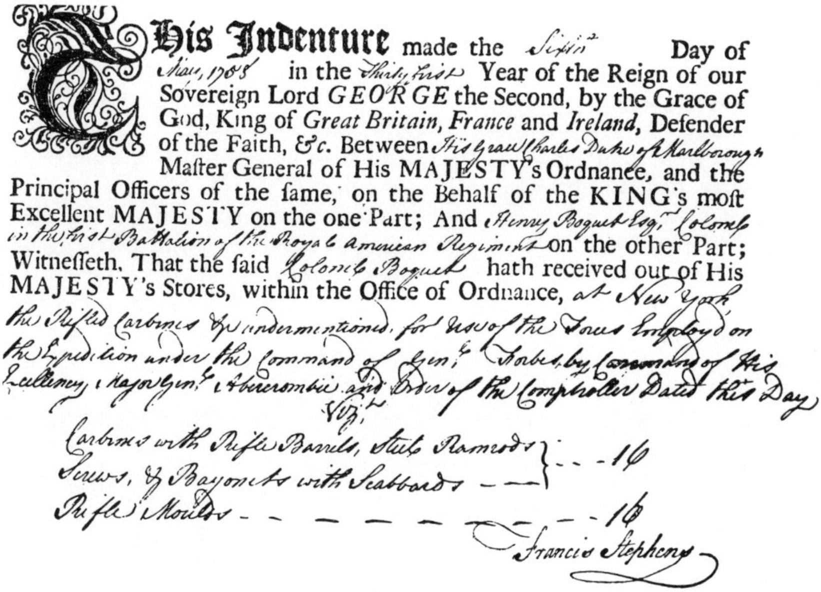
This Indenture made the Sixth Day of May, 1758 in the Thirty first Year of the Reign of our Sovereign Lord GEORGE the Second, by the Grace of God, King of *Great Britain, France* and *Ireland,* Defender of the Faith, &c. Between His Grace Charles Duke of Marlborough Maſter General of His MAJESTY's Ordnance, and the Principal Officers of the ſame, on the Behalf of the KING's moſt Excellent MAJESTY on the one Part; And Henry Boquet Esqr. Colonel in the first Battalion of the Royal American Regiment on the other Part; Witneſſeth, That the ſaid Colonel Boquet hath received out of His MAJESTY's Stores, within the Office of Ordnance, at New York the Rifled Carbines &c. undermentioned, for use of the Forces Employed on the Expedition under the Command of Genl. Forbes, by Command of His Excellency Major Genl. Abercrombie and Order of the Comptroller Dated this Day Viz.

Carbines with Rifle Barrels, Steel Ramrods Screws, & Bayonets with Scabbards ... 16

Rifle Moulds ... 16

Francis Stephens

FIG. 10.—The original indenture issuing sixteen rifles to Col. Bouquet from the Ordnance store at New York in 1758. Add. MS. 21640. British Museum.

to seek supplies in Germany. A few German rifles were purchased and given preliminary trials. On 13th October, 1775, the London newspaper *The Craftsman* reported:

> "Yesterday Morning some of the parties of the Guards, who had been learning the exercise of bush fighting, had a sham attack on Kensington Gravel Pits, which their officers called Bunkers Hill; some of the soldiers were called riflemen and had a target fixed to exercise their dexterity at, but alas! there was not one hole in it. However, they made the thistles fly that surrounded it and peppered the gravel pits with a vengeance."

At the end of the year, Viscount Townshend, the Master General, expressed himself satisfied with the experiments and asked Lord George Germaine, the Secretary of State, to obtain the King's permission for the purchase of 1,000 German rifles. As a justification of this number he pointed out that:

> "the Highlanders who have many Marksmen and Deer Killers amongst them are particularly desirous of having 5 of those pieces per Company. I am persuaded they would be of great use in America. Colonel Harcourt desires also the same proportion and I would submit whether every Battalion engaged in the Service should be provided with this much boasted weapon of that Country."

With the situation growing desperate—the American riflemen were wreaking havoc with the British troops—he did not wait for the Royal reply and, in January, 1776, sent a preliminary order for 200 rifles to Col. Faucitt the British agent at Hanover, instructing him to ensure that none were made of cast iron, and also to obtain a sample of the gunpowder commonly used for the rifles (WO 46/10).

Having placed orders for 200 rifles where he could expect a quick delivery, Townshend then opened negotiations with the Birmingham trade for the remaining 800. A rifle was sent to William Grice, the gunmaker, so that he could make an official pattern. After this had been approved, the Ordnance Viewer, John York, placed orders for 200 rifles each with Grice, Benjamin Willetts, Mathias Barker and Galton & Sons, the price being agreed at three guineas per rifle.

One is tempted to identify the pattern rifle with the rifle in the Tower (Plate 26). With a heavy octagonal barrel, squared buttplate and sliding wooden patch box lid, it has been copied closely from a German model. The lock is signed by Grice and the barrel is stamped with William Grice's mark, a Crown over WG. Both Ordnance proof marks and the V and P marks of some private proof house in Birmingham appear on the barrel, which is 36 in. long and rifled with eight grooves. The trigger guard of this rifle is a reconstruction.*

The rifles were soon in production and William Clachar, Editor of the *Chelmsford Chronicle*, on a visit to Birmingham wrote this account in his diary:

> "The Gun manufactory is pretty; the forging, scraping and boreing pleas'd me much. The Rifle Guns are handsome pretty pieces, 800 are nearly finish'd on government account at three pounds three shillings each. A Gentleman, with one of them at a distance of 150 yards shot a Ball 6 times out of 8 within the circumference of the crown of my hat; at 400 yards he shot within half a yard of the mark".
> (JAHR, Vol. XVII, p. 234)

The Guards, too, were still busy practising and their aim had improved so that the *Scots Magazine* could report on 3rd February that some of them shooting in Hyde Park were able to hit a small target at 300 yards.

It was these tales of markmanship that caught the imagination of the sporting British public and became the talk of the London coffee houses and clubs. The feats of the American riflemen were described

---

* Specimens of these muzzle-loading rifles, identified by makers' and government marks, have been found in North American collections. They have Short Land pattern furniture, no butt box, and barrels with swivel rammers similar to the rifle on Pl. 33 (1).

in detail in the press, and open admiration was shown towards riflemen taken prisoner. However, if the civilians were enjoying the new topic of conversation, Townshend was finding the subject a wearisome one. Howe, in America, was clamouring for rifles and light three-pounder artillery. Col. Faucitt had written to say that it was essential for a finer sort of powder to be produced for the rifles. Orders were given to the Royal Laboratory to arrange for the latter and pressure was brought to bear on the gunmakers. Eventually Grice reported that he had finished a hundred rifles and from Stade (Lower Saxony) came the news that a similar number of German rifles had passed a proof of double loading, and awaited shipment. But with the manufacture of the muzzleloading rifles proceeding smoothly at last, there was a sudden change of plan.

On 27th April, 1776, the *Scots Magazine* reported that Townshend and some other officers had attended the trial of a rifle invented by Capt. Ferguson of the 70th Regt. Its performance was first compared with the common musket and then a larger audience was invited down to the wind-swept marshes of Woolwich to witness what, considering the conditions, must surely rank as one of the greatest feats in the annals of shooting. On 1st June, 1776, the following account was published in the *Annual Register*, the *Gentleman's Magazine* and most of the London newspapers:

> "Some experiments were tried at Woolwich before Lord Viscount Townshend, Lord Amherst, Generals Harvey and Desagulier and a number of other officers with a rifle gun upon a new construction, by Capt. Ferguson of the 70th Regt.; when that gentleman under the disadvantages of a heavy rain and a high wind performed the following four things, none of which had ever before been accomplished with any other small arms. 1. He fired during 4 or 5 minutes at a target, at 200 yards distance at the rate of 4 shots each minute. 2. He fired six shots in one minute. 3. He fired four times per minute advancing at the same time at the rate of 4 miles in the hour. 4. He poured a bottle of water into the pan and the barrel of the piece when loaded so as to wet every grain of the powder and in less than half a minute fired with her as well as ever without extracting the ball. He also hit the bulls-eye at 100 yds, lying with his back on the ground and notwithstanding the unequalness of the wind and wetness of the weather, he only missed the target three times during the course of the experiments."

The effect was immediate. On 24th June, the Master General decided that no more muzzleloading rifles should be made, "as a new construction of Capt. Fergusons is approved and who is authorized by his Lordship to give directions to the Workmen which must be implicitly followed".

Ferguson, born in 1744, was the second son of an Aberdeenshire laird, James Ferguson of Pitfour, and first saw service as a fourteen-year-old Cornet in the Scots Greys in Germany. Never of robust health, he was invalided home from 1762–68. He then joined the 70th Regt. in the West Indies but he was again stricken by illness and returned home in 1774. It was probably then that he began designing his famous breechloading rifle. Before considering the action of this rifle, a few words on the history of breechloading rifles are necessary.

The rifle never achieved the popularity in Britain that it did on the continent, where suitable game was still plentiful in the eighteenth century. Only in Scotland was there an opportunity for its proper use. Few sportsmen, therefore, were versed in the art of correctly loading a rifled barrel with tight fitting wad and ball, and a curious result of this was that many of the rifles that were made in this country had some form of breech action which could be easily loaded with loose ball and powder. Benjamin Robins, writing "Of the nature and advantages of Rifled Barrel Pieces" in *Transactions of the Royal Society*, 1747, remarked on this:

> ". . . the rifled barrels which have been made in England (for I remember not to have seen it in any foreign piece) are contrived to be charged at the breech, where the piece is for this purpose made larger than in any other part. And the powder and bullet are put through the side of the barrel by an opening which when the piece is loaded, is filled up with a screw."

The idea of loading a gun by the breech instead of at the muzzle can be traced back to the early days of firearms and there were many ingenious mechanisms devised for this purpose. The employment of a screwed plug was popular; it could be inserted on top, at the side, or underneath the barrel. The latter arrangement was most convenient, as the plug could be connected to the trigger guard which acted as a lever. But it had two disadvantages: the gun had to be turned upside down for loading; and the task of unscrewing the plug and returning it to its correct position could not be performed in a hurry. The solution to this was to run the plug vertically through the barrel so that, on the trigger guard being turned, the plug descended, leaving a loading aperture on top. Into this could be dropped first a loose ball and then a charge of powder. The screw plug became, in effect, a breech plug and many of the early examples suffered from the lack of necessary strength to withstand the charge.

One of the first gunmakers to employ this idea was Daniel Lagatz of Danzig, but his plug was primarily a safety device cutting off the barrel from a complicated magazine breech action. He was followed by the French engineer Isaac de la Chaumette who, between 1700–18, invented improvements for guns, bayonets and powder flasks, which were published in *Machines et Inventions Approuvées par l'Académie Royale des Sciences*, Paris, 1735. In 1704, he produced his "Fusil qui se charge par la culasse" (Fig. 11), which Ferguson was to reproduce over seventy years later with but minor improvements.

La Chaumette came to London as a Protestant refugee in 1721 and lost no time in obtaining a Patent (No. 434) to cover "Divers Engines,

10. Evolution of the flat lock. *Top:* Dog-lock of George I dated 1715.
Middle: Dog-lock of 1710 converted by removing the dog and filing the
notch off the cock. *Bottom:* Musket dated 1720 (a sealed pattern).

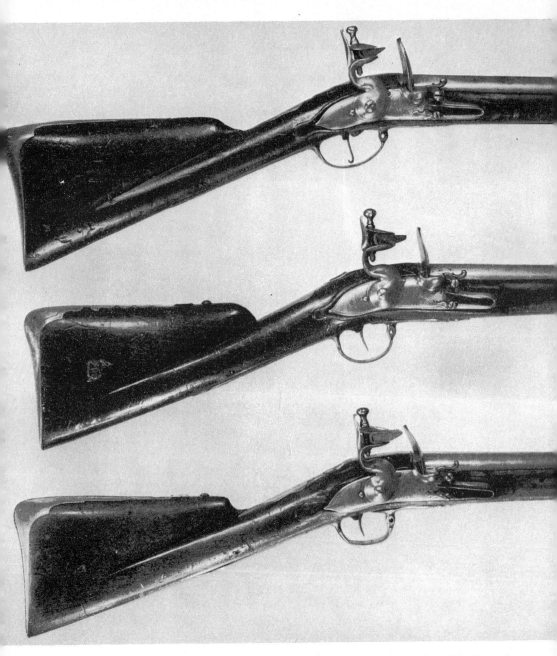

11. The early Brown Bess. *Top:* Iron-mounted musket dated 1718. *Middle:* Sealed-pattern musket with iron mounts by Wooldridge dated 1722. *Bottom:* Brass-mounted musket dated 1728.

Page 74

12. With knobs on! *Top:* Musket by Joseph Clarkson marked KANE A No. 1. *Middle and Bottom:* Two Dutch-made muskets bearing the cypher of George I. All with curious swellings on the butt.

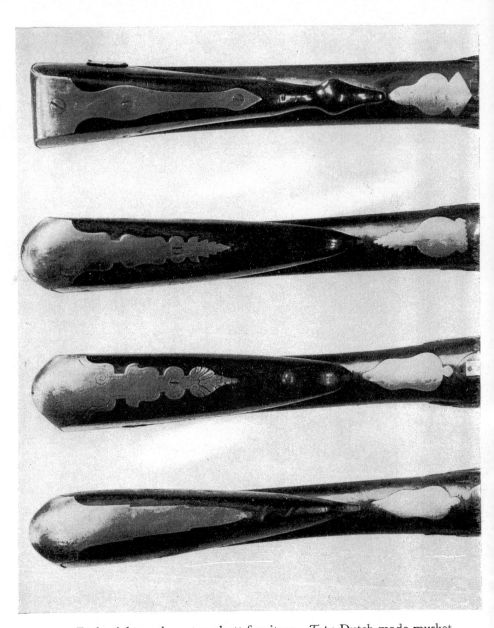

13. Early eighteenth-century butt furniture. *Top:* Dutch-made musket.
(2) Musket made by James Freeman for Royal Welsh Fusiliers. (3) Wooldridge's musket of 1722. (4) Iron-mounted Brown Bess of 1718.

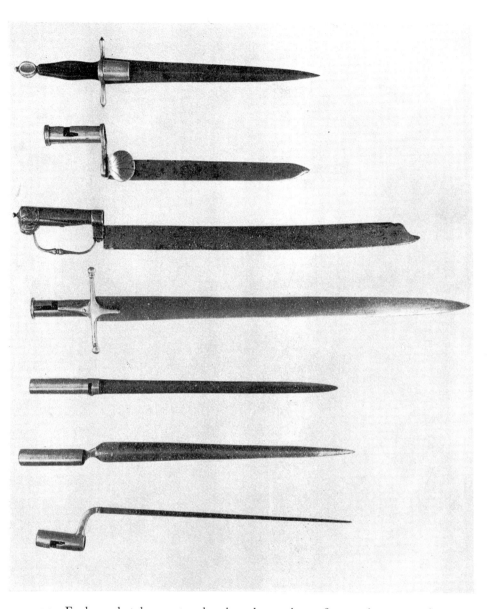

14. Early socket bayonets; showing the variety of types in use at the beginning of the eighteenth century. The top one, looking like a plug bayonet, from the *Collection of J. F. R. Winsbury, Esq.*, has a brass socket at the side.

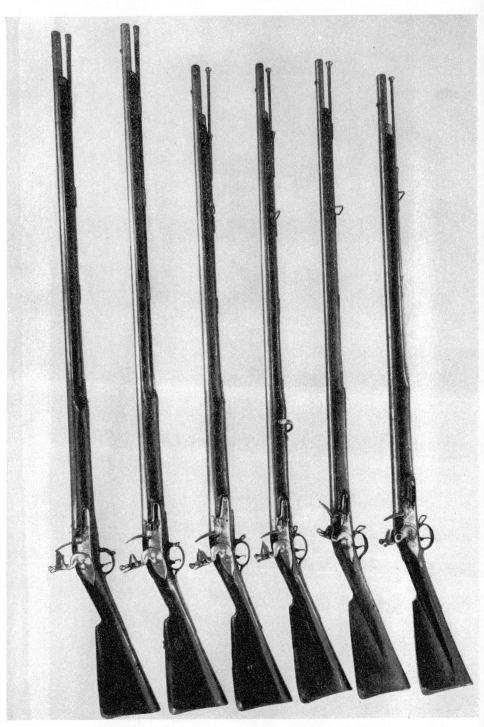

15. Land Pattern arms. *Left to right:* (1) Long Land musket dated 1731 (46 in. barrel). (2) Sealed pattern Long Land musket of 1746 (46 in. barrel). (3) Short Land musket dated 1762 marked MILITIA NEW PATTERN (42 in. barrel). (4) Heavy Dragoon carbine (42 in. barrel). (5) Light Infantry carbine dated 1759 (42 in. barrel). (6) India Pattern musket (39 in. barrel).

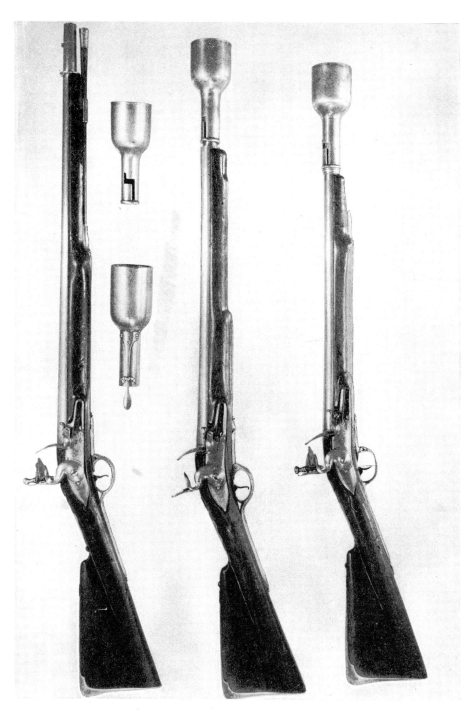

16. Grenade guns. *Left to right:* (1) Dated 1740 and marked ROYAL
ARTILLERY. The larger cup underneath has a clip fitting and belongs
to a gun made by Wooldridge in 1739. All the others have bayonet-type
slot fitting. (2) Dated 1747. (3) Dated 1728. The last two guns have
special counter-balanced sights built into the side plates.

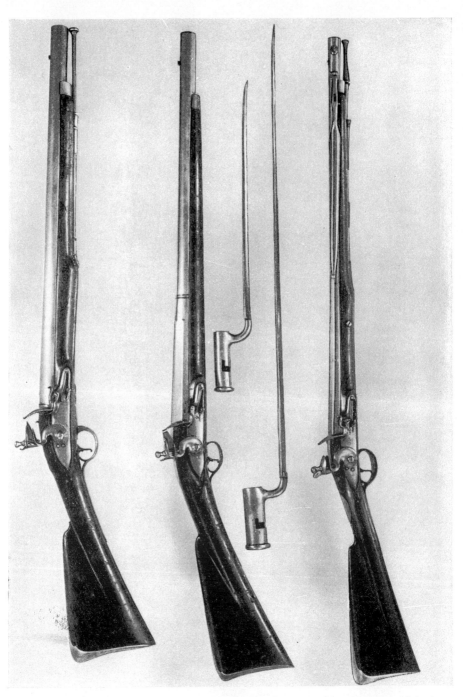

17. *Left to right:* Large-bore carbine by John Probin, *c.* 1780. (2) A similar carbine with its long bayonet compared with the normal size, *c.* 1750. (3) The 28 in. barrel carbine with folding bayonet, *c.* 1780.

Machines and Instruments". Then, on 27th October, the following advertisement appeared in the *Daily Courant*:

"Whereas His Majesty has been graciously pleased to grant his Royal Letters patent date the 12th August last, to Mr. de la Chaumette, Ingenier etc. for several useful and curious Inventions and among the rest for a new kind of Weapon and for all sorts of Guns and Firearms which fire at least five times quicker than the Arms now in use.

A publick Tryal of the said Firearms is to be made at the Artillery Ground in Bunhill Fields on Thursday the 2nd. November next, between 10 & 11 in the Forenoon; and any Person desiring to be furnished with such Guns and Arms may enquire at White's Chocolate House, St. James's Str."

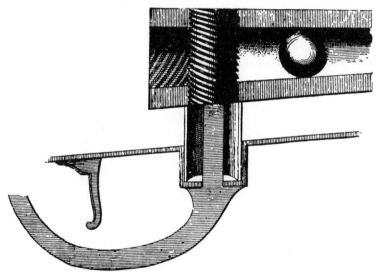

Fig. 11.—La Chaumette's breech action. From the illustration in *Machines et Inventions Approuvées par l'Académie Royale des Sciences.*

Although no account of the trial was published, its success was sufficient to disturb the members of the Gunmakers' Company. A special meeting of the Court of Assistants of the Company was called on 5th December, 1723, when it was learnt that "some Person or Persons had obtayned a Patent for the sole makeing of a new invented handgun of which a considerable Quantitye had been made and more bespoke to the great prejudice of the Trade". The Company tried to contest the legal powers of the patent and went so far as to refuse to prove the guns, thus rendering them liable to seizure. However, some of the members were obviously implicated in the enterprise and under their pressure the matter was dropped (GMB).

The foremost maker of la Chaumette's guns was his compatriot,

E

Bidet, whose name appears in the Gunmakers' Proof Ledger from 1721–31. Several examples of his breechloading guns exist, the finest being that made for George I, now in the collection of H.R.H. the Duke of Brunswick.*Apart from its handsome decoration of chiselled steelwork and silver inlay, the gun is notable for two improvements introduced by Bidet. A quick thread on the plug enables the breech to be opened with one turn of the guard, and a movable stop prevents it from being overturned and extracted in error.

Historians will, however, most appreciate the inscription on the barrel which reads:

> "*Carabine Nouvelle*
> *La Chaumette a produit ce foudroyant tonnerre*
> *De touts ses protecteurs on benira le sort*
> *Puis que c'est le moyen de terminer la guerre*
> *Et d'etablir des siecles d'or.*"
> New. Carbine
> La Chaumette has made this terrible gun
> All its patrons will be blessed.
> For it is the means of ending war
> And establishing the Golden Age.

The Board of Ordnance remained unimpressed by this prophecy and I have found no evidence that they gave the new gun any trial. The idea of fast loading had, however, an obvious appeal to the military, and Marshal Saxe gave this type of action considerable publicity when he advocated its use in carbines—"je veux que tous mes soldats aient des fusils avec un dez à secret"—and in a wall piece named the Amusette. (*Mes Rêveries*, Amsterdam, 1757.) It is doubtful whether any were actually made for the French Army, and the historian Carlyle dismissed the book as "a strange military farrago, dictated as I should think under opium. . . ." Nevertheless the action was frequently used on sporting guns and, in 1761, the *Annual Register* reported the trial of an Amusette in Dublin, firing a half-pound ball to a range of 800 yards.

By Ferguson's time, then, the action was well known, but, to use Townshend's own words, was "thought liable to clog and when out of order is very difficult to be mended or replaced in the hurry of service". As we have seen, Ferguson successfully demonstrated that he had overcome these defects. An order for one hundred of his rifles was given to the same four gunmakers already employed on the muzzleloaders, and Ferguson journeyed to Birmingham to supervise their manufacture with William King, the Master Furbisher, who undertook to prove them.

The rifles, breechloading and muzzleloading, are usually entered together in the gunmakers' bills as:

"Rifled guns with plugs and bayonets   £4 o o
           without   do   £3 3 o"

* This royal gun is now in the Royal Armouries, HM Tower of London (No. XII.5685).

From the Ordnance Bill Books in which they appear I have compiled the following production figures:

	Muzzleloaders	*Fergusons*
William Grice	200	25
Benjamin Willetts	192	25
Mathias Barker	78	25
Galton & Son	200	25
	670*	100

The Bill Books also include payments to John Wilkinson, the Master Armourer, for bullet moulds for the rifles at a shilling each. The number of Ferguson rifles made is confirmed by the bill of William Sharp for the following engraving work:

"Numbered only Rifled Guns thrice numbered 100 @ 3d. — £1   5   0
  „   „   Belt Plates for rifled men   200 @ 1d. —   16   8
  „   „   Bullet Moulds   12 @ 1d. —   1   0"

By September, 1776, the rifles must have been finished for on 1st October the vigilant reporter of the *Scots Magazine* noted that Ferguson was at Windsor Castle, with some men from Lord George Lennox's Regiment, demonstrating his rifle before the Royal Family. On this occasion Ferguson is reported to have told the King that he could fire seven shots a minute, adding pleasantly "that he would not undertake in that time to knock down above five of his Majesty's enemies".

On 22nd November, Ferguson applied to the Ordnance for permission to take out a patent on the grounds that it would be "the only means of Securing for the service of Government the few hands who by four months Constant attention have with difficulty been brought to make Arms upon that Construction and prevent these Arms from falling into bad hands". Official approval was granted, his Patent (No. 1139) passed the Great Seal on 2nd December, 1776, and was finally enrolled the following 29th March.

It is to Ferguson's credit that he admitted that his screw plug action had been tried before, but emphasized that it had failed for want of several improvements. The main purpose of his patent, while including several other breech actions and a special four groove rifling and an adjustable rearsight, was to safeguard these improvements.

"The improvements are First, a projection of the barrel towards the guard to receive the screw plug long enough to allow the plug to descend sufficiently low occasionally to be cleaned after much firing without coming entirely out of the grooves, by which means the difficulty, loss of time and embarrassment of hitting the proper grooves (in occasions of hurry and danger) to re-enter the plug is avoided.
Secondly that part of the screw plug which forms the breech of the

* Additional research has revealed that Willetts and Barker did eventually deliver all their rifles.

barrel is made smooth and hollow by which means it neither retains so much of the smoak or foulness, nor in going round does it lodge it into the female screw so as to clog it and impede the motion of the plug.

Thirdly there are various channels cut across the outside of the screws of the plug in such directions as not to communicate and occasion any part of the charge to blow out at the same time that they are contrived to go along the whole surface almost of the female screw in mounting and descending, thereby loosening and receiving any foulness that may have lodged.

Fourthly, there is a hollow or reservoir behind the screw plug at the breech of the barrel into which the smoak which had forced its way through the grooves is thrown, when the plug turns round so as to clear the grooves or female screw from being clogged by the foulness that might otherwise lodge in them."

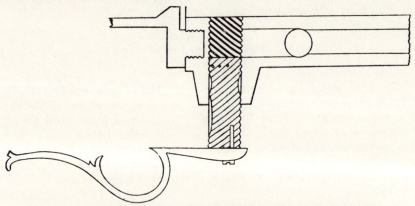

Fig. 12.—One of the drawings from Ferguson's Patent (printed specification), showing his screw-plug breech. Note that the chamber and ball have a larger diameter than the barrel.

With the completion of the rifles, the matter passed out of the hands of the Ordnance and the Secretary for War, Viscount Barrington, took control. First he directed the Officer Commanding Chatham Barracks to form a detachment of one hundred men and N.C.O.s, mainly from the recruits of the 6th and 14th Regiments. On 6th March, 1777, Ferguson was placed in command, issued with a supply of powder and carbine balls, and began an intensive course of training. His Commanding Officer (Lt.-Gen. Trapand of the 70th Regt.) was notified that "Capt. Ferguson is to return to the Regt. at the end of the Campaign unless Sir Wm. Howe should have a further occasion for his services". Finally, Gen. Howe in America was notified of the impending arrival of a Corps of Riflemen bringing with them a supply of green cloth for uniforms (WO 4/99, 4/273).

At the end of March, Ferguson was at Portsmouth waiting the sailing of transport, and his arrival in America was not reported until 24th May by Howe, who added: "from the Experience of so intelligent an Officer

I am hopeful this Corps may be essentially serviceable". He attached the Riflemen to the column under Gen. Knyphausen in the attack on Brandywine Hill on 11th September. As the long column moved into battle with its train of artillery, it was guarded on the flanks by the 71st Highlanders, whilst in the van were Ferguson's Riflemen and the Queen's Rangers under Major Wemys. They fought several actions with superior forces of American riflemen and played a major part in the success of the battle. In doing so they suffered heavy casualties and Ferguson was wounded in the arm. Knyphausen sent a commendation to Howe, who in view of Ferguson's incapacitation decided to disband the Riflemen and incorporate them in the light companies of their old regiments. At the same time he assured Ferguson that he would "adopt any plan that can be effected to put you in a situation of remaining with the army under his command".

It was a bitter blow for Ferguson, but his sturdy spirit prevailed and his arm was saved from amputation, although he was never to recover its full use. His subsequent service was short and tragic, and it is only necessary here to sketch it briefly. In the autumn of 1778, he commanded a combined naval and military force in a successful and savage attack on Little Egg Harbour. In 1779, he formed a small corps of loyalists known as the American Volunteers. They sailed for New York with the expedition under Sir Henry Clinton and assisted in the siege and capture of Charleston. Although disabled, Ferguson was a remarkably active officer, leading his men in many daring raids and sometimes, on his own, reconnoitring enemy territory or engaging in field fortification. In 1780, then a Major, he was appointed Inspector General of Militia in Georgia and Carolina with the acting rank of Lieutenant-Colonel. It was at the command of the first battalion of this militia that he was finally defeated and killed at the Battle of King's Mountain on 7th October, 1780.

While it is thus easy to trace his movements, the fate of his rifles remains a mystery. Some writers have suggested that the American Volunteers were armed with them but there is no evidence to support this. Examination of existing specimens of the rifle only adds to the confusion. It is true that many of these are sporting weapons but it is strange that all the military examples differ in dimensions and other features. Probably the only one that can be reasonably identified as one of the original hundred is the rifle now in the Morristown National Park Museum. This has an overall length of 49 in. and a 34 in. barrel of ·68 in. cal., rifled with eight grooves. Ferguson does not seem to have adopted his patent four-groove rifling for any of his rifles. The lock is engraved with the Royal cypher and Tower, and the barrel is stamped with the Ordnance proof marks and the initials MB and IW, probably the marks of Mathias or Matthew Barker, and his partner John Whately. Just behind the brass plug, on the barrel, is stamped a mark of a Crown over PF, which may well be Ferguson's own mark struck when he was supervising the manufacture. The tang is numbered 2.

A revolving sling swivel is inserted where the sideplate should be, the other swivel being in the normal position near the muzzle. The stock is cut away for a bayonet, the stud being placed underneath the end of the barrel.

Another rifle of similar design is the specimen in the Smithsonian Institution, Washington, which by tradition is the rifle given by Ferguson to Anthony de Peyster, his second-in-command. This is complete with the original bayonet having a blade 25 in. long and 1½ in. wide. It has an overall length of 50 in. and a barrel of 33 in. with eight grooves, like the first example, but the bore is said to be of ·60 in. cal. Both barrel and lock are engraved with official marks and the name of the maker D. Egg. Although Egg was not one of the four original contractors, he was responsible for the rifle used by Ferguson in the first trials and another one made as a pattern for the Tower, both being paid for by the Ordnance. He also made the silver mounted rifles used by Ferguson personally, now in the collection of W. Keith Neal, Esq., and the truly magnificent rifle in the Windsor Castle Collection, (Laking Cat. No. 420) which was made for the Prince Regent.

Most of the Ferguson rifles which bear a gunmaker's name are of too fine a quality to suggest their issue to the ordinary rank and file. The carbine in the McMurray Collection is a good example. Of very similar appearance to the Morristown rifle, the barrel has been reduced to 28 in. and the overall length to 44 in. Although the lock is engraved with the Crown and Royal Cypher, the barrel has been proved at the Gunmakers' Company Proof House and is marked HUNT 17. Five-groove rifling has been employed in this barrel. The lock is also signed HUNT on the tail behind the cock. This presumably refers to Joseph Hunt, the London gunmaker, who was not employed by the Ordnance until the end of 1777. The mounts and the plug are made of white metal and there is an adjustable backsight on the lines of the patent—refinements which suggest that the rifle was made for a Volunteer Company. Both this carbine and another in the Keith Neal collection—marked HUNT 14—have stamped on the barrel behind the plug the letters FERGUS, perhaps some requirement of the patent (Plate 25).

Like most of the Government's new weapons, the Ferguson rifle was also taken into the service of the East India Company. In my own collection is a fully stocked Ferguson rifle made by Henry Nock and dated 1776 on lock and barrel. It is also marked with the insignia of the Company. The relevant records of the Company having been destroyed, one can only guess for what purpose it was made, but the absence of a bayonet suggests that it was an experimental issue to cavalry. The butt is marked with the serial number 15. The barrel is 29 in. long, of ·60 in. cal. and is rifled with eight grooves. The plug is made of brass with engraved ornamentation on top. An interesting refinement to the lock is a brass insert on the steel or hammer spring apparently intended to give the steel a smoother action (Plate 24).

The reader may well ask why, if the Ferguson rifle performed so well

---

* This rifle is now in a private collection in the USA.

in its trials and in battle, no more were made or that the issue was not extended to other units. There were two main reasons. First there was an inherent weakness in the stock, which had to be cut away to take the plug housing at the very place where it was already narrow and liable to fracture; the result can be seen in some of the existing specimens which are cracked across the stock between the lock and the trigger guard. Secondly the operation of the rifle required some skill and the standard cartridge could not be used.

When the Duke of Richmond became Master General, therefore, he engaged Durs Egg to prepare two carbines with a breechloading action in which a cartridge could be used. Egg was paid £31 10s. for these in 1784, one carbine being kept in the Ordnance Office and the other presented to the King. The latter may be the carbine in the Windsor Collection (No. 255) which has silver mounts dated 1784. The Ordnance Bill refers to them as "Two new invented Carbines to load at the breech with long spear Bayonets etc., and two new Breech frames etc. as the first made ones broke in proving the second time".

These carbines were examined by Boards of General Officers in July, 1784 and January, 1785, who recommended that a number of them should be sent to four regiments of Light Dragoons for experiment. In February, 1785, Egg, who had also been engaged on a rifled cannon at Woolwich, was given an order for thirty carbines, ten with barrels of 2 ft. 4 in., ten of 2 ft. 9 in. and ten of 3 ft. 2 in. These were "to load at the Breech, to have long Bayonets, the barrels to be bronzed and the Locks to be of Hennems Construction. Half of each Length to be rifled and the other half to be unrifled" (Plate 23). The prices ranged from £4 to £4 14s. according to the length of the barrels and whether they were rifled. For the first five made, which included one with a 2 ft. 6 in. barrel, he received £15 15s. each. In the same bill was a carbine of ordinary design, but "with a long Bayonet to fix both ways". Before considering these carbines, we must review Hennem's part in the undertaking.

Jonathan Hennem was an arms contractor who held the lease of the Armoury Mills, Lewisham. In 1784, he produced a flintlock of conventional appearance but which was a clever example of a screwless lock (Fig. 13). The springs and moving parts were held to the lockplate by means of clips and spigots instead of screws, and could be easily removed by a "spring lifter" tool. The 20th Regt. was armed with muskets fitted with these locks and the inventor accompanied the regiment to Ireland to train the soldiers in their use. They appear to have answered their purpose and Hennem was granted an award of £100 together with his expenses. He was also given the main contract for the locks. The idea of dispensing with screws was carried still further when Hennem produced a musket with his lock held to the stock by an ingenious catch (Tower Armouries XII–104).

The Egg carbines were issued to the 7th, 10th, 11th, 15th, and 16th Light Dragoons in 1786, but their reports were not received until May,

1788 (WO 26/33, 71/11). The delay can be understood when we consider the unusual design of the carbine. The breech consists of a tip-up chamber, which could be loaded in the usual way with the common cartridge, which is locked in position by a lever which clips into two projections on top of the barrel. Apart from the use of a screwless lock the carbine was also noteworthy for the barrel being held by bands instead of being pinned to the stock. Another startling feature was the long, socketed spear bayonet, which when not in use could be reversed and fitted back to the carbine with its point safely housed in a clip attached to the front of the trigger guard. The long spear bayonet was also used on a few muzzleloading carbines. Although Egg appears to have claimed the breechloaders as his own invention, they were

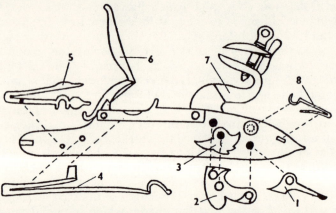

FIG. 13.—Hennem's lock dismantled. (1) Sear. (2) Bridle with swivel catch. (3) Tumbler. (4) Mainspring. (5) Steel spring. (6) Steel. (7) Cock. (8) Sear spring.

actually copied from the design of Giuseppe Crespi of Milan. They were used by the Austrian cavalry from 1770–79, being discarded because the mechanism was not gas-tight.

All the reports on the carbines differed, but it was generally admitted that the rifled barrels had performed best (two reports speak of ranges of 500 yards) and the Board decided that the carbine with a 2 ft. 4 in. rifled barrel should be chosen for further experiment. Having expressed the view that the movable chamber might be susceptible to wear, they suggested that information on this point might be obtained from the Minister at the Court of Vienna. They agreed with the cavalrymen that the long bayonet could be improved and that a folding bayonet might be better. The Egg breechloading carbine in the Scott Collection, Glasgow, has been fitted with such a bayonet, perhaps as a result of the Board's findings; but the intention to experiment further with the carbines does not seem to have been carried out. As we shall see in the next chapter, the Duke of Richmond, the most inventive of all the Masters General had become interested in another lock, another gunmaker, and another system of firearms.

Before leaving the subject of the Crespi or Egg breechloaders, it may be mentioned that a similar action with a tip-up chamber was patented in London and Paris by Urbanus Sartoris. He solved the problem of the gas leak by fitting an interrupted-screw joint between the chamber and the barrel. The latter had a large folding handle and could be turned and moved forward to unlock the breech. Although Sartoris patented an improved version in 1819 and a few well-constructed carbines were made, the Ordnance gave him no encouragement and his London business (he described himself in his Patents as a merchant) went into liquidation in 1826.

CHAPTER V

THE last quarter of the eighteenth century and the first quarter of the nineteenth can be said to be the heyday of the English gunmaker. Whilst on the continent the quality firearm was often a mere vehicle for a profusion of gold and silver decoration, the English gun was designed primarily as an efficient weapon. Nevertheless, the astonishingly accurate barrels gauged by eye alone, and the delicate lock mechanisms set in graceful walnut stocks, had a beauty of their own. It was inevitable that this should be reflected in the manufacture of military firearms. But whereas the virtues of the great sporting gunmakers like Joseph Manton, Joseph Egg and Henry Mortimer have been extolled in the books of Hawker and Thornton, and the later gunmakers, Greener and Baker, have spoken sufficiently for themselves, proper credit has never been given to the activities of such craftsmen as Durs Egg and Henry Nock in the field of military firearms. Durs Egg has already been mentioned, although the brief account of some of his activities does not do justice to his lifetime's work as a contractor to the Government for all kinds of firearms and swords.

Henry Nock was in the same category of gunmaker, capable of creating magnificent presentation pieces on the one hand and on the other of organizing a series of workshops with a firearm production running into thousands. An engineer as well as an artist, his attempts towards the mass production of firearms have never been fully appreciated. He was born in 1741, but his first appearance in the Ordnance records was in November, 1770, when he submitted a new pattern musket for approval. The main improvement appears to have been in the lock, about which the Officers of the Small Gun Office in the Tower observed "that the Steel Sears and Tumblers are improper for Tower Musquets or any other Military Locks; that the Pan of the Lock is rather too short and bored too deep, the main Spring pitched too forward and the nib too thin, but that the Size and Weight of the Lock will do very well".

At the commencement of his career, Henry Nock was a gun-lock smith, and he describes himself as such in the Patent (No. 1095) which he took out in April, 1775, together with the gunmaker William Jover and a gentleman called John Green. Part of the patent referred to a concealed lock with an ingenious gas escape. Also included was the false breech by which a barrel could be more easily removed from the stock for cleaning, a device which he was to incorporate in his military musket. He was, however, sufficiently established to undertake the manufacture of Ferguson rifles for the East India Company already described. In 1777, he was supplying bayonets to the Ordnance and in the following year he was associated with the Birmingham makers, Samuel Galton, Benjamin Willetts, William Grice and Thomas Blakemore, in a company formed for the supply of locks (WO 46/11). It was a short-lived association broken by dissensions between journeymen, masters and the government department. Shortly after this, Nock secured the first contract for a gun which was to set him on the road to success.

In July, 1779, a certain James Wilson, appeared before the Board of Ordnance with "a new Invented Gun with seven barrels to fire at one time". It was by no means a new invention, as firearms with groups of barrels can be traced back to the fourteenth century, but the gun passed its first test at Woolwich, a Committee of Officers agreeing that, while it was not suitable for the Army, "it may be useful on board Ships to fire from the Round Tops". Henry Nock was given an order to make two "seven barrelled rifle guns such as may be fit for the common uses in service". These two multiple rifles were approved by the Admiralty who proposed the following rates of issues to their ships:

74 gun ships inclusive	20
64–60 gun ships inclusive	16
50–44 gun ships inclusive	12
Frigates of all sorts	10
Sloops	8

For some reason not stated, the Ordnance then decided that the barrels of these guns should be smoothbore instead of rifled, and this change of plan was accepted by the Admiralty with equanimity. Wilson then intervened to suggest that Nock should be given an order for twenty guns to be used in a sea-going trial on board the *Phoenix* at Portsmouth. While this suggestion was carried out, his attempts to participate in the trials were firmly rebuffed. Following a reward of £400 granted him in May, 1780, Wilson took no further part in the manufacture of the seven-barrelled guns.

Nock's experience of their construction now stood him in good stead, and he successfully underbid several other London gunmakers to win a contract for 500 guns at £13 each. He was allowed £15 for the two trial pieces, which were the only ones to be rifled. Throughout 1780 Nock delivered the guns in batches from 20 to 50 at a time until the order was satisfactorily completed. There was then a lull in the manufacture, due apparently to difficulties experienced by the Navy, the original charge of powder, 2½ drams, making the recoil of the

seven barrels excessive. After some experiments by the Royal Laboratory, this charge was reduced to $1\frac{1}{2}$ drams and the common musket
powder substituted for the more powerful rifle powder first issued.

No further orders for seven-barrelled guns were given until October,
1787, when the Naval Depot at Chatham submitted an indent for 100.
Nock again received the contract at the same price as before but,
although he later offered to supply them at the reduced figure of
£10, it appears to be the last instance of their manufacture. Nock was
thus their sole maker and an analysis of the Ordnance Bill Books
reveals that he produced a total of 655 guns at a cost of £8,519 (JAAS,
Vol. I, p. 182).

The guns are described in these bills as "Pieces with Seven Barrels
each with steel rammers, brass furniture and Double Bridle locks
unrifled". As a general description very little need be added to this.
The whole gun weighs approximately 12 lb. and is $3\frac{1}{2}$ ft. long. The
barrels, engraved with their maker's name, are 20 in. in length, and
of approximately 32 bore—the official size of the bore was ·46 in. and

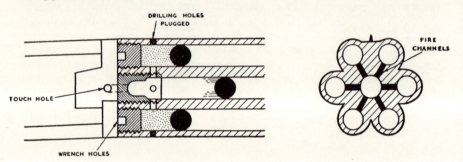

FIG. 14.—Side and cross-sections of Nock's seven-barrel gun.

balls of $46\frac{1}{2}$ to the lb. were used, supplied in kegs of 1,000. A six-round-
one formation was adopted for the barrels which were brazed together
with a sighting rib bearing a foresight only soldered down the middle
of the top two. Once the lock is removed, the barrel assembly can be
unscrewed from the central spigot at the breech, very much after the
fashion of the turn-off cannon-barrel pistols of the Queen Anne period.
This spigot is the vital part of the gun and contains a bell-like chamber
which is connected to the touch-hole. From this chamber six radial
channels lead to the outer ring of barrels (Fig. 14). These channels
have had to be drilled with the barrels in position and so each barrel
has on its outer surface a drilling hole which has been carefully plugged
without apparently causing any weakness. It is also provided with a
screwed breech-plug with a square indentation to take a suitable
wrench, the flush position being noted by a numbered mark. To a gun
difficult to produce, therefore, must be added the disadvantage of an
ignition system which was completely hidden once the barrels were
screwed into position.

Two varieties of locks have been noted. The most common type was designed so that all the interior springs were behind the cock, and the steel spring was L-shaped, so that the front of the lock plate could be fitted tight against the side of the barrel, making a reasonably weatherproof join. It was a form of back-action lock with a shortened mainspring which must have weakened the lock's power. Probably for this reason the second type of lock was introduced, its only departure from the conventional design being the reversal of the normal steel spring. This lock had the unusual refinement for a military firearm of this period of having its mainspring attached to the tumbler by a swivel.

The seven-barrelled guns were issued to Howe's fleet for the relief of Gibraltar in 1782, the Admiral recieving a personal issue; and they formed part of the armament of H.M.S. *Pandora* when searching for the mutineers of H.M.S. *Bounty* in the South Seas in 1791. But many naval commanders, including Nelson, disliked such weapons being used aloft because of the risk of fire to the sails. When, in 1805, James Wilson, then a Captain of Marines, suggested that the guns should be re-introduced for the use of Sea Fencibles he was informed that they had been "long considered obsolete".

The guns did achieve a short period of popularity as sporting weapons, and Nock made some particularly fine specimens, including a silver-mounted gun and pistol for the King.* The *pièce de résistance* was, however, the double seven-barrelled gun made by Dupe & Co. for Col. Thornton which he illustrates in *A Sporting Tour through Various Parts of France*, 1806. Now in the Musée d'Armes, Liège, the fourteen barrels bear the proud inscriptions of "Perdition to Conspirators" and "With this alone, I'll defend Robro Camp 1795" (JAAS Vol. I, p. 178).

The first success of Henry Nock as an Ordnance contractor in 1780 was followed by a lean period after the war in which the production of military firearms was naturally curtailed, and he turned to the sporting market. In 1784, he became a freeman of the Gunmakers' Company by redemption, and set up a shop at No. 10, Ludgate Street, near St. Paul's Cathedral. By this time, however, a new Master General of the Ordnance had been appointed, the Duke of Richmond, Lennox and Aubigné.

The new Master General, appointed in April, 1782, was a man of tireless energy and enthusiasm, of whom Edmund Burke wrote: "Your Grace dissipates your mind into too great a variety of minute pursuits all of which from the natural vehemence of your temper, you follow with almost equal passion". His pursuits included the study of fortification and the design of military firearms and equipment. In spite of a busy social and political life, his travelling bills show that he was constantly on the move between his country seat at Goodwood, his office at Westminster and the proving grounds at Woolwich. During his term of office he introduced new ammunition wagons, horse harness and a revolutionary type of musket.

The Duke's interest was first attracted by the screwless lock of

* A seven-barrelled swivel gun made by Ezekiel Baker for the Prince of Wales in 1804 is at Windsor Castle.

Jonathan Hennem, described in the previous chapter, and at one time he obviously visualized the general adoption of this lock. Although Henry Nock secured a small order for these locks, his offer to supply the standard type of lock was met with the reply that the Board contemplated an alteration in the flintlock. To this refusal may be attributed his determination to produce his own screwless lock. With the Master General's encouragement he succeeded in producing a new lock which he fitted to 39 muskets all incorporating new features. His bill dated 19th June, 1786, was certified by the Duke who also authorized an additional award of £100 for the lock's invention. The bill, interesting for its details of working conditions, reveals that Nock derived some inspiration from Prussian sources.

"172/8797 Allowed 19th. June 1786

To Henry Nock the sum of Three Hundred & One pounds 11/9d. for making & compleating 39 Pattern Muskets of sorts, & including £100 for his time, Trouble & Ingenuity for bringing the new invented Lock to so much Perfection as p. Master General's Order 29th. May 1786, & Certificates; vizt.

		£	s.	d.
1 Man 27 Weeks making Locks, Tools etc. from June 17th. 1785 to May 13th. 1786 @ 21/- p Week		28	7	0
1 Man 13 do do @ £2 2s p Week		27	6	0
1 do 13 do do @ £1 1 do		13	13	0
3 do 13 do do @ 18s do		35	2	0
Men sundry times boring & filing Pipes & Furniture filling bayonets etc.		4	10	6
1 Man reducing & rectifying Barrels 37 Days @ 5/-		9	5	0
11 New Musquet Barrels	@ 14/-	7	14	0
Rough Stocks		2	17	6
Brass Work		4	10	0
39 New Rammers & Screwing Heads		3	18	0
39 Worms	@ 8d.	1	6	0
Sets Nails & Triggers			9	9
Stopper Blanks Leather & Flints			6	6
39 New Bayonets	@ 2/3	4	7	9
Smoothing & Burnishing Barrels	@ 6d		19	6
32 Buff Leather Strings	@ 18d	2	8	0
39 Scabbards	@ 20d	3	5	0
7 Prussian Frames & Cover for Locks		3	13	6
7 Prussian Slings			17	6
39 Sets forging & reforging for Locks & Guns		8	15	6
7 Bayonets to be returned into store	@ 2/3		15	9
1 Man 26 days Stocking & restocking Muskets	@ 4/-	5	4	0
2 Men 23 Days each setting up & making off do	@ 4/-	9	4	0
1 Man 39 Days finishing Musquets & bolting do	@ 3/-	5	17	0
1 do 23 do false breeching Looping Barrels	@ 4/-	4	12	0
Making 7 Prussian Locks Steel Screws & Tumblers	@ 9d ea	3	3	0

1 Man 27 Weeks for Files Oil Fire & Candles

	@ 2/– pwk	2	14	0
5 do 13 do do	@ 2/– do	6	10	0
		£201	11	9

For his Time, Trouble and Ingenuity in
bringing the Invention of the new Lock
to so much Perfection, p Master General's
Order 29th May 1786   100   0   0

£301   11   9 ”

(WO 52/21)

Five of the new muskets were shipped to Gibraltar for trial, and
the Duke continued his experiments. Another gunmaker, Walter Dick,
was given a similar award for another new lock. In both the Nock and
the Dick lock the mainspring was utilized to move the cock and the
steel, but whereas Nock's lock was totally enclosed and screwless,
Dick's lock had an open exterior mechanism with only the sear and
tumbler protected by a cover.

As well as seeking a better flintlock, the experiments were aimed
at reducing the weight of the British Army musket without impairing
its fire power. Thomas Blomefield, the Inspector of Artillery, conducted
a series of trials with musket barrels of different lengths and bores.
Various experimental muskets were used, many of them made by
Henry Nock. One of his bills, dated 22nd January, 1787, was for nine
new pattern muskets "with Rollers to the Locks for the Hammer to
act upon and Chains to the Cocks and Main Springs".

One of these muskets was further described as a "double barrel
Musquet with two Locks and the upper Barrel rifled". This undoubtedly
describes the gun still in the Tower (Plate 27). It has several interesting
features. First there are its two barrels; the lower one of smooth 14 bore
and 39 in. long, and the upper of slightly smaller bore 20 in. long and
rifled with eight grooves. The side-by-side locks are operated by double
triggers, which are separated by a brass division to prevent the accidental discharge of the rear "set" trigger. The locks are basically what
were to become the standard Nock lock, as illustrated on Plate 32.
The only differences are in the method of attaching the sear spring to
the plate, the shape of the roller lever, and the catch which retains
the front of the inside plate. The heavy barrels, stamped with the mark
HN, have a break-off breech and are held to the stock by substantial
pins, both practical points which were to be adopted for Nock's
musket.

According to Deane's *Manual of Firearms* (p. 54), the Austrians armed
their light frontier troops with similar double-barrelled guns but they
were withdrawn on account of their weight and inconvenience.

Another of Nock's experimental muskets in the Tower (Plate 28)
has an unusual breechloading mechanism in which a reloadable

cartridge takes the charge. The breech is opened by pulling up the ring seen in the close-up. This ring, which also acts as a back-sight, lifts up a spike which runs right through the barrel, cartridge and stock forming a secure lock. When the spike is fully withdrawn, a backward pull on the ring removes the cartridge from the breech. It looks complicated but in practice the breech has a swift and smooth action. The removal of the locking spike also sets the gun's safety device. This is a flat spring next to the trigger guard which prevents the trigger from being moved and the lock from being accidentally fired whilst loading is in progress.

This breechloader and some of the other experimental muzzle-loaders are fitted with a more complicated version of the Nock lock. This is not recessed into the stock and, to afford better weather protection, it is fitted with an additional interior brass cover. The outer lock-plate is kept in position by a large screw whose head is a distinguishing feature of this lock.

The experiments with different muskets continued throughout 1788 and 1789, both Walter Dick and Jonathan Hennem making contributions. In April, 1790, the Master General appears to have made up his mind and he tentatively circulated the members of a Board of General Officers with what he called "Considerations on the Expediency and Expence of Altering the Musquets of the Army" (WO 71/12). Considering his enthusiasm for the new guns, he made a very fair assessment of the difficulties of the project. The proposed changes would mean entirely new arms, as the existing ones could not be adapted, and a change in the position of the ramrod meant new motions for the regulation musketry exercise. He estimated that the new musket and bayonet* would cost £2 1s. against the old £1 15s. 6d. With a stock of 197,371 army muskets, the cost of an immediate change would be £404,610 15s., so he suggested a gradual replacement. The length and weight of the musket were to depend on whether infantry were to fire standing three- or two-deep. He concluded his report with nine questions concerned with whether the calibre of the ball should remain at $14\frac{1}{2}$ or be reduced to 16. The Officers' opinions are not known, but in June the Duke arranged for them to witness a performance of the proposed musket's powers.

Instructions to the Board show that six muskets made by Henry Nock were used in this trial, and that balls of $14\frac{1}{2}$, 15 and 16 to the pound were fired. The Duke had taken the precaution of first testing Nock's musket with 16-bore balls against the regular infantry musket's $14\frac{1}{2}$-gauge. These dimensions refer, of course, to the diameter of the ball. Allowing for the windage, i.e. the gap between the ball and the barrel, said to be 11/100 of an inch, the bores of the barrels were respectively 13 and 11.

On 10th June, the *St. James Chronicle* reported:

"Yesterday at noon his Royal Highness the Duke of York and the Duke of Richmond with several General Officers were in Hyde Park trying and

---

* Although the new bayonet is not described in the records, it was a socket bayonet with a locking ring after the French pattern (*see* fig. 27).

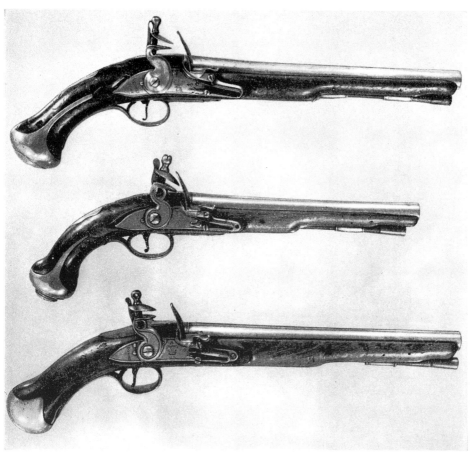

18. *Top:* Pistol dated 1738, marked 2 TROOP-H-G-Gds. *Middle:* Pistol dated 1759 with masked butt and 10 in. barrel. *Bottom:* Sea Service pistol with 12 in. barrel and belt-hook (not visible in photograph).

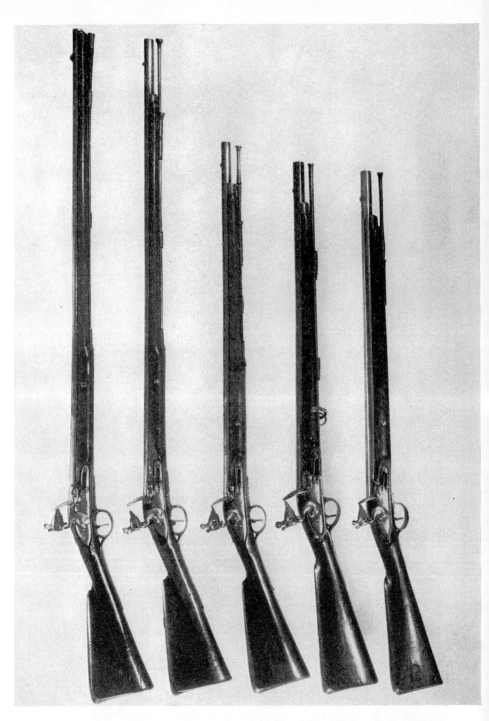

19. Cavalry carbines. *Left to right:* (1) Fully stocked carbine dated 1762, with 3 ft. 1 in. barrel and wooden rammer. (2) Light Dragoon carbine of 1756 pattern with 3 ft. barrel. (3) Elliott's carbine with 2 ft. 4 in. barrel, *c.* 1780. Note the slotted rammer. (4 & 5) Two Pattern 1796 carbines with 26 in. musket-bore barrels.

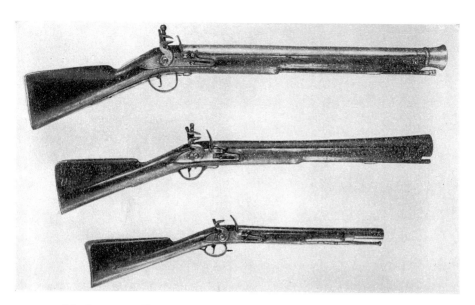

20. Musketoons. *Top:* Heavy musketoon with flat lock dated 1721, the brass barrel bearing Charles II proof marks. *Middle:* Sea Service musketoon with flared iron barrel, early brass mounts and a later lock. *Bottom:* Burgoyne's musketoon with 16 in. oval-mouth barrel.

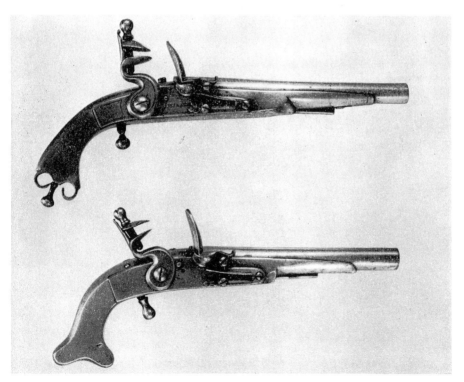

21. Birmingham-made pistols for the Highland regiments. *Top:* All steel pistol by Isaac Bissell. *Bottom:* Pistol with gun-metal stock probably by John Waters.

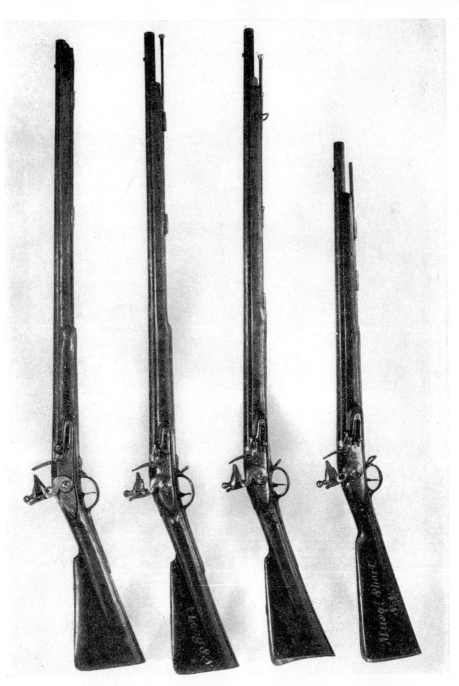

22. Black Sea Service muskets. *Left to right:* (1) Fully stocked musket with wood rammer, flat lock dated 1745. (2) Long Sea Service musket with 3 ft. 1 in. barrel, *c.* 1780. Both these muskets have heavy brass mounts of 1710–20 pattern. (3) India Pattern musket cut down for Sea Service, *c.* 1800. (4) Short Sea Service musket with 2 ft. 2 in. barrels. Made up from old materials, *c.* 1820.

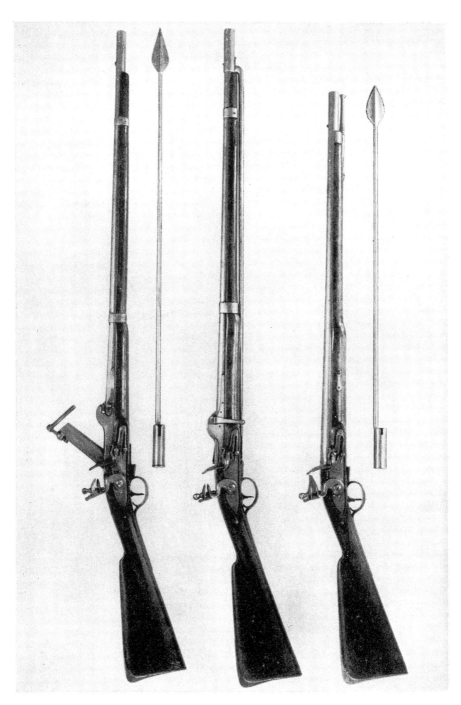

23. Spear carbines. *Left to right:* (1) Egg breechloader with breech open and spear detached. (2) Egg breechloader with Hennem's lock; the breech closed and the spear sheathed. (3) Muzzleloading carbine with similar spear bayonet.

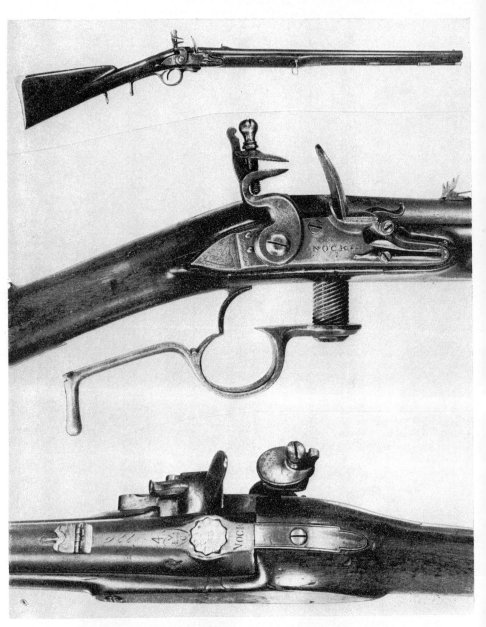

24. *Top :* Ferguson rifle made by Henry Nock for the East India Company. *Middle :* Close-up of lock with breech open. *Bottom :* Top of the barrel with breech closed. Both lock and barrel are dated 1776.

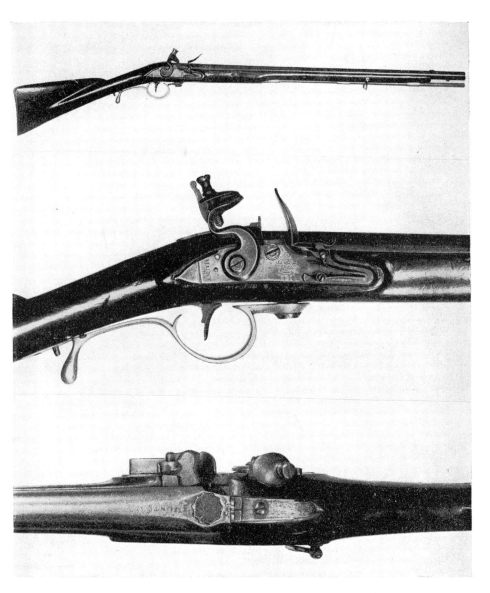

25. *Top:* Ferguson rifle made by Joseph Hunt for a Volunteer regiment. *Middle:* Close-up of the lock with breech closed. Note the special backsight. *Bottom:* Top of barrel with breech closed. *Collection of J. H. and John C. McMurray.*

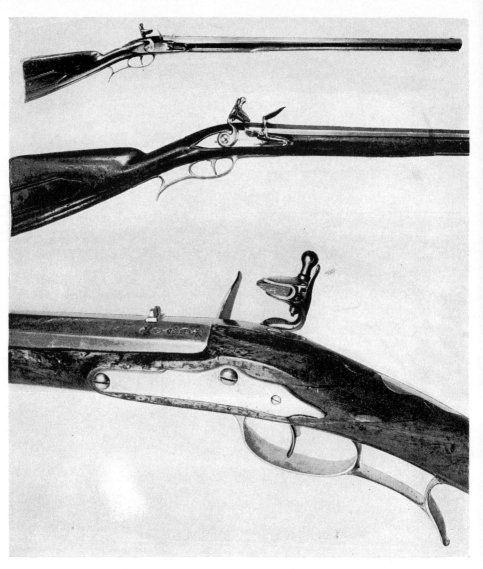

26. *Top:* Rifle by William Grice. *Middle:* Close-up of lock of Grice rifle. *Bottom:* Side view. The trigger guard is a reconstruction.

proving several new patterns of Soldiers Muskets. They are about three inches shorter than the usual size; and although lighter in every respect will do execution at as great a distance as those used at present."

The findings of the Board of General Officers are not known, but approval must have been given for by August the Ordnance were confident enough to inform their storekeepers that Land Service muskets could be issued for naval service if necessary, "it being in contemplation to supply the Army by Degrees with others of a Different Pattern". Orders were given to Nock and to Hennem for the "New Pattern Musquets 13 ball to the lb. with steel rammers", some with "rammers to the butt" and some with "rammers to the muzzle". These muskets were later classified officially as the Duke of Richmond's two Patterns.

In the first type the rammer, instead of resting on a stop at the end of the trigger guard, was pushed downward through the stock until it came to rest on the inside of the buttplate. Its other end finished halfway up the stock under the barrel. At this point the stock was swelled out to make a convenient grip for the hand, a large rammer pipe also being fitted. As there was no need for any other pipes, the stock was tapered off towards the muzzle. This had the advantage of transferring some of the muzzle weight back to the butt. Any overall reduction in weight was, however, offset by the use of a slightly larger Nock lock 6¼ in. long. The second type was supplied with a rammer in the normal position.

Both gunmakers found difficulties in the manufacture of these novel guns. Nock did not make his first deliveries until the beginning of 1792. Hennem, whose workmen were not so experienced, was a year later and as a result had his contract cancelled. Three guineas each were paid for the first deliveries but, with his workshops properly tooled up, Nock offered to supply the guns at £2 11s. with the normal rammer, and £2 12s. 6d. for the rammer to the butt model. On Boxing Day, the Board finally agreed to this offer and gave Nock an order for 10,000 muskets consisting of 20 warrants of 500 each, payment for each warrant to be made within a month after delivery had been certified. Even with these favourable terms, Nock does not appear to have delivered any of the new muskets in 1793. This was probably due to the vast amount of work which was passing through his hands.

During all the years of experiments, he had also been engaged on the normal business of an arms contractor supplying the Ordnance, the East India Company, Volunteer companies and export merchants. As well as his shop in Ludgate Hill, he had a series of workshops in Whitechapel capable of any manufacture from the smallest part of a pistol to the largest wallpiece. Thousands of small arms were sent to him for repair and he supplied hundreds of brass cannon locks for the Navy. His skill as an engineer was widely recognized and the task of constructing any new pattern tool, jig or gauge was generally

F

entrusted to him. Another novel weapon produced by him was the pistol for the Royal Horse Artillery (Plate 29).

This regiment was raised in January, 1793, and Nock was asked to supply them with 80 double-barrelled pistols at £8 each. They are the only arms that can be positively identified from a description in the Bill Books. This reads:

> "Pistols for the Horse Artillery. Double barreled, one of the Barrels Rifled 18 ins. long 13 Balls to the lb., one detant Trigger, a slide in the Left Hand Tumbler, folding elevating sight, a Shifting Butt & a Steel Rammer & the Barrels browned."

The shifting butt was what we now call a detachable butt.

These pistols were probably modelled on the hundred pistols "with moveable butts" made for Lord Townshend's Norfolk Volunteers by the Ordnance in 1783. Townshend refers to them as "stocked in the German Manner, being more portable than carbines" (WO 46/18). A more illuminating observation is found in the description of this troop of cavalry, which was raised in 1782, in *The British Volunteer*, 1799:

> "They carried but one pistol, but this was a double barrelled one, and was capable of being fitted with great facility to a but which hung from the right shoulder, by means of which they could take good aim at any opposed object. The other holster contained ammunition and a sufficiency of provision for one day."

Curiously enough, the Ordnance Minute Books show that Nock was the contractor who supplied the butts of these pistols at 10s. per pair.

Unlike his double-barrelled gun Nock placed the barrels of the Artillery pistols side by side. The left-hand barrel is rifled with nine grooves and its lock is released by the rear trigger which can be set by being pushed forward. The small grip of the pistol and its excessive weight—7 lb. 12 oz.—make it almost impossible to use with one hand. With the butt in position, however, it can be used like a carbine. The steel ramrod is housed in an unusually large brass trumpet pipe.

The time spent on designing and making all these special weapons was bound to have its effect and at the end of 1793 the Ordnance found itself in a desperate plight for arms. During all the years of experiment no large-scale manufacture of muskets had been undertaken. They now resorted to the time-honoured procedure of importing arms from the continent. However, these were not the kind of arms that they liked to place in the hands of their line regiments. Having committed themselves to the introduction of a new musket, they turned every kind of moral pressure on the one man capable of producing it. Eventually Henry Nock was summoned before the Board of Ordnance and was persuaded to guarantee delivery of the Duke of Richmond's muskets at the rate of 200 in February and March, 600 in April and 1,000 each month until the order of 10,000 was completed. The Board in their

turn undertook to pay for each delivery of materials or complete arms
"in Ready Money and with the least possible Delay".

As an added incentive the price was increased to £2 14s. 6d., but
Nock did not succeed in keeping his promise. The Ordnance Bill
Books (as far as they are complete) show his annual production as
follows:

1794	1,206
1795	794
1796	750
1797	600

As all these bills refer to "Land Musquets New Pattern with rammer to
the muzzle, Barrels Browned", it seems that the first model musket
with the rammer to the butt was abandoned. What was then the
second model musket which was so difficult to manufacture? An
examination of this firearm reveals what a superior weapon it was,
probably the finest military musket ever made. The barrel, 42 in. long
and of 13 bore, has the false breech and break-off plug of Nock's first
patent. It is secured to the stock with substantial pins, which fit into
square lugs under the barrel and are specially shaped and slotted so
that they can be easily removed. The rammer is a straight steel one
held in position by a hidden spring in the bottom guide. A very plain
stock was used, the graceful Brown Bess style being superseded by a
design incorporating little or no comb, with the minimum of brass
furniture. The emphasis is entirely on the mechanical efficiency of the
gun, which weighed approx. 10 lb.

The lock (Plate 32) is what may be called the standard model
Nock lock. Its fitting to the stock is copied from that used on sporting
guns. Only one screw is used, which is threaded into the cock pivot or
centre, while the front of the lock hooks into a screw in the lock cavity of
the stock. The lock itself has many unusual features. It is screwless
except for the screw controlling the jaws of the cock. All the parts are
held between two plates which are easily dismantled. To do this, the
interior locking plate is freed from a small catch, swivelled slightly and
then pulled off. Once the mainspring is unhooked from the link which
connects it to the cock, the remaining parts simply lift off their respec-
tive pivots. This leaves the main plate, to which are attached the pan or
flash shield and the steel. If required, the dowels holding the shield can
be pushed out. The lock was made in two main sizes, a large one 5½ in.
long for muskets and carbines, and a small one 4¾ in. long for rifles and
pistols. Of these four arms, only the carbines and some of the rifles were
fitted with pan shields.

Mention of carbines brings us to the year 1796. On 21st March, a
Board of General Officers, convened to examine a complaint about the
arms used by Dragoons, made the following recommendations:

"The Firelock at present in use for the Heavy Dragoons having been
long considered as very inconvenient, useless and cumbersome, the Board

recommend in place thereof a carbine of 26″ in the Barrel and Musket Bore and that until such New Carbine can be provided by the Ordnance the Barrel of the present Dragoon Firelock should be cut down to the above size 26 ins so as to be reduced to a Carbine; a Swivel Bar added to it with a bend in the upper part will give an additional convenience in the carriage and to be carried But downwards. The Bayonet also to be reduced to 15 inches.

It is also recommended by the Board that only one Pistol per Man be used in the Regiment of Heavy Cavalry the Barrel of which to be 9 ins long and that the bore of the Carbine and Pistol be the same calibre viz 16 serviceable balls to the lb—the same as in the regiments of Infantry.

And that the pistol ramrod be made of iron and fixed to the holster pipe.''

(WO 71/12)

Similar proposals for the Light Cavalry were made on 9th April. The bore of 16 to the lb. described as that used by the infantry presumably referred to the size of the ball used in the Duke of Richmond's pattern musket. Although this small size bullet was soon replaced by the normal 14½ bore ball, the proposal for the standardization of the military bullet was carried into effect, and for a few years all new small arms were of musket bore.

Nock was called on to produce patterns and gauges for the new carbines and pistols, but the Ordnance this time did not confine their orders to one man or to one type of lock. Although the first batch of carbines and pistols were made by Nock in 1797 and his screwless lock fitted, the following year large contracts were divided among the gunmakers of London and Birmingham, and the office pattern lock was issued for their use. During his efforts to produce the Duke of Richmond's musket, however, Nock had delivered to the Tower considerable numbers of separate locks. These were now issued to some of the gunmakers for setting up into carbines. A number of these carbines are in the Tower and in private collections. Some with the Nock lock are illustrated and will be seen to vary slightly. In fact, different regiments seem to have introduced modifications. Not all of the carbines have the swivel bar with a bend in it. There are two series of carbines in the Tower with straight bars; those with Nock locks are marked 2 D.G. (2nd Dragoon Guards) and those with the ordinary lock 3 D.G. (3rd Dragoon Guards). Many of the carbines are of inferior finish, refinements such as the special barrel pins and breech being absent.

As the rammer of the new cavalry pistol was to be carried in a holster, there was no provision on the pistol for it, and the absence of pipes and slots gives it a curious unfinished appearance. The only furniture is a small plain trigger guard. The Patt. 1796 pistol with the ordinary lock was made for 19s. 6d., but I have never seen one.*The use of a Nock lock on the pistol increased the price to 30s., and it must be admitted that this short pistol with its 9 in. barrel and wide stock is an ugly and clumsy weapon. That illustrated (Plate 29), although similar to the Government model, was evidently made for a Volunteer Company, as it has a brass barrel and no official markings.

---

* Most Patt. 1796 pistols with the standard flintlock were stocked and set up with a steel rammer. See Pl. 43.

Locks made for the Ordnance with pan shields have the maker's name engraved in block letters on the middle of the plate and GR and Crown on the shield. When there is no shield, the royal mark appears in the middle and Nock's name is placed vertically on the tail of the lock. Those made privately have the maker's name in script and the front of the lock is embellished with a sun-burst decoration.

A lock which is often confused with that of Henry Nock was the one patented by Sir George Bolton, at one time a tutor to the Royal Family. On 23rd March, 1795, he took out a Patent, No. 2041, for what might aptly be called the "Bolting" lock. Although the inventor adopted a variety of the enclosed lock because of its strength, the main purpose of his patent was devoted to a special bolt which took the place of the normal sear and was designed to prevent the lock from being accidentally fired. As he affirms in his book, *Remarks on the Present Defective State of Firearms etc.*, which he wrote in the same year: "Since the ball in rifle-barrels requires so great a blow to drive it down, unless the precaution of bolting is taken there must be very great danger of jarring the cock out of its place". The cock on his lock was fitted with jaws which could be turned from side to side by a large knurled knob so that the lateral angle of the flint could be quickly adjusted to give a better spark. Some of these locks were made by Thomas Fisher of High Holborn for sporting use, but they were never seriously considered by the Ordnance.

With Nock's failure to produce sufficient numbers of the Duke of Richmond's musket, the enterprise finally came to an end in 1798, and one of the last tasks of Henry Nock before his death in 1804 was to alter them to another pattern. Approximately 300 of the rammer to the butt model were made and some 3,000 of the standard model.

Although ten years of experiments had left the store of small arms in a dangerously low condition and the result was that inferior and foreign arms had to be introduced. Henry Nock's efforts were not entirely wasted. He set a standard of workmanship which was to influence the manufacture of the later firearms for the regular service. In 1832, when a new cavalry carbine was being considered, one of Nock's carbines made for the 2nd Dragoon Guards was examined and it was stated that "they had been in use for 35 years, have scarcely ever been known to be out of order or to require repair, and when properly flinted, have very rarely been known to miss Fire".

It was the locks on these carbines which caused most interest, and George Lovell, the foremost designer of military percussion arms, wrote:

"These locks were invented by the late Henry Nock, who was certainly the very best Gun-maker of his time, and introduced many valuable improvements in the construction of military arms;—They are part of several thousand that were prepared under the orders of the Duke of Richmond when Master General of the Ordnance and were originally intended for a Musquet of particular construction known as "The Duke of Richmond's Pattern" which was afterwards abandoned on account of the Bore being smaller than the regular English Calibre although it was larger than the French. The locks were then converted to the use of Carbines and Pistols for Heavy Cavalry.

These kind of Locks were manufactured somewhat in the same manner as the French "Platines Identiques"—the several parts were made by different artificers in Moulds, Guages and Tools and fitted together by a separate set of men. They are formed entirely without Screws; all the Pivots being fixed by small pins in the outward Plate and bearings on the inner one, so that the Cock, Hammer and Sear work quite free upon fixed centres and on the accurate fitting and true perpendicular position of these Centres with reference to the Plate the whole of the improved action of these Locks depends.

I entirely agree with General Dalbiac in his opinion of the excellence of their construction, and I do not hesitate to state that they are the best Military Flint Locks that have come under my observation. It is true they give a somewhat cumbrous appearance to the stock, but the principal Bar to their general use is their high Price and the difficulty of procuring workmen capable of making them in sufficient numbers to meet the Demands of the Service at large."   (WO 44/677)

The name of Henry Nock may mean nothing to the modern soldier, but it has been perpetuated in curious fashion, the flat breech end of the Lee-Enfield rifle barrel, similar to that used by Nock on many of his guns, being known officially as the "Knoxform".

CHAPTER VI

THE INTRODUCTION OF THE RIFLE

UP to the end of the eighteenth century, the Ordnance, on the few occasions when it had experimented with the use of rifles, had always showed a marked preference for breechloaders. In 1794, however, the British Army was involved in a spate of fighting brought on by the French Revolution. At home, there was an enormous increase in the number of Fencible and Militia Regiments and, to use the words of Fortescue, "there sprang up an infinity of Volunteer corps, infantry, artillery and light horse". To this vast throng of amateur soldiers was added a motley collection of foreign levies, emigrants and volunteers: La Chatre's Loyal Emigrants, the Prince of Salm's Light Infantry, Hompesch's Hussars, the York Rangers and the like. Many of these men were experienced in the use of the short, thick-barrelled rifles of the continental Jäger. Some brought these arms to this country and the demands of others for similar weapons led the Ordnance once more to seek supplies of rifles.

Henry Nock, Joseph Grice and Durs Egg are known to have sent in patterns of rifles from 1796–98, but only Egg appears to have received a contract. The exact number is not known but, in May, 1796, the Board agreed to pay his "fair and just demand" of £3 15s. for each "rifle musquet". The Minute Books, as usual, give no further information but the Egg rifle can be reasonably identified with the specimen in the Jac Weller Collection (Plate 39). This is similar in size to the India Pattern musket (see Chapter 7) with an overall length of 54 in. but it has the plain stock of the Nock pattern musket. The 39 in. barrel is rifled with nine narrow deep grooves to a bore of ·704 in. and is fitted with a plain rearsight. Because of the rifling, a heavy steel ramrod is provided and to house it the stock is slit from muzzle to trigger guard in the fashion of the Nock carbine and some Baker rifles. Both lock and barrel are marked D. EGG, with the Crown and GR on the former.

As usual, the Ordnance turned to Germany to augment its supply and, in August, 1798, through the agency of Paul and Haviland Le Mesurier, ordered 5,000 Prussian rifled muskets with bayonets at 35s. each. At that price good quality weapons could not be expected, and the Master Furbisher, Jonathan Bellis, examining the first batch of 2,000 in November, 1799, reported that 223 were broken and those that were serviceable were inferior to the original samples. The price was accordingly reduced to 33s. It was probably these rifles which were issued to the foreign units in this country and to the 5th Battalion of the 60th Regt. formed from the remnants of several foreign regiments in 1798. Rifles were also issued to the 3rd Battalion of this regiment in 1800 and to the 7th Battalion in 1813. The cheap German rifles did not suit everyone and a Dutch Corps under the Hereditary Prince of Orange were allowed to make a special purchase of 1,012 German rifles, for which the Ordnance paid £2,600, stipulating, however, that a dozen of the rifles should be lodged in the Tower as patterns.

Familiarity with the foreign riflemen removed some of the Englishman's distrust of the muzzleloading rifle, and the changes which were taking place in European tactics forced the military to reconsider their ideas on rifle companies. In August, 1795, Sir Ralph Abercromby, commanding a West Indies expedition, went so far as to ask for "a Corps of Riflemen" and suggested that, as there were no British troops properly trained, they might be raised from Darmstadt troops (WO 6/25). It was another three years before the War Office decided to consider the matter seriously. William Fawcett, the Adjutant General, gave his approval to the publication of *Regulations for the Exercises of Rifleman and Light Infantry*, an English translation of a German work by Baron de Rottenburg, who was concerned in the formation of the 5th Battalion 60th Regt. Jonathan Bellis was also asked to give his opinion on a suitable rifle for a proposed Corps of Riflemen.

The last instruction may seem strange when we know that Egg had already supplied rifles, but his pattern had been, in effect, a rifled musket. The Army quite obviously decided that what it wanted was a rifled carbine of the kind carried by the continental Jäger companies, but of English manufacture. The offer of William Bolts to supply 6,000 foreign cavalry carbines with rifled barrels and a sabre to fix on the barrel and act as a bayonet was refused; but it shows what the Ordnance had in mind. English gunmakers were invited to send in samples of rifled barrels, among them being the Birmingham makers Thomas Stokes, William Rock, John Trueman and Thomas Russell.

While the Ordnance were thus organizing a supply of the rifles, the Commander-in-Chief faced the task of forming a proper body of men. In January, 1800, the Adjutant General wrote to Col. Coote Manningham informing him that the Duke of York proposed to place him in command of a Corps of detachments from fourteen Line Regiments, "for the purpose of its being instructed in the use of the Rifle and in the System of Exercise adopted by Soldiers so armed" (WO 3/21). Opinion on the wisdom of this move was by no means unanimous and Cornwallis, writing in February, 1800, gave his opinion that "only a tenth part of the Corps should be armed with rifles and that the others should be trained as light infantry and brigaded for the present with the light companies of Irish Militia" (Charles Ross, *Correspondence of Cornwallis*, 1859, III, p. 177).

Manningham, who had enthusiastically forwarded some suggested principles for an establishment of the Rifle Corps, was informed that it was neither a permanent nor a distinct Corps but a "Corps of Experiment and Instruction" (WO 3/32). However, after months of argument the matter was resolved. In October, 1800, the Corps of Riflemen was properly established with effect from 25th August. By the end of the year, an appropriate green uniform and other accoutrements for the eight companies were authorized (WO 4/181/2).

The question of what type of rifle should be carried was not so easily settled. There is no official report of the trials that took place and we have to accept the word of Ezekiel Baker, the Whitechapel gunmaker. In his *Remarks on Rifle Guns*, he describes how his rifle barrel 2 ft. 6 in. long with a quarter-turn, seven groove rifling was chosen from several English and foreign rifles during a trial at Woolwich on 4th February, 1800. A claim for travelling expenses by the Master Furbisher confirms that a series of experiments on rifles did take place at Woolwich during the first week in February. Some time in March, the Board of Ordnance gave Baker an order for pattern rifles and barrels. The following month he supplied two rifle barrels at 24s., four exterior barrel gauges at 10s. 6d. each, and twelve interior gauges at 5s. each. Although the inference is that only his barrel was approved and that he was not necessarily the designer of the stock, etc.—he certainly makes no claim to this in his book—nevertheless he was the first gunmaker to send in complete rifles and there is no doubt that the rifle which we now call the Baker is correctly named. On 30th September Baker submitted a bill which included the following:

"Musquets Rifled and Barrels Browned
Musquet Bore with boxes, sword bayt. & scabbards		6 @	97/-
,, ,, ,, ,, without bayts.		10 @	86/-
,, ,, without boxes or bayts.		43 @	82/-
Carbine Bore with boxes & without bayts.		2 @	86/-
,, ,, without boxes or bayts.		70 @	82/-
Wood Mallets small		59 @	2½d. "

From the outset we are presented, therefore, with several types of rifles, the main distinction being in the bore. The musket bore was, however, soon discarded and Baker, in his *Remarks*, recalls: "I made some rifles of equal dimensions to the muskets, in order that they might be supplied if necessity required, from any infantry regiment that might be near them. They were, however, strongly objected to by the commanding officer, Col. Manningham, as well as all the officers of the regiment, as requiring too much exertion and harassing the men from their excessive weight."

Two large-bore rifles of this period are shown on Plate 33. The first is not the true Baker type although it is similar in general appearance. The barrel, 2 ft. 4 in. long, is rifled with eight deep-cut grooves and the calibre is slightly over musket bore. There is a flat along the top of the barrel on which are set a folding leaf backsight and an iron foresight. At the muzzle two holes have been drilled in the sides of the barrel for what may have been a swivel fitting. Both trigger guard and butt box are not of the Baker pattern.

The second rifle must, however, be one of the first musket-bore Bakers. The barrel has the standard length of 2 ft. 6 in., with seven grooves and a calibre of approximately ·70 in. and is fitted with a less elaborate folding backsight. At the muzzle end a bar is brazed on the side to take a sword bayonet. The stock is well shaped at the wrist and the deep curved trigger guard forms a reasonable grip. For additional support a cheek-rest has been raised on the left of the butt. The brass mounts are plain, with an oval escutcheon, one small and one large trumpet pipe for the steel rammer, and a flat S-shaped side plate. The butt box as designed for these early models is 6 in. long, the lid covering two recesses—a circular one for patches and a rectangular one for the tools which were issued with the gun. These consisted of a ball drawer and wiping eye and a small lever to fit a hole drilled in the end of the rammer. They were supplied for 1s. 6d. a set.

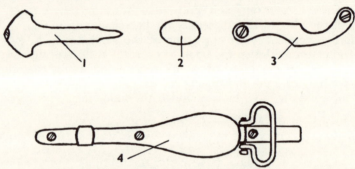

FIG. 15.—Baker rifle pattern furniture. (1) Butt tang. (2) Escutcheon. (3) Side plate. (4) Trigger guard.

The carbine bore model, apart from its calibre of ·625 in., is identical to the above, although the rifle illustrated is later in date and the butt box is smaller (Plate 33).

Originally it was intended that the barrels should be made in two qualities at the rate of 3,000 per month. A Board's order of 9th March, 1800, recommended this rate of production with the following prices:

> For barrels made of the best Gun Iron forged from the skelp the price of 13/– each.
> For barrels made of the best Gun Iron twisted the whole length of the barrel price 20/– each.

The normal Ordnance system of manufacture was thus set in motion. Barrels, plain and twisted, and locks "with steel sears and tumblers for rifled musquets in the soft state" were sent to London where they were set up by Egg, Nock, Baker, Pritchett, Brander, Wilkes, Wright, Barnett, and Harrison & Thompson. These gunmakers shared the first order for setting up 800 rifles at 36s. with boxes and 32s. without.

As was natural at the beginning of a new arm, modifications were constantly being made. In September, an additional order for 100 rifles was placed, "to consist of the pattern last approved by Colonel Manningham". No description of the pattern is given beyond the fact that the butts were to have boxes. It seems likely that most of the early models made without boxes were subsequently fitted with them. Nock and Baker contracted to do this conversion in 1801 at 3s. 4d. per rifle and were allowed to send their workmen into the Tower for the purpose. The same men were also given the job of fitting "flies" or detents into the tumblers of the locks.

Another unexplained model was made in September, 1801, when 800 "Rifles of the Pattern required for the Regiments in the West Indies" were ordered from the London gunmakers, Nock getting the major share. Half of these were to have "Boxes in the But and Bars for Sword Bayonets" at £3 6s. and the other half without for £2 19s.

The sword bayonet designed for the Baker was based on a German model, with a flat blade 23 in. long, one cutting edge and a brass handle. Henry Osborne the Birmingham contractor, was responsible for the prototype and the first consignments. He ran into trouble with these and, in March, 1801, complained to the Ordnance that he had sustained a loss on "the Rifle Bayonets not suiting the purpose they were intended for". It is possible that the bayonet shown on Plate 34 may be one of the first pattern. The knuckle-bow has a square-cut corner found on very few of the bayonets and there is a hole in the grip, presumably for a sword knot. In November, Osborne submitted a bill for 100 bayonets at 11s. each and for six "Skeleton sword bayonets as patterns for fitting the sword bayonets to rifle musquets" at 21s. each.

It was inevitable that the new interest in rifles should spread to the Volunteer Associations. These small companies of gaily clad warriors, to be called into action only in the event of invasion, were formed from the inhabitants of the various wards, hundreds, parishes and other districts and from members of business companies, and trades, getting their names from those sources. Meeting in taverns, coffee houses and churches, they vied with each other in the splendour of their attire. Supplying their own uniforms, they normally applied to the Ordnance for arms and accoutrements, after obtaining official recognition. What that department was prepared to issue was, however, not always of the best standards. Some Corps preferred, therefore, to provide themselves with arms of a "superior construction".

In April, 1798, Col. Charles Herries, commanding the London & Westminster Light Horse Volunteers, asked for an issue of Harcourt's carbines. As these carbines were being kept for a special assignment, he was offered the cheap India Pattern musket instead. The Colonel evidently did not think much of this idea, for we read in *Loyal Volunteers of London & Environs*, published by Ackermann in 1799, that his 7th, 8th, and 9th Troops were dismounted and armed with "a Rifle-barrelled Gun of a new construction, which will do execution at a great distance; and their Broad swords are so contrived as to serve occasionally as Bayonets". Herries, in his *Standing Orders* of 1805, refers to rifle instruction by a Sergeant Armourer, "who has served many campaigns as Serjeant in a corps of German Yagers".

The *Loyal Volunteers* also illustrates a private of Sadler's Sharp Shooters, a corps formed under the direction of James Sadler, "a very ingenious Machinist, inventor of the celebrated War Chariot, in which two persons, advancing or retreating, can manage two Pieces of Ordnance (three-pounders) with alacrity, and in safety, so as to do execution at the distance of two furlongs," and armed with his "Patent Gun and long cutting Bayonet." Sadler did produce some special cannon—two were tried by the Ordnance in 1796, were placed in the Royal Military Repository, and were taken over by a Volunteer corps in 1803—and his War Chariot formed the subject of a coloured print by Rowlandson: but his gun has never been identified and there is no Patent in his name.

A printed prospectus (dated 23rd August, 1803) of the Duke of Cumberland's Corps of Sharp Shooters informed applicants for member-ship—they were elected by ballot and paid a guinea subscription—of the type of rifle to be purchased: "The Barrel to be 2 ft. 9 in. in length which is to carry a sized ball of 30 to the pound—iron ramrod—bolt lock and scroll guard—sword bayonet 23 inches long in the blade with brass handle, lacquered or gilt to fasten to the side of the piece." Gentlemen were, in order to prevent accidents, cautioned that "no Hair-triggers will be allowed and every lock should be provided with a Bolt. . . ." The same prospectus advised enthusiastic marksmen that "there will be Ball-Firing on Thursday at Six o'clock in the Morning, Such Gentlemen as chuse [*sic*] to attend will muster upon the Ground to the Left of the Paddington Canal, between the first Bridges, when Rifle Pieces and Ball will be provided, The Gentlemen to bring their own Powder" (HO 50/78).

Three typical examples of the rifles used by these volunteers are shown on Plate 36. All of them have similar barrels to the Baker rifle, approximately 30 in long with seven-groove rifling, but the stocks and accessories have been fashioned to individual requirements. The first rifle by S. Wallis, believed to have been used by the Great Packington Volunteers, has a Baker type butt box and sideplate, a folding aperture rearsight and a bayonet-stud under the muzzle. The bayonet, with a blade just over 2 ft. long, is not unlike the bayonet later adopted by the Sappers and Miners. The second rifle is a very fine-quality piece by the London gunmaker Staudenmayer, all the mounts and the hilt of the sword being gilded. The latter has an ingenious fitting which slips over the muzzle and was held by a locking ring, now missing. The third rifle is a rather plain specimen of Henry Nock's work used by the

Cambridge University Volunteers. Some of Nock's rifles made for Volunteers are fitted with his screwless lock and patent breech (Plate 30) and have an unusual lead-in to the muzzle, the first five or six inches of the barrel being smooth-bored.

The Baker rifle designed for infantry was soon considered as a cavalry weapon. On 30th September, 1801, Baker submitted a bill for "Carbines rifled for the Life Guards" supplied complete at 97s. and 89s. without boxes. The first price was the same as that charged for the original musket-bore infantry rifle and suggests that the infantry weapon with little modification was adapted for the use of this élite cavalry. Unfortunately no dimensions of the carbine are given but in September, 1812, when a further batch was ordered, the prices of the various processes of manufacture are given as Setting Up—£1 4s.; Lock—7s. 11d.; Bayonet—2s. 9d.; Ramrod—2s.; Barrel—17s.; Rifling—7s; Apparatus—1s. 2d.

Much of Baker's success was due to his friendship with the Prince of Wales and it was his royal patron who encouraged the development of a special cavalry rifle. Baker illustrates two targets in his book said to have been fired on 4th June, 1803, during a comparative trial of two barrels 20 in. in length at a distance of 200 yards. One barrel was made by Henry Nock. This had a bore of 16 balls to the pound, rifled with a twist of a half-turn in two feet and a charge of 105 grains of powder. The other, by Baker, of 20 bore, had a quarter-turn rifling and a smaller charge of 84 grains. The trial was not without its element of drama, for Baker had been apprenticed to Nock, who was now nearing the end of his life. The result was a defeat for the older man, whose barrel could only register four hits out of twelve against Baker's nine hits. On the evidence of one trial, the Ordnance were not likely to recommend the universal adoption of a rifled carbine for cavalry, but a fortnight later Baker was given an order to supply forty of these carbines at four guineas each for the Prince of Wales's regiment, the 10th Light Dragoons.

In 1805, further trials were made with 20 in. barrels by Baker and three other gunmakers, Arnold, Gill and Egg. For some reason Baker departed from his principles; he increased the twist of his rifling to half-turn, and thereby achieved the worst result. Durs Egg's barrel with a quarter-turn rifling was a clear winner, but no pronouncement appears in the Minute Books of the Ordnance other than a note of the price to be paid for twisted barrels (unrifled) for the 20 in. Prince of Wales pattern carbine, 14s. each delivered in London, and 15s. each delivered in Birmingham. It is clear, however, that production of the new barrels was started immediately. By March, 1806, the Inspector of Small Arms at Birmingham reported that 4,327 infantry and 4,693 cavalry barrels were complete ready for rifling, and over 10,000 of each kind in process of manufacture. He was told that 3,000 of each were to be set up, and the rest to be completed except for rifling and retained in store. Swivel rammers were also ordered at 2s. 9d. each.

Whether Baker's barrel was adopted or not, he seems to have taken

the major part in the setting up of the cavalry rifles, at least for the
10th Light Dragoons. At first, they were built like miniature Baker
infantry rifles with the same pattern brass furniture. The small well
wrought barrels are fitted with swivel rammers and the locks have a
safety bolt behind the cock, both devices which were being incorporated
on all the carbines and pistols from 1805 onwards. The cavalry rifle
illustrated (Plate 40) has Baker's name on the lock and barrel. At a
later date he altered the design of the stock, giving this reason in his
book: "I have found by experience that the swell of wood underneath
the stock similar to a pistol has a much better purchase to the trigger
hand than the steel or brass scroll guard, which is usually attached to
guns of every description". In January, 1813, he received an order to
set up 500 of the rifles at 40s. each and these were apparently issued
to the 10th Light Dragoons in November as a special experimental
armament. The new stocks were so successful that, in 1827, more of the
regiment's carbines were restocked in this manner, although the
Commanding Officer insisted that the locks had their safety bolts
removed. The carbine on Plate 40 is engraved "XRH" on the butt
tang and is one of these later models.

It is difficult to judge the extent of the issue of Baker rifles as they
are given no official name in the records. In 1806, rifles were issued to
the 1st and 2nd Light Infantry Battalions of the King's German Legion
on their arrival in England from Ireland, but a complaint in May of
the next year that the rifles of the 8th Battalion were of three different
calibres suggests that German rifles were involved (WO 3/192/3).

There was by this time no shortage of rifles and their issue was
extended to the militia regiments of Shropshire (1810), Pembrokeshire
(1811), and Carnarvon (1812), (WO 3/199/203). Nevertheless the
demands being made on the gunmakers for the standard musket and
carbine meant that every source of supply had to be tapped. The
Ordnance officers in Dublin were asked to arrange for manufacture of
rifles locally and the comparative prices between that city and London
were revealed.

LONDON   DUBLIN

Infantry Rifle

	£	s.	d.		£	s.	d.
Barrel	1	8	6	Barrel 24/-			
Lock		8	9	Rifling 6/-	1	10	0
Setting up complete				Lock forging 2/2			
except for bayt.	2	0	0	Lock Filing 6/10		9	0
				Setting up complete			
	£3	17	3	except for bayt.	3	1	9
					£5	0	9

Cavalry Rifle

	£	s	d			£	s	d
Barrel	I	I	0	Barrel 17/–				
Lock		15	0	Rifling 5/–	I	2	0	
Rammer		2	9	Lock forging 2/2				
Setting up				Lock filing 14/1		16	3	
complete	I	15	0	Setting up				
				complete	3	4	0	
	£3	13	9		£5	2	3	

From the date of its introduction in 1800 to the end of the Napoleonic Wars in 1815 the lock of the Baker rifle, like that of all the other arms of the period, underwent several changes. Starting with a typical rounded eighteenth-century form of lock with a swan-neck cock, it was subsequently fitted with the flat lock and ring-neck cock of the New Land Series, then a flat lock with a safety bolt and raised pan, and finally a return to the rounded shape when the Government factory at Enfield started making the rifles. The presence of any of these locks on a rifle cannot, however, be used too strictly in the dating of a piece owing to the system of taking different batches of materials out of store for the final process of setting up.

As far as can be judged the stocks of Baker rifles fall into two classes. The earlier ones have large butt boxes containing two compartments, and the rammers fit into the normal hole drilled into the stock. In the second type, the stock is not drilled but slit for a rammer housing, and the butt box is a smaller edition with a plate 4½ in. long (Plate 35). This contains a rectangular compartment for tools only, which suggests the discarding of patches and the use of cartridges only. With the patches went the wooden mallets which seem to have had a very bad reception. While it would appear that these slit-stock rifles are a later variety the same design of stock is found on many of the 26 in. barrel carbines introduced in 1796 and of course on the Egg rifles mentioned at the beginning of this chapter. It was a practical device which helped to prevent the jamming of the rammer in the stock under wet or dirty conditions.

In the Tower Armouries there are several slit-stock Baker rifles with no butt box, on which the line of the stock runs straight from the toe of the butt to the trigger, instead of being shaped above the trigger guard (Plate 35). The barrels of these rifles are not stamped with the government mark and, as they are engraved with company markings and the letters A.R., one is tempted to ascribe them to the Ayrshire Rifle Regt. of Local Militia—referred to as the Ayrshire Rifles. In March, 1810, their commanding officer, Lt.-Col. Hamilton, was allowed the regulation price of muskets for rifles which he had provided for his regiment on condition that they were to be considered public property. A plain fixed backsight is normally found on these straight slit-stock rifles.

The development of the Baker rifle was inevitably bound up with that of its bayonet. Apart from its initial modification at the hands of Osborne, the sword bayonet with its flat blade and rounded knuckle bow appears to have continued unchanged until 1815. But on 19th May of that year, the Adjutant General wrote to the Board of Ordnance to draw their attention to the disadvantages which riflemen had endured in the recent fighting, due to the lack of a suitable bayonet; "the Sword at present attached to the Rifle being on various accounts by no means so efficacious a weapon as the Bayonet" (WO 3/212). It was not actually stated on this occasion but it becomes apparent from later reports that there were difficulties in shooting the rifle with the bayonet fixed.

It was a strange defect, brought to the notice of the Ordnance in 1835 by Lt.-Col. Eeles of the Rifle Brigade, and it formed the subject of a report by George Lovell in the following year when he was experimenting with percussion rifles. He tried out eighty-five flintlock rifles fitted with sword bayonets and found that they could not be fired properly with the bayonet fixed "through the rush of fluid from the muzzle catching under the cross guard and grip of the bayonet with such force that the strongest and best springs are broken or bent after two or three rounds, or the hook in the Bar so battered that it will no longer hold".

However, to return to 1815. The Commander-in-Chief directed that a pattern rifle should be prepared "leaving the sight of the Rifle in its present state and totally unconnected with the bayonet; the holder or hitch of which should be on the lower side of the barrel". The sword was still to remain part of the equipment, for which no doubt the riflemen were duly grateful. Letters and diaries of that time show that the rifleman liked his little sword—it was very handy for chopping wood. At the end of May, a rifle and two swords were sent to the Commander-in-Chief for his approval, a sword bearing the insignia of the 52nd Regt. being recommended. The latter was duly chosen with the proviso that it "would be rendered still more eligible by being made applicable to the purposes of a Saw, in the same manner as the Swords of Light Infantry Serjeants of the Coldstream Guards".

I have not been able to identify this sword, 5,000 of which were ordered in November at 12s. 6d. each. In the photograph of Baker bayonets (Plate 34), one sword bayonet is shown with a saw back, but it is unlikely that this was the new sword, such a simple modification would surely have been mentioned.* There is, however, little doubt about the new bayonet. It was of the socketed type with a locking ring. On 10th July, 5,000 new rifle bayonets were ordered from fifteen Birmingham contractors at a price of 2s. 11d. each, "including collar and spring".

Arrangements were made for the necessary alterations to the rifles. Those of the 3rd Battalion, 95th Regt. were directed to be sent to the Tower. The 5th Battalion, 60th Regt., who were now armed with Bakers, were told to send theirs to Dublin. In August, a supply of 200

* It was probably the short sword with a brass stirrup-hilt and saw-back blade which is usually described as a Pioneer sword. Its pommel is a stylised version of the lion-headed 52nd Regt. sword.

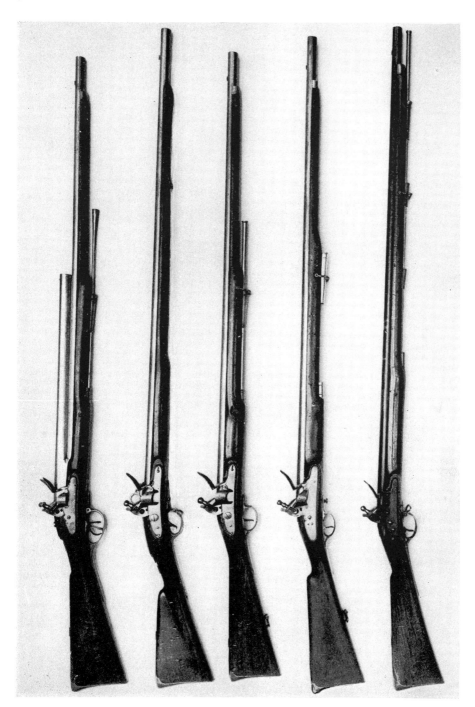

27. Nock's muskets. *Left to right:* Experimental double-barrelled gun, with the upper barrel rifled. (2) Breechloading musket. (3) Duke of Richmond's pattern musket, rammer-to-the-butt model with experimental lock. (4) Rammer-to-the-butt-model with standard Nock lock. (5) Duke of Richmond's pattern musket, rammer-to-the-muzzle model.

28. Close-up of Nock's breechloading musket. The breech open with the chamber in the loading position.

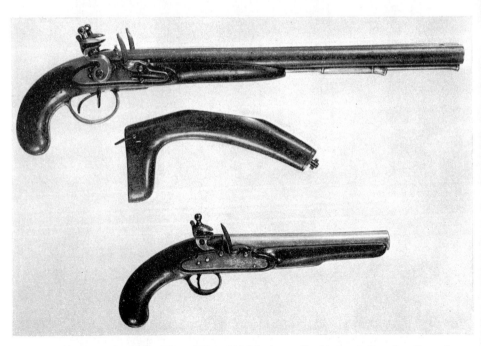

29. Nock's pistols. *Top :* The double-barrelled pistol for the Royal Horse Artillery with the detachable butt underneath. *Bottom :* Brass-barrelled pistol with Nock lock and 9 in. barrel.

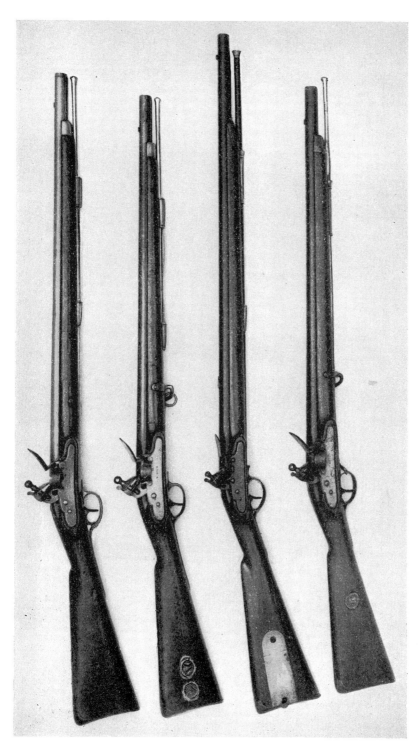

30. Nock's carbines. *Left to right:* (1) Carbine made for the Queen's Light Dragoons. (2) A sealed pattern marked No. 3. (3) Rifled carbine made for a volunteer company, fore-end damaged. (4) Sealed carbine marked No. 5.

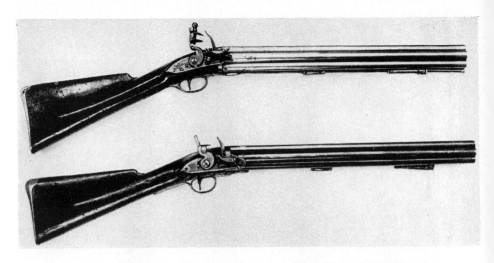

31. Nock's seven-barrelled guns. First and second models.

32. The Nock lock. *Top left:* The 5½ in. model for carbine and musket. *Middle:* The same lock shortened and adapted to take two stock screws. *Bottom:* The 4¾ in. lock for pistol and rifle. *Right:* The 5½ in. lock dismantled.

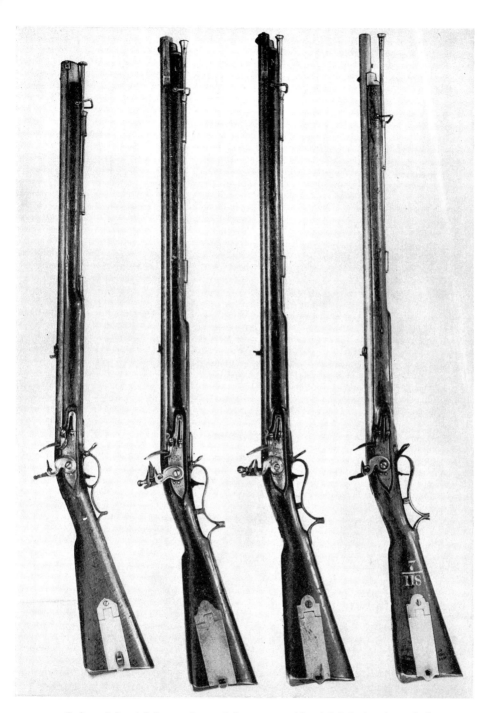

33. *Left to right:* (1) Large-bore eight-groove rifle. (2) Musket-bore Baker rifle. (3) Carbine-bore Baker rifle. An early model with large butt box. (4) Baker rifle adapted for socket bayonet.

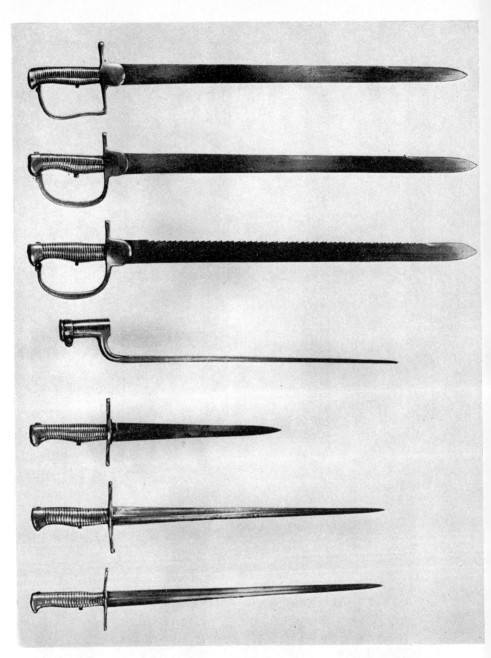

34. Baker rifle bayonets. *Top:* Original (?) sword bayonet. (2) Standard sword bayonet. (3) Sword bayonet with saw-back blade. (4) Socket bayonet with locking ring. (5) Experimental hand bayonet. (6) First model hand bayonet. (7) Final light model hand bayonet.

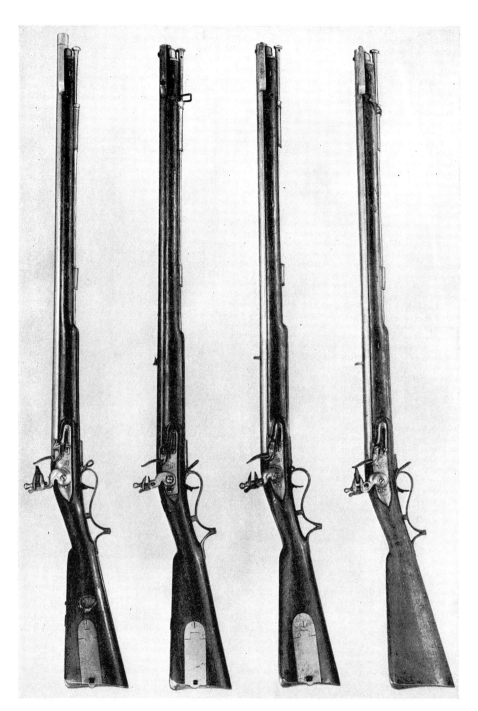

35. Late model Baker rifles with slit stocks and rounded butt-box plates.
Left to right: Sealed pattern of 1823 (?). (2) Rifle with bolted lock and
raised pan. (3) Rifle made at Enfield. (4) Rifle by W. Ketland with
straight grip and no butt box, marked A. R. (Ayrshire Rifles?).

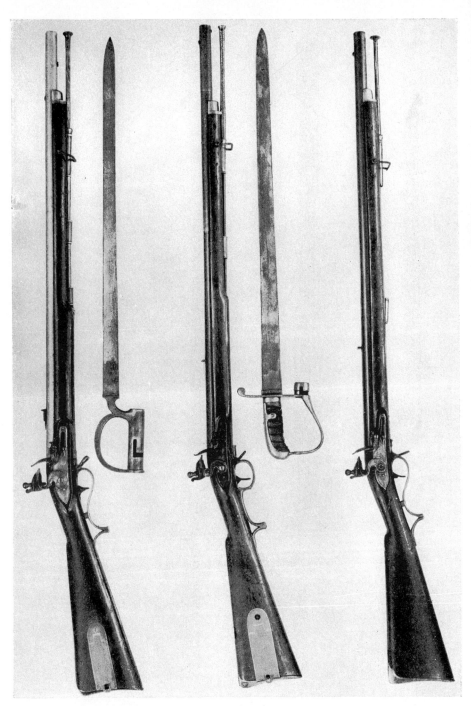

36. Volunteer rifles. *Left to right:* (1) By S. Wallis. (2) By Samuel Staudenmayer. (3) By Henry Nock. All with 30 in. barrels of carbine bore and
seven-groove rifling.

new pattern rifles was sent to Paris for the 2nd Battalion, 95th Regt., to replace those damaged in the Battle of Waterloo. Further evidence concerning the new bayonets was provided in 1819 when the arms factory at Enfield undertook the conversion of 500 rifles from the Tower and, in a dispute between the Gun Finishing Department and the Barrel Department as to who should do the alteration to the stock and barrel, a reference was made to the fitting of "Common Bayonets instead of Sword Bayonets". The position was finally clarified in the following year when 565 obsolete bayonets made for the Duke of Richmond muskets were made applicable, "with a very little alteration", to infantry rifles being set up at Enfield, to save the cost of new ones.

A Baker rifle converted to a socket bayonet is illustrated on Plate 33. It will be noticed that the large trumpet pipe has been moved nearer the lock, the stock cut off at a point where the old bayonet bar commenced, and a nose band fitted. The alteration to the barrel was simpler. The bar was cut off—on the rifle illustrated the marks of the two bar supports are still visible—a bayonet stud was brazed on underneath, and the foresight moved from its position $\frac{3}{4}$ in. from the muzzle to about 3 in. down the barrel, "to give room for the collar of the Bayonet". At the same time the foresight was made higher. This unfortunately gave rise to several complaints about sighting the rifles.

Perhaps for this reason—or it may have been the high cost of the conversion—the use of a socket bayonet on the Baker rifle was soon discontinued. In May, 1823, the preliminary arrangements were made for the provision of 10,000 rifles with "Bayonets with Brass Handles". Five thousand were to be rough stocked and set up at Enfield with barrels made at Enfield. The remaining 5,000 were to be set up by the London gunmakers with barrels supplied by the Birmingham trade. Of the 10,000 locks necessary, half were to come from Birmingham and the balance from Enfield. The sighting, rifling and browning operations were to be confined to a few London men. The bayonets, now called hand bayonets, were simply a combination of the brass grip and spring of the old sword bayonet with the triangular blade of the common musket socket bayonet. By this means a bayonet was provided at little expense and without the need for changing the bar fitting already on the rifle.

Every attempt was made on this occasion to secure a well-made arm and the thirty odd Birmingham barrel-makers, under contract to make the barrels in lots of 150 at 15s. per barrel, were told that they "must be made of the best twisted Stubb Iron and strictly kept to weight, Guage etc. according to the Pattern, to be 2 feet 7 in. in length and from 4 lbs. 2 oz. to 4 lbs. 4 oz. in weight, to be delivered in the plain unrifled state and to be very carefully bored to the inside Guage sent. And the Breech Pins must not be of a smaller Screw than the Pattern." The necessary gauges and the two complete pattern rifles were sent to Birmingham. The rifle on Plate 35 may be one of these. It has

G

a Board of Ordnance wax seal on the butt and the barrel is 2 ft. 7 in.
long and unrifled, a line being engraved an inch from the muzzle to
indicate the final length after rifling. Appropriately the first 600 of the
new rifles were issued to the 1st Battalion 95th Regt. in September,
1823.

In June, 1825, Lt.-Col. Brown of the Rifle Brigade complained that
the hand bayonet with the brass grip was too heavy and submitted one
with a buckhorn handle. While this was rejected as being too susceptible
to damage, Jonathan Bellis, the Master Furbisher, was instructed to
lighten the existing bayonet. At first he produced the one shown on
Plate 34 with a flat blade 10½ in. long weighing 1 lb. 4 oz. This, however,
reduced its efficiency as a weapon. Finally he cut down the size of
the brass grip so that even with the full length triangular blade the
weight was brought down to about 1 lb. (officially 15½ oz.) (Plate 34).

Baker, of course, did not lack competitors. The first challenge was
made in 1801 when a breechloading rifle by James Wilkes, the sword
cutler and gunmaker of Covent Garden, was given extensive trials by
Col. Manningham at Caesar's Camp, Bagshot. Two more rifles were
ordered and the gunmaker asked to adjust the sights and "to form the
Plughole at the Breech precisely of the same size as the Calibre of the
Rifle". The trials of the rifle came to a conclusion in May, 1805, with a
payment of eleven guineas to the so-called inventor. I use that adjective
as the Wilkes breechloading action (Plate 37) was simply a screw plug
let into the top of the barrel with a link to prevent its loss—one of the
oldest of ideas.

Another breechloading rifle to receive an early rejection was
Hulme's rifle. In May, 1807, a Committee of Field Officers authorized
the construction of twenty of them at a cost of five guineas each, but
no further action appears to have been taken. It was certainly a better
action then Wilkes's, but again it was an adaptation of a very old
device, a vertical rolling breech operated by a side lever. This was
copied directly from the so-called Lorenzoni action of the seventeenth
century without that gun's magazines of powder and ball in the butt.
The Hulme rifle was a single-shot weapon, the lever operating the
breech only, which in its open position could be loaded through a
hole in the top of the brass frame. The rifle illustrated (Plate 37) is
stamped PATENT, although no Patent was registered in the name of
Hulme or Helme, as it is often spelt. The butt tang is also engraved
"No. 23 (71) HULME'S RIFLE". The barrel is of ·6 calibre and has
seven-groove rifling.

The Ordnance kept a close watch on the activities of other countries
where rifles were concerned. It awarded £200 to Capt. Hassebroick,
an engineer of the King's German Legion, in 1813, for his trouble in
bringing forward an undisclosed invention of a breechloading rifle
(WO 44/627). In May, 1828, it ordered three copies of the "Pattern
American Rifle" to be made and tested against three others "with
every improvement it will admit of". But these were still early days in

the study of the problems of the rifle, and the state of official knowledge can be judged by the fact that the Ordnance were led to undertake a full-scale trial in 1822 of muskets firing rifled balls, on the theory of Lt.-Col. Miller of the Rifle Brigade "that it is not the impetus communicated to the Ball from the Barrel that gives it its spiral motion but the Air being forced through the Spiral indentations on its sides in its flight".

The last manufacture of Baker rifles took place in 1838 when some 2,000 were set up by the London gunmakers, being rifled and sighted by Baker, Beckwith, Squires and Pritchett. This was done to use up materials in store, although some locks had to be made to make up the numbers. In spite of the introduction of the Brunswick percussion rifle, the Baker flintlock continued in service for some years, mainly with colonial regiments. In 1841, the Ceylon Rifle Regt. and the Royal Canadian Rifle Regt. were both issued from the Tower with the flintlocks, although the latter issue was a temporary one only, pending the provision of percussion arms. As late as 1851 the Baker was reported in use in the Kaffir Wars.

CHAPTER VII

THE LATER FLINTLOCKS

HISTORIANS, Fortescue in particular, have always blamed the Office of Ordnance for the scarcity of arms which this country always faced whenever war broke out. They forget that the Ordnance was a Government department depending on Parliament for a vote of funds which was never sufficient to cover its immediate needs; that it was obliged to keep its contractors waiting for money, yet at the same time insist on the highest standards of workmanship. When the Duke of Richmond commenced his experiments with Henry Nock in 1785 it was understandable that he should regard the period of peace as an opportune moment to try and improve the regulation musket. To some extent he must be blamed for allowing these activities to continue beyond a reasonable time, but no one could have foreseen the extent of the military activity that was to follow the French Revolution. When he realized the dangerously low level to which the store of arms had fallen in 1793, he did everything in his power to remedy it. He harried the Board to get their contractors to fulfil the terms of their contract and, if necessary, to place new ones.

But it was too late. Every gunmaker in the country was overwhelmed with orders and knew only too well that private customers paid better than the government. In July, 1793, the Ordnance took its usual counter-measure by ordering 10,000 foreign muskets, this time from M. Lassance of Liège. But in the following month the Secretary of the Board was obliged to confess that "everything that could induce the Artificers to go has been tried. . . . I fear were other Persons to be employed it would not advance the Business for as we have now no Locks in Store and few Barrels (none for carbines) they would have to get all these Articles from B'ham before they would begin to set up or engage Workmen, and even these Workmen would be decoy'd from other Masters who are now working for the Ordnance."

The Ordnance had now reached an *impasse*. As each week went by the demand for arms mounted, but, in spite of the large orders which had been given to the contractors, a mere trickle of arms came into the Tower. Richmond resolved on desperate measures. On 11th October he wrote to the Home Secretary, the Rt. Hon. Henry Dundas:

"There is not in Store more than what is necessary to supply the Warrants already issued for Land Short Musquets which is the Firelock generally in use . . . . Ten thousand have been bespoke from Liege and we are under treaty for another Ten Thousand. But all our Workmen have failed us in respect to the time they had agreed to send in supplies. And the People at Liege are very dilatory."   (HO 50/370)

He explained how the gunmakers blamed the strictness of the Ordnance inspection and the strength of the proof powder which burst too many barrels, but thought that the real trouble lay in the numerous orders which they had from Ireland and the East India Company. He suggested that the Government should ask that Company to sell its stock of new arms and any others under contract to the Ordnance, and then refrain from further orders until the Government was properly supplied. He also suggested that trade muskets suitable for the Militia of Canada and West Indies should be bought from merchants.

This was an astute move on Richmond's part, for Dundas had been instrumental, earlier in the year, in securing parliamentary approval for the renewal of the East India Company's monopoly. Richmond sent another letter on 24th January, 1794, in which he drew Dundas's attention to the fact that the militia in Canada numbered 29,337 but had only 8,617 fusils for arms. There were no arms to spare in the Tower and the 10,000 stand of arms ordered from the Liège gunmakers were a doubtful asset ("they cannot work to a pattern and although the bore is the same, scarce any two of the musquets are similar") (HO 50/371).

Dundas was now moved to exert his influence and on 6th February a note came from East India House to say that the Court of Directors did "most readily consent" to the ceding of arms to the Government A vast transfer of firearms then took place. The Company's warehouses in London were emptied, arms in transit on the roads and canals were diverted and an East Indiaman *en route* for India in the Channel was brought into Portsmouth, where 5,000 stand of arms were taken from its holds. At the end of the year the East India Company had delivered to the Ordnance 28,920 muskets, 2,680 fusils and carbines, 1,342 pairs of pistols and 300 wall pieces (WO 1/892). 256 chests of French pattern muskets belonging to the Birmingham contractors Galton and Whately, lying in their London warehouses, were also purchased—5,120 at 25s. each.

In subsequent years, although the East India Company regained control of its arms manufacture, it was on several occasions called on by the Ordnance to supply arms. In 1808, the cost of these amounted to £19,844, and, in 1813, 1,000 pairs of Cavalry pistols and 10,000 muskets cost the Government £2,505 16s. 8d. and £19,217 12s. 2d. respectively.

Throughout 1794 and 1795 all gunmakers were given *carte blanche* to send in as many India Pattern and trade muskets as they had in stock or could manufacture. The Ordnance viewers in Birmingham

were told to contact cabinet makers, wheelers and carpenters to per-
suade them to turn over to the rough stocking of guns. Two
Ordnance agents, Capt. Miller and Maj. Trotter, were sent abroad to
make more purchases, Miller to Gothenburg and Copenhagen, and
Trotter to Hamburg. The result of all this activity was soon noticeable
in a return of the number of muskets in the Tower made in July, 1794.
In the main category of musket described as the "Short Land Musket
with steel rammer" the following varieties were present:

New Pattern [Duke of Richmond's?]	42 in. barrel	934
Regular Service	42 in. barrel	2,989
„ „ India Pattern	39 in. barrel	5,908
Trade		4,441
Liège	different	3,639
Danish	Lengths	4,630
French		4,481

(HO 50/371)

The Brown Bess with its well tried barrel and lock was thus dis-
placed in numbers by cheap arms of various shapes and sizes. Later, in
1827, the Master Furbisher was to complain: "[in 1794] the small
Number of Arms thus remaining in Store obliged the Ordnance to
procure Arms wherever they could find them as well as to suspend the
regular Views and Inspection of Arms, as formerly manufactured for
the King's Service, by which means a great number of Arms of inferior
quality were submitted into the Service which has been attended with
a source of trouble and difficulty to this day" (WO 44/541).

As far as possible, the inferior weapons were not issued to British
regular troops, but were used to arm the many foreign units in England,
and allies abroad. In August, 1796, the Ordnance were able to notify
the Chevalier d'Almeida that 12,000 muskets, 3,000 carbines, 3,000
pairs of pistols and 2,000 swords were ready for dispatch to Portugal.
For the year ending March, 1797, an account of money owing for
small arms showed the following sums had been spent:

	£	s.	d.
To the Gunmakers	57,293	1	11
For Foreign Arms	74,250	0	0
East India Company	103,193	9	4
	£234,736	11	3

(WO 46/25)

In 1797, the Ordnance felt that it must try and maintain some
standard musket and, with so many of the East India Company's guns
already in its hands, it resolved to adopt their 39 in. barrel musket as
its main weapon. Orders were given to the Midland contractors to
furnish what materials they had in hand of the regular pattern and then
turn over to the supply of "Musquets of the India Pattern with chambered Barrels". Prices for the complete muskets were agreed at 32s.

for payment in 1 month, 32s. 9d. for payment in 2 months and 33s. 3d. for payment in 3 months. A spare lock was to be supplied with each gun at 7s. each. Presumably this was for the benefit of the London gunmakers who were brought in for their usual task of rough stocking and setting up materials issued from the Tower. Prices for this work were 13s. 9d., 14s. 6d., and 15s. for payment in 1, 2 and 3 months respectively.

By the adoption of the India Pattern musket the Ordnance introduced what is often called the 3rd Model Brown Bess, a misleading classification. In the normal way the authorities would never have countenanced the adoption of such an inferior quality arm. As already mentioned, the gunmakers preferred making it to the regular model because it was easier to put together and was not subject to such high standards of view and proof. The brass furniture was of plainer pattern; the sideplate had no tail; the trigger guard was less elaborately moulded, and the shorter barrel enabled one rammer pipe to be discarded. Although the stock was shaped with the Brown Bess type of butt, the walnut was of the inferior heart and sap quality.

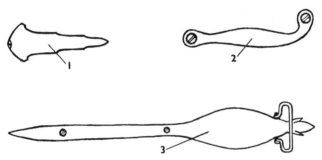

FIG. 16.—India pattern furniture. (1) Butt tang. (2) Side plate. (3) Trigger guard.

With the musket went the carbine, of which a few were ordered for Sergeants in 1807. At least one musket and several wall pieces from the original batch of arms transferred from the East India Company are still in the Tower. As will be seen from the photograph (Plate 46), the Government musket has been copied exactly from the Company's model, with the Royal Crown and Cypher replacing the private trade marks. The Sergeant's carbine is merely a smaller edition of the musket with a 37 in. barrel of carbine bore.

In the eighteenth century, the locks of the East India Company's firearms were engraved with their trade mark; a heart-shaped shield quartered by a diagonal cross with the initials V.E.I.C. (United East India Company) in the quarters. An earlier shield mark, in which there is no cross, the initials E and I being contained in two semi-circles, is often found stamped on the stocks of their guns—apparently a store-keeper's mark. Before 1708, a circular mark bearing the initials

G.C.E. (Governor and Company of East India Merchants) was stamped on their goods, although I have never seen it on a weapon. This mark was surmounted by a Christian cross, which, being resented by pious Muslims as a symbol of alien religious propaganda, was subsequently replaced by the figure four, itself an old merchants mark. (See John Irwin, 'Insignia of the English East India Company', *Journal of Indian Textile History*, No. IV, 1959, pp. 78–9.). Early in the nineteenth century, the Company adopted a proper heraldic crest— a lion, *rampant-gardant*, holding a crown—as its mark for firearms (Appendix E.)

The commencement of the manufacture of rifles meant another drain on the gunmaking resources of the country so that, despite the turn over to the production of the new musket, the Ordnance were still short of arms. Their agent Miller, now a Major, sent over a pattern musket from Hamburg which was passed as fit for "extra service" and he was instructed to buy as many as he could for 27s. each. The Ordnance had learned, however, to distrust these samples, and to save arms being dispatched which either did not come up to the standard of the sample, or were not fit for service, it was decided in February, 1800, to send two viewers from the Tower to Hamburg to prove and inspect the arms there. Cautiously, it was noted "as their Status in Life renders them not beyond the Reach of Corruption, a superior officer should go with them" (WO 1/782). Another source of supply, the merchants Le Mesurier, had their contract for 20,000 foreign muskets increased to 30,000.

The Peace of Amiens brought some respite to the hard-pressed Ordnance officers and they once more considered the introduction of a new regular-service musket. The failure of the complicated Duke of Richmond's musket obviously influenced them in deciding to adopt the very plain musket and subsidiary weapons known as the New Land Series. Manufacture seems to have started sometime in 1802. In November, Henry Nock's offer to make "locks of the new pattern" at the rate of 5,000 per annum at 9s. each was refused, but a similar offer from Baker and Negus was accepted. The following year the process of manufacture of "the Musquet of the New Pattern" was speeded up, orders being spread over a larger number of contractors. Miller was sent to Birmingham to buy as many locks and barrels as possible for the setters-up in London. Barrels were to cost 11s. 6d., proved in Birmingham, and 12s., proved and delivered to London. The setting up charge was to be 13s., plus 9d. for the engraving and hardening of the lock, and 6d. for filing the barrel.

The new musket was a plain but well-made arm. The brass furniture consisted of the Duke of Richmond's Pattern buttplate with its small tang and plain trigger guard held by a single screw. The India pattern sideplate was used, secured by a wood screw in its centre. The steel rammer with a swell at the muzzle end was positioned by two small pipes and a long trumpet pipe. As with the 1796-pattern carbines, no

tail pipe was fitted. The high comb and long wrist of the Brown
Bess were replaced by the simple stock of Henry Nock's guns. Another
feature of Nock's guns—the flat keys to hold barrel to stock—was also
retained, but the break-off breech was not fitted. The 42 in. barrel
had only a bayonet stud acting as a foresight. Other small parts of the
musket were brought more in line with the sporting weapon; the trigger
was housed in a box trigger-plate instead of being hung from a pin.

The lock had a flat plate $6\frac{1}{2}$ in. long and a flat ring-neck cock, some
of which had an accentuated front curve, giving them a pot-bellied
look. The mainspring on these locks was different from earlier locks.
Instead of being secured to the plate by a screw, a tenon on the fixed
end of the spring engaged with a notch in the thick edge of the plate.
While some of these locks were free of any decoration, many had a

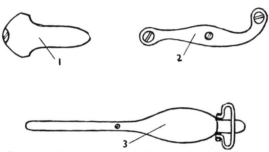

FIG. 17.—New Land pattern furniture.   (1) Butt tang.
(2) Side plate.   (3) Trigger guard.

small sprig of engraving on the tail of the lock and sometimes on the
cock. Following in the tradition of Henry Nock, each lock plate was
checked with a pattern to ensure that the tumbler and screw holes were
properly aligned.

The moment a new musket was successfully under way it was
inevitable that other new arms should be considered to accompany it.
On 27th June, 1803, the Adjutant General sent the Secretary of the
Board a pattern of a gun which the King had decided should be adopted
by the 52nd and other Light Infantry regiments, with the accompanying
instructions: "The Barrel shall be browned, a grooved sight shall be
fixed at the Breech end of the Barrel and a Canvas Cover similar to
that used by the Austrian Troops shall be provided for the purpose of
covering and protecting the Butt and Lock of each Piece" (WO 3/152).

The resumption of war with France, however, prevented the immediate execution of the royal wish. Although some muskets were
altered for the use of the 52nd Regt. by Henry Nock, the Master
General had to inform the Commander-in-Chief in August, 1804,
"that the extreme pressure of business at present in every branch of the
Ordnance Dept. precludes the possibility of the sort of Fuzee you
propose being furnished for the Light Infantry Regiments". But a

promise was made to produce the gun whenever circumstances permitted. A year later, barrels for the "New Pattern Light Infantry Musket" were ordered. No further mention of their manufacture is made until July, 1810, when the prices for setting up the New Land and Light Infantry muskets in London and Birmingham were agreed at 25s. and 26s. respectively. Only one in ten of the muskets assembled was to be of the Light Infantry pattern.

This second gun in the New Land Series had the same lock and style of stock as the musket, but the barrel was cut down to 39 in. As an aid to the markmanship expected from light infantry, a plain slotted backsight was fitted at the breech end of the barrel and a scroll trigger guard acted as a pistol grip (Plate 42). The small proportion of these lighter muskets originally ordered was revised in the following year in the light of the need for more light infantrymen, and, on 28th October, 1811, 20,000 Light Infantry barrels were ordered from thirty-one Birmingham contractors. The large musket lock used on these first-issue light infantry guns was later replaced by a lighter lock only 6 in. long.

The apparent long delay between the ordering of the first batch of barrels in 1805 and the setting up in 1810 was probably due to the more pressing need for other arms. In August, 1803, Brownlow Bate, who had managed the Ordnance work in Birmingham during the previous war, returned there to join forces with Miller, now a Colonel, who was busy on arms of the regular pattern, to re-establish the manufacture of the India Pattern arms. A full agreement was drawn up on 28th March, 1804, in which separate terms were granted to 11 gunmakers (for rough stocking and setting up), 18 barrel makers, 20 lock makers, 7 bayonet makers and 11 rammer makers. Each contractor had to sign a covenant not to perform military work for any other party except the East India Company without the permission of Col. Miller, who was appointed Inspector of Small Arms in charge of the whole operation.

It was also made clear to them that no variation would be considered in the prices for the various processes which were:

Stocking and Setting up	—	16	0
Lock Hardening etc.	—		9
Barrel	—	7	8
Lock	—	6	6*
Bayonet	—	2	6
Rammer	—		8

$$£1 \quad 14 \quad 1$$

A similar agreement was made with nine flint makers of Brandon in Suffolk for the supply of 356,000 flints per month. Prices for these were one guinea per thousand for musket flints, and one pound for the same number in carbine and pistol size. These were to be supplied in the proportion of 50 carbine and 50 pistol flints to every 1,000 for muskets.

* This was composed of 4s. 7d. for filing, 1s. 3d. for forging and 8d. contractor's profit.

With the re-opening of their premises in Birmingham, and a proper establishment of viewers and furbishers there under Col. Miller, the Ordnance gained a reasonable control over the gunmaking industry for the first time. The production of India Pattern muskets rose steadily from 1804 to reach a peak in 1813 and finally to cease in 1815 with the end of the war. The full figures for these years were given during a Court of Enquiry in 1824 (WO 44/519).

1804	—	37,879
1805	—	42,468
1806	—	60,525
1807	—	58,323
1808	—	83,895
1809	—	147,785
1810	—	180,452
1811	—	219,661
1812	—	267,654
1813	—	278,932
1814	—	157,347
1815	—	68,790
		1,603,711

Although the standards of viewing and proving these muskets were less exacting than those applied to the regular pattern, they were nevertheless sufficient to account for the rejection of some thousands of barrels. Gunmakers were always adept in disguising minor flaws and imperfections in their work, and an interesting side-line of their trade was revealed in 1806. On 17th June, Samuel Galton and some other Birmingham gunmakers complained to the Ordnance that, in consequence of the abolition of the Slave Trade, "they were shut from the Market at which they had been enabled to dispose of the Barrels which were rejected by the Ordnance". The Board were very sympathetic and agreed to increase the price of India Pattern barrels by 10d. and allow an additional 4d. for better filing and forging, providing supplies were also increased.

Possibly with a view to absorbing some of the sub-standard barrels, the manufacture of "extra service" muskets of inferior quality was set up in 1809. It was also an opportunity to use up poor quality gun stocks. As the war dragged on, the supply of proper walnut had become a matter of some concern to the extent that an attempt was made to grow walnut trees on the thirty odd Ordnance stations in England and Wales. The quality of "extra service" stocks can be judged by comparing their cost of 1s. 6d. against the first-quality Tower stock of 4s. 10d. Even so, it was judged necessary that the wood should be sound and "free from shakes" and not "Cross in the Hand". The venture only lasted three years and, as the Birmingham production figures show, was not important:

1808 — 1,922
1809 — 1,534
1810 — 2,225
        ———
        5,681

Manufacture was not confined to the Midlands and the London gun-makers Ezekiel Baker, William Parker, Thomas Reynolds and Durs Egg also supplied these muskets complete at 31s. each. In 1814, 16,672 extra service stocks were reported in store at the Tower.

It was a period when the Ordnance offered every kind of financial inducement to the trade, and the gunmakers were not slow to take advantage of it. In September, 1808, the "Manufacturers of Materials" under the chairmanship of Theodore Price held a protest meeting in the Stork Tavern, Birmingham, as a result of which they applied for 6d. increase in the price of locks. Once more the Ordnance agreed on the assumption that more locks would be forthcoming. In the following year, Mr. Price, as chairman of a "Committee of Gunmakers", proudly announced that 200 men and apprentices had been drawn into the lock-making industry by the offer of premiums, and the Ordnance with great affability donated a hundred guineas towards this fund.

Although the price of the India Pattern musket fluctuated, the pattern of the gun, with the exception of the cock, remained unchanged throughout its manufacture by the Ordnance. The swan-neck type was replaced by the ring-neck or "throat hole" type at the end of 1809, for the reason that it was "stronger and more durable and would simplify the Manufacture of Locks", and an increase of 2d. in the price was granted.

With all this official encouragement, many of the gunmakers began employing machinery, and the effect of this was not long in coming. In July, 1814, the Tower was found to be so full of arms that incoming India Pattern muskets had to be diverted to Edinburgh, Chester, Dover, Chelmsford and Tynemouth for storage. The contractors were warned that production of this pattern would have to be diminished progressively over the next three years and then manufacture turned over to the New Land Series of arms. In March, 1815, Napoleon's last efforts in Europe caused a momentary alarm and the Ordnance gave the India Pattern priority again. But in July, with peace restored, it abruptly cancelled all orders and reduced the output of its factories at the Tower and Lewisham.

Once more the Ordnance turned its attention to its neglected New Land Series. In December, 1812, the pattern of a carbine had been designed for Gentleman Cadets of the Junior Department of the Royal Military College. Two hundred of these were made in 1817 and the same pattern was apparently adopted for the Cadet forces of the Royal Naval College, Portsmouth and the Marine Society in 1819 This Cadet's carbine was a smaller edition of the New Land musket with a

34 in. barrel of carbine bore. There were also slight variations in the brass furniture; the side plate had no wood screw in the middle and there was a small shield thumbplate or escutcheon. It was also the only gun in the series to have a tail pipe for the rammer, and for some reason the barrel keys and slots used on the larger guns were replaced by the old method of pins and loops (Plate 42).

It is difficult to establish how many of the New Land muskets were made, and to what extent they were taken into service by the army. The one illustrated on Plate 42 is engraved GREN^{dr} GD^s No. 71, and it is probable that only a few selected regiments like the Guards received an issue of the musket. In 1823, 800 were ordered to be set up at the Enfield factory, and it was here that the last gun in the series, the Sergeant's carbine, was produced in May, 1832 These carbines were the result of the decision made in July, 1830, to issue Sergeants of infantry regiments with fusils instead of pikes. They were produced by converting 800 light infantry muskets "with small locks", the barrels of which were reduced to a length of 33 in.

The India Pattern and New Land Series of arms so far described formed the bulk of arms made in the last period of the flintlock, but they were accompanied by a mixture of carbines and pistols not always easy to identify from the records. Orders given to Col. Miller in 1813 name the following arms in production:

> India Sergeant's Carbines
> Artillery Carbines
> Eliott's Light Dragoon Carbines
> Musket bore Carbines for Cavalry
> Short Cavalry Carbines
> Pistols with Swivel Rammers
>   Carbine Bore Regular Pattern
>   Musket Bore Regular Pattern
>   Carbine Bore 9in. or Dumpling

The India Pattern carbine has already been mentioned. The Artillery carbine was evidently very similar for, in February, 1828, 527 of them were altered by the simple expedient of cutting two inches off the length of the bayonet blade, "which would make them similar to those of the India Sgts. Carbines". Eliott's carbine had altered considerably from the arm bearing General Eliott's name described in Chapter 3, but it still retained the same barrel length, weight and carbine bore. The fact that there were both carbine and musket bore carbines illustrates the vacillating policy of the military towards the type of arm to be carried by the cavalry. The decision of 1796 to maintain one carbine and pistol of musket bore for Light and Heavy Cavalry was obviously not adhered to for long. The advent of the infantry and cavalry rifle of carbine bore seems to have brought a revival of a smoothbore carbine of the same calibre.

The main carbine in use was, however, the short cavalry carbine with a 16 in. barrel. It was known as the Paget carbine, taking its name from General Henry Paget (1768–1854), who is credited with its design. There is no mention of its association with this great cavalry leader at the time, but as Colonel of the 7th Light Dragoons he may well have assisted in its preparation. Later, as the Marquis of Anglesey, he was Master General of the Ordnance from 1827–28 and 1846–52. Two examples of this carbine are illustrated (Plate 40). The barrel has a V backsight on the tang and a long sloping foresight, and is held to the stock by keys and slots. The stock and furniture are plain and the side bar or rib has a backward bend. The carbine with a folding stock bears the regimental markings of the 16th Queen's Light Dragoons and may have been a regimental conversion.

The three main features of this carbine, which were found on many of the pistols, were the swivel ramrod and two modifications to the lock—a safety bolt and a raised pan. It is impossible to decide from the records of the Ordnance who was responsible for these or the exact date when they were introduced. Bolt locks were under construction for the Ordnance as early as 1806, when some 12,000 were made. They were fitted to the short cavalry carbine when it was issued to certain Light Dragoons regiments late in 1808 (WO 3/195). Five thousand new pistols were also set up with the same lock as the carbine, and pistols with wood rammers were hastily converted to swivel rammers.

The majority of pistols had 9 in. barrels and they began as a development of the plain 1796 model of Henry Nock. The idea of carrying the ramrod separate does not seem to have been popular and, in July, 1801, 2,000 pairs of Light Dragoon pistols of "the old pattern" were ordered. The top pistol on Plate 43 has the Nock type stock without a buttplate, but has been fitted with a steel ramrod in a rather complicated tail pipe. In January, 1810, the Birmingham contractors Willetts and Holden offered to supply 500 pairs of pistols of a design submitted by them with a lock having "a raised pan". This was a pan found on most sporting weapons for the purpose of keeping the lock waterproof. In the normal lock with a flat pan, rain or moisture on the fence at the rear of the pan seeped into the priming powder. With the raised pan, channels on either side diverted any water down past the pan.

The swivel rammer and raised pan were retained on most of the remaining pistols, but the bolted lock was an additional expense not always considered necessary, nor was it always welcomed by the soldiers. It is a pity that the Ordnance books do not afford full identification of these pistols, as several intriguing names are recorded. The "Dumpling" pistol with a 9 in. barrel of carbine bore was apparently built for "extra service". It was supplied with a swivel rammer and raised pan in 1812 at a cost of £2 4s. 2d. per pair. The following year there are several references to a "Russian" pistol, which one assumes was based on a Russian model. In 1814, the "Squirrel" pistol for "extra service" is mentioned, but this may be another name for the "Dumpling". In the same year a considerable number of sea service weapons were ordered mainly for the use of the large Coast Guard and Preventive

Services. Some of the pistols made for them were considerably shortened in 1822, the barrels of one type which has been noted being only 4½ in. long.

It is strange that the policy of standardizing the bore of all arms in 1796 was so quickly discarded, for its benefits were obvious. The re-introduction of different bores during the Napoleonic Wars soon presented problems, particularly to cavalry regiments, some of which had carbines of one bore and pistols of another. The matter was already complicated by the use of different cartridges, the charge necessary for a pistol being less than that for a carbine. In many regiments it was the custom to use musket cartridges and to shake out half the powder when loading the pistol, but if the soldier forgot to do this in the heat of the battle, the pistol could be blown out of his hand. The flintlock itself was by no means perfect and caused some concern by its high rate of misfires.

A Board of Officers under Sir Richard Hussey Vivian was convened by the Commander-in-Chief in July, 1827, to study these problems. Their report, made in October, 1828, recommended the establishment of one carbine for light and heavy cavalry and the abolition of the pistol (WO 44/677). In the following year several carbines were submitted for their approval. They included one of Nock's original carbines, a very similar carbine by William Moore, the London gunmaker, and a specially made carbine by the new Master Furbisher, Charles Manton. Manton, a relative of the immortal "Joe", was appointed in March, 1829, on the death of Jonathan Bellis. At his examination for the job, it was revealed that he had not served an apprenticeship and his experience was confined to the making of "best guns used by the opulent class". As might be expected, Manton immediately tried to introduce some of the features and quality of high-class sporting weapons into the military arm. In a musket he submitted to a Select Committee in 1829 two improvements were described as "fronting the hammer with steel" at a cost of 1s. and the fitting of a roller to the hammer spring for 1s. 6d. While these improvements were appreciated, the extra expense was not thought justifiable. Manton then concentrated on his carbine.

His first model was made by Ezekiel Baker—on Plate 54 the resemblance between Baker's own carbine and that of Manton's design is noticeable—at a cost of £4 14s., but it was modified several times before it succeeded in meeting the wishes of the Board. Six of the carbines were made and issued to the 15th Hussars for trial in 1830. Handling and firing on horseback then revealed other faults; it was too long, the swivel weak, and the backsight not as effective as the old one. A safety bolt was also recommended, as one Hussar had accidentally fired his carbine while trotting. In January, 1832, another six carbines were made with shorter barrels, bolted locks and a scroll guard instead of a pistol grip. Conflicting reports were received of these carbines, and at least one regiment, the 10th Royal Hussars, armed with rifled carbines by Baker, would not countenance any change at all. However, in April, 1833, the various reports were analysed as to the barrel, bore and pattern preferred. Manton's carbine with a smooth barrel of carbine bore was given the majority vote and a sealed pattern placed in the Principal Storekeeper's office.

The Manton—or Pattern 1833—carbine owes much to Nock and to Baker. To the latter's influence can be traced the form of the barrel and fore end of the stock, with its very short swivel, and the sideplate and rib are identical to that on Baker's 1822 carbine. The barrel, 20 in. long, has the Nock break-off and fitted to the tang is a distinctive scoop backsight. The lock is a partial return to Nock's enclosed lock in that the hammer pivot is enclosed within the plate and is operated by the pressure of the short side of the mainspring.

The pattern carbine was submitted to the Commander-in-Chief and finally to the King, who admired it and said he would like to see the Lancers armed with it as well. The Ordnance were, however, careful to point out that 10,000 carbines would be needed to re-arm all the cavalry and lancer regiments and thought it unwise to risk any expense until the percussion trials were complete (WO 44/677). But, on 12th November, 1834, they authorized the manufacture of 1,000 of the carbines. In the following July, arrangements were made for half to be set up at Enfield and the other half by twelve London gunmakers. Although the date 1835 appears on the carbines, they were not completed until 28th June, 1837, when the final batch of 411 were reported ready for distribution, 297 having been supplied in February, 1836, to the 9th Lancers and 292 to the 7th Dragoon Guards in March, 1837. A very fine example of the flintlock arm, the Manton carbine was overtaken by the percussion era, and the 1835 batch were the only ones made.

Another carbine of the late flintlock period of which only a few were made, but which is of special interest, is the double-barrelled Cape carbine. In December, 1821,* a pattern carbine for "a Troop of Colonial Cavalry at the Cape of Good Hope" was ordered to be made at Enfield under the joint direction of the Storekeeper, George Lovell, and the Master Furbisher, Jonathan Bellis. All materials were said to be available at the factory except for the left-hand lock, and the total price with twisted stub barrels was estimated at £5 1s. 2d. In March, 1822, 136 were ordered and a year later another 116. This last batch was completed in February, 1824, and a pattern deposited in the Tower (Plate 66).

The flintlock Cape carbine was the first of a series of which the rest were all percussion examples. It was a heavy fearsome gun with 26 in. barrels of ·733 in. calibre, and even its co-designer, George Lovell, was worried about the recoil. He feared that the discharge of one barrel would dislodge the adjoining ball, and advocated the use of special felt wads. The usual scroll guard and swivel rammer *en vogue* were fitted. As there was no sideplate, the 10 in. long runner bar was pinned to the

---

* The carbine was suggested by Lord Charles Somerset in June, 1820, but was then rejected by the Duke of Wellington.

37. Close-up of breechloading rifles by Wilkes (*Top*) and Helme.

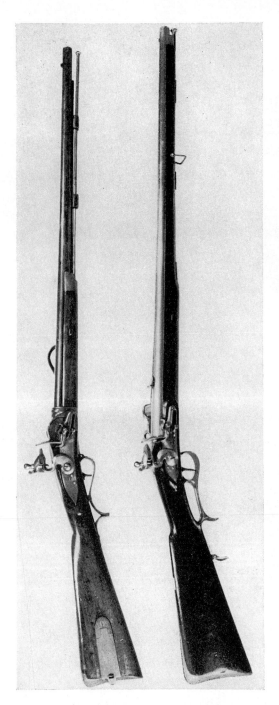

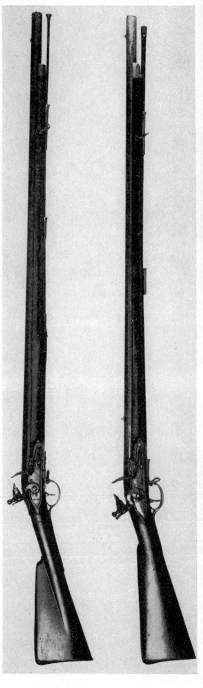

38. *Left:* Breechloading rifle by Helme. *Right:* Breechloading rifle by Wilkes.

39. *Left:* India Pattern musket made for Volunteer company by William Parker. *Right:* Muzzle loading rifle by Durs Egg with slit stock and heavy steel rammer, both with 39 in. barrels.

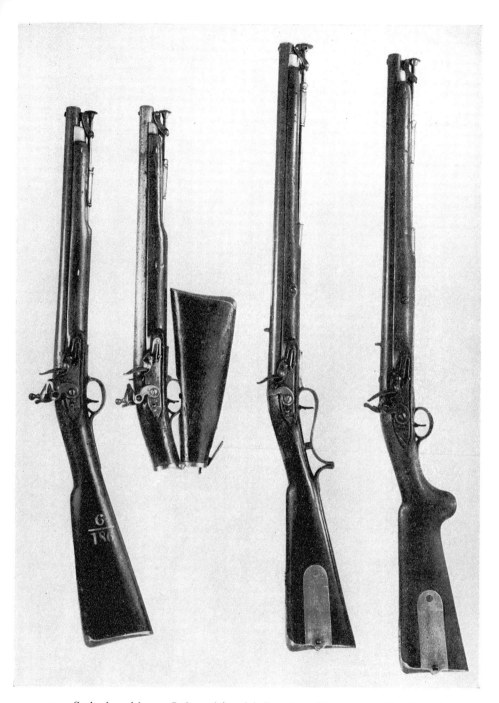

40. Swivel carbines. *Left to right:* (1) Paget carbine with 16 in. barrel.
(2) Paget carbine with folding butt, marked Q L D (Queen's Light
Dragoons). (3) Baker cavalry rifle with 20 in. barrel. (4) Baker cavalry
rifle with pistol grip, marked X R H (10th Royal Hussars).

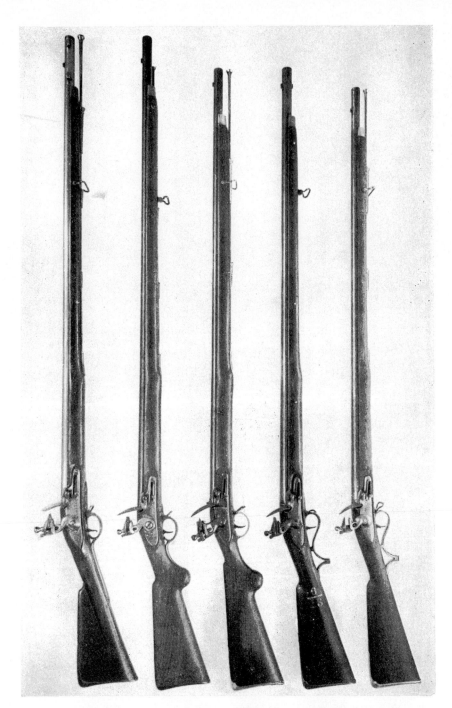

41. Baker's muskets. *Left to right:* (1) With special clip-on bayonet fitting. (2) With pistol grip and rammer to the side. (3) With a combination percussion lock and flintlock. (4) Presentation inscribed musket of 1822, the lock with an adjustable circular spring. A special bayonet and side rammer are fitted. (5) Carbine made for the East India Company.

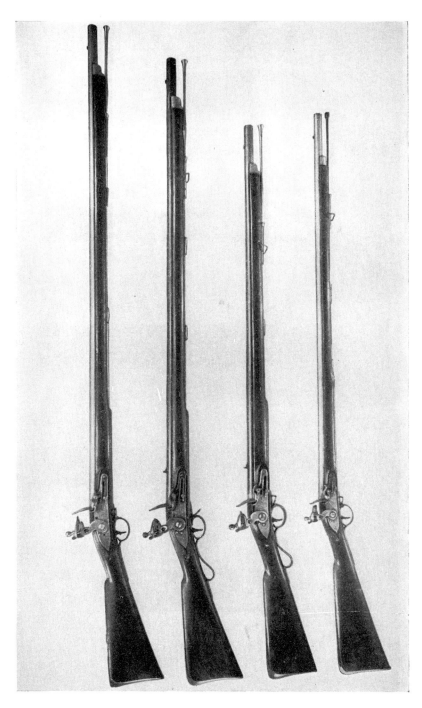

42. New Land Pattern arms. *Left to Right:* Musket with 42 in. barrel.
(2) Light Infantry musket with 39 in. barrel. (3) Sergeant's carbine with
33 in. barrel. (4) Cadet's carbine.

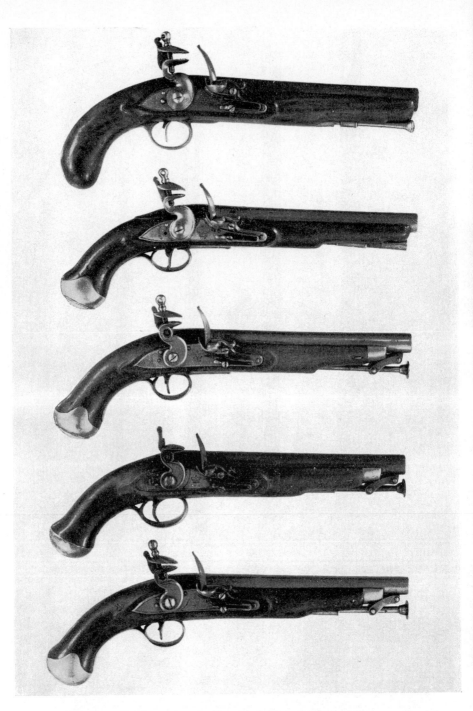

43. Flintlock pistols with 9 in. barrels. *Top:* Modified Patt. 1796. (2) Light Dragoon. (3) New Land Pattern with raised pan and swivel rammer. (4) William IV pistol with bolted lock, etc. (5) Sea Service pistol of William IV (this has a belt hook not visible in the photograph).

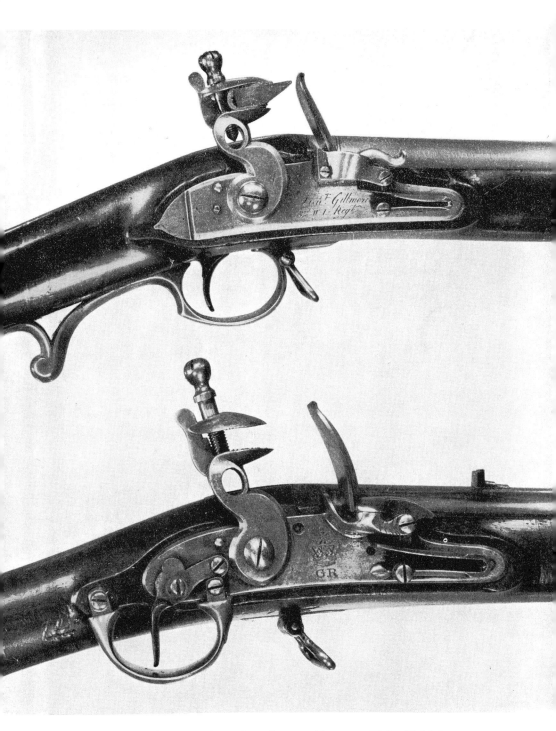

44. *Top:* Close-up of Gillmore's musket. *Bottom:* Close-up of John Noble's musket. Note the external trigger and guard.

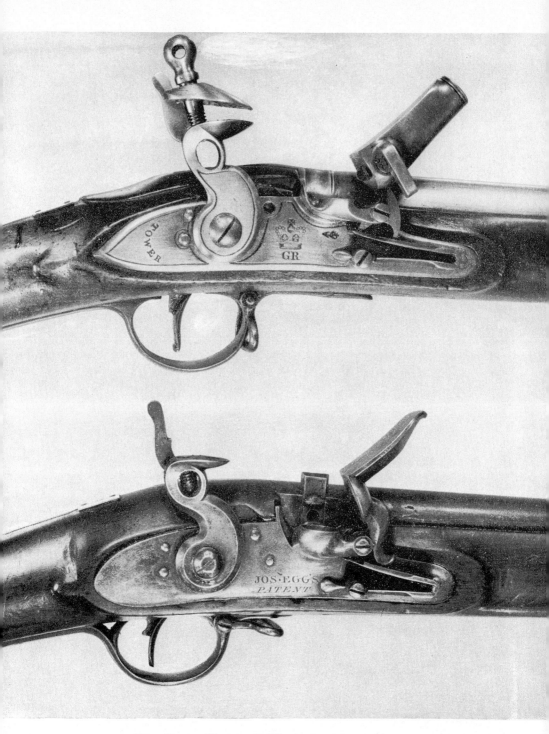

45. *Top:* James Thomson's flintlock with magazine primer. *Bottom:*
Joseph Egg's waterproof flintlock. The touch-hole cover is raised.

stock at both ends. The barrel tang incorporated the scoop backsight later adopted by Manton for his carbine.

Official attempts to improve the flintlock, culminating in the Manton carbine, have been described, but there were many ideas put forward by private individuals, gunmakers, soldiers and other inventors. Foremost in these endeavours was our old friend Ezekiel Baker. From 1800, when his rifle was adopted by the British Army, until his death in 1836 he was constantly inventing and, it must be admitted, blatantly advertising some new gun or accessory. In 1810, the Society for the Encouragement of Arts, etc. awarded him their Silver Medal for an improved cavalry pistol (see *Proceedings*, Vol. XXVIII, pp. 199–206). At first sight it was merely a well-made pistol with a swivel rammer and a bolted lock. Every part of it was, however, cleverly designed for some special purpose. The rammer could be left in the barrel to hold the ball in place; the touchhole and pan were self-priming; the safety bolt came into operation automatically at half-cock; the hammer was lengthened to stop the pistol from being cocked when replaced in its holster, and so on.

Many of his muskets were fitted with pistol grips, but those he made under contract for the East India Company have the rifle type trigger guard instead, which was considered stronger. Another feature of Baker's muskets was a ramrod which started in the normal position in front of the guard but twisted to the left as it reached the muzzle. With this went a special bayonet. Baker had a particular liking for intricate locks. His cocks often have special jaws to ease the insertion of flints, and the plate sometimes has two holes drilled in it for no obvious reason. They were so placed that, when the springs were compressed, a nail inserted in the holes acted as a cramp for their easy removal. A small screw often screwed into the edge of the plate below the cock was "a regulating screw" to adjust the tension of the mainspring.

Baker was one of many gunmakers who showed no love for the new percussion locks but he did design several transitional locks, being combinations of percussion and flintlock actions. In Jackson's *European Hand Firearms*, Plate LXIII, there is illustrated a combination lock by Baker dated 1821. This with a slight modification was patented the next year by Sampson Davis (No. 4648); he called it his "Devolving Lock". Baker fitted another of these locks to the magnificent musket now in the Tower of London (Plate 41). It can be used as a flintlock, and a percussion hammer is fitted to the side of the cock. As this descends, a lever and claw holding the cap in position on the nipple is knocked out of the way. The touchhole is controlled by an automatic shutter. Engraved on the trigger guard is the weight of the arm 9 lb. 8 oz. and the lock is dated 1832. According to the Ordnance Minute Books, two muskets with Baker locks "to fire either flint or percussion" were included in the percussion trials of that year. They were an advantage in situations where the soldier or sportsman might run out of percussion caps.

H

Most of Baker's muskets were far too complicated to win the approval of the Ordnance, although in 1834 they thought highly enough of a set of arms submitted by him to offer to purchase them, "so that the improvements applicable to flintlock or percussion arms are not lost". Baker rather haughtily informed them that they were not for sale. He had previously presented them with a musket, carbine and pistol, whose barrels were engraved with the grandiose legend:

DEPOSITED AT THE ROYAL REPOSITORY AT WOOLWICH BY PERMISSION OF HIS GRACE THE DUKE OF WELLINGTON, MASTER GENERAL OF THE HONOURABLE BOARD OF ORDNANCE BY EZEKIEL BAKER, GUNMAKER & ARMOURER TO HIS MAJESTY GEORGE THE 4th. 1822.

One of the most successful of private ventures to improve the flintlock was that of George Dodds and his "Royal York Gun-Lock". This lock was examined at Woolwich sometime in 1803 and in the following year the Society for the Encouragement of Arts etc. awarded its inventor a Silver Medal and ten guineas (it is illustrated on Plate VIII of Vol. XXII of their *Proceedings*, 1804). Later, in a printed leaflet, Dodd describes how in that year the Ordnance ordered 800 to be set up in New Land muskets but only half that number were completed. In 1805, Dodd took out Patent No. 2825 for his lock, describing himself as an engineer of Great Ormond Street. The East India Company experimented with them and gave them a good report. With this encouragement, Dodd asked the Ordnance, in April, 1813, to reconsider them. Another 100 muskets were made and issued to the 2nd Battalion of the 1st Foot for trial, but there the matter ended (WO 44/624).

Dodd's lock was a very clever adaptation of the normal lock mechanism, whereby the lock when set at half-cock could not possibly be released. In this position, the more pressure on the trigger the more the vertical sear bit into the tumbler. Like many other ideas, it was feasible on the drawing-board but difficult to put into practice. William Parker of Holborn was one of the gunmakers given the job of making and setting up these guns. Although he was allowed the high price of 14s. for each lock, he complained of the "great difficulty and loss of time in the getting up of the lock and hanging the trigger". The diagrams of the lock's action (Fig. 18) show what a delicate task this must have been.

The trouble with most inventions, even if designed from a practical point of view, was that by solving one problem they frequently raised another. John Noble, a Superintendent of the Enfield factory, was impressed by the number of guns returned for repair with their stocks broken in the region of the lock. He reasoned that this was due to the weakening influence of the trigger slot and guard recesses and accordingly produced a gun with the trigger and guard attached to the outside of the lock (Plate 44). Twelve were made for trial but were rejected almost immediately because they were so clumsy to handle (WO 44/631).

One of the faults of the flintlock was the frequent breaking of the flint. If this happened during an action, there was little chance of the soldier getting the stiff jaws of the cock unscrewed and a new flint inserted in time. The fire power of a company could be considerably reduced. One solution advanced was a cock with a detachable head, but this was found to work loose. Sir Howard Douglas, whose father had been responsible for the introduction of the flintlock into naval gunnery, submitted a lock in 1817 whose cock had a double pair of jaws facing in opposite directions and held in position by a wing nut. If one flint broke, the other could be swivelled to the front in a matter of seconds. Although the idea was Douglas's, the design of the lock was probably that of Henry Nock, who co-operated with him in 1804. After various trials the lock was approved, but its application to small arms was

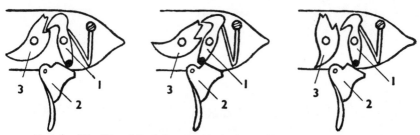

Fig. 18.—The "Royal York Gun-Lock" mechanism in the half-cock, full-cock, and released positions. (1) Sear. (2) Trigger. (3) Tumbler.

thought inadvisable, the backward-facing flint causing damage (Plate 47). As a lock for naval cannon, however, it had an immediate success and the Admiralty ordered its gradual introduction (WO 44/540).

Another failure of the flintlock was due to water getting at the powder, either in the pan or through the touchhole into the barrel. Joseph Egg, a master at devising ingenious locks, submitted a gun to the Ordnance in 1816 which had an air-tight slide over the touchhole shut down by closing the pan cover and opened by the action of the tumbler in firing (Plate 45). This musket underwent a most vigorous trial. Ten rounds were fired with the lock dipped in water between each round, four rounds with the lock first dipped in water with the pan open and priming put in afterwards, three rounds with the lock watered after each loading and priming, and, finally, twenty rounds were fired rapidly to see whether the slide would be effected by heat No misfires having occurred, the gun was loaded and the breech submerged in water for ten minutes. When the priming was renewed, the gun fired perfectly (WO 44/624). Twenty-five New Land and twenty-five India Pattern muskets were converted for trial but, not having the specially made barrels of Egg's original gun, several of them burst in proof. On the evidence of this imperfection, the guns were apparently rejected.

Egg's protestations at this decision were not as persuasive as those of Joe Manton, whose glib tongue once extolled his own waterproof lock with the words: "It will fire under water, indeed, so long as you keep the muzzle out of the water, you may if you like use the stock as an oar in pushing your sporting punt forwards; the gun will still go off for certain." (Lacy, *The Modern Shooter*, 1842, p. 539). All Egg received for his trouble was his expenses of £55 0s. 2d.

The failure of the priming was the bugbear of all soldiers, as it meant opening another cartridge. The Ordnance would therefore, have welcomed a satisfactory form of magazine primer. In 1813, James Thomson submitted a steel or hammer which had a chamber capable of delivering about twenty primings by turning "a small cylindrical grooved pin" in its base. The release mechanism, when fired, rapidly expanded with the heat and quickly jammed. With a slight alteration, however, it was passed and fitted to twelve muskets which were issued to the 2nd Battalion of the 9th Foot (Plate 45). Their experience convinced the Ordnance that there were several disadvantages and—something no one had thought of—the need for a powder horn to refill the magazine. This was enough to warrant its rejection. Thomson patented his magazine, however, in March, 1814 (No. 3784).

Probably the most expensive experimental musket made was that of Joseph Albert Gillmore. As a Lieutenant of the 3rd West Indies Regt., he had witnessed the disadvantages of both rifle and musket, and his gun was an attempt to combine the quickloading of the musket with the accuracy of the rifle. He set out his views in a printed pamphlet and persuaded the Ordnance to have a gun specially constructed in the Government factory in 1815. As this did not meet with his approval, he obtained permission for Messrs. Forsyth & Co. of Piccadilly to make one to his specification, which they did for the sum of £40.

There is nothing particularly outstanding in the appearance of the gun (Plate 44), and only minor improvements are embodied in the stock and lock. The 39 in. barrel was, however, built on a revolutionary principle. Gillmore's theory was that, by using a special cartridge in which the ball was embedded in a cup or wad, the standard musket ball could be used in a barrel two sizes smaller. (The musket barrel was approximately 12 bore and the ball $14\frac{1}{2}$ to the lb.) By reducing the windage, as it was called, more accuracy could be obtained and the charge reduced by a third. Unfortunately Gillmore, in his enthusiasm for a lighter gun, went still further and the gun finally produced fired a ball of 18 to the lb. While agreeing that it was a fine weapon the examining committee refused, therefore, to consider any change in the standard musket bore, and Gillmore had to be content with a commendation and a payment of £60 for his expenses. The gun was originally furnished with a special bayonet and tangent backsight, now missing. As an opinion on the intelligence of the British soldier, the Committee's comments on the backsight are worth recording: "It cannot be expected that the Common Soldier could attend to the adjustments necessary to derive any benefit from its adoption" (WO 44/626).

The inventive spirit that produced so many varieties and modifications of the flintlock also lent itself to the production of some strange combination weapons. Pistols were added to swords, daggers and lances, and the musket, already, one would have thought, of sufficient weight, was linked with the pike. The last was a revival of the ideal of the "Double-Armed Man" fostered by William Neade and others early in the seventeenth century. At a surprisingly late date, two attempts were made to interest the Ordnance in pike-muskets; in March, 1833, by Com. W. D. Evance of the Royal Navy (WO 44/624), and in March, 1844, by Maj.-Gen. W. Morison of the East India Company's Madras Artillery* (WO 44/539). Evance's musket had a folding pike after the fashion of the folding bayonet, but Morison's pike could be detached, if necessary, being held by a ring and a slotted catch on the stock. Both weapons were rejected, although it was noted that they could be "formidable weapons in desultory and irregular warfare". The East India Company, however, made a small number for trial. In this category of firearm *curiosa* can be placed the hand rocket launchers inspired by the rocket artillery of Sir William Congreve. A variety of experimental launchers seems to have been made, usually in the form of a brass or copper tube with a flintlock igniter, and fired in the manner of the modern bazooka. A selection of these firearms is illustrated on Plates 50 and 51.

Before leaving the subject of the flintlock, I will deal briefly with the events leading to the introduction of browning of gun barrels in 1815. In the records of the seventeenth century many guns were described as russeted, but by the eighteenth century the majority of barrels were kept polished or bright. In fact, Orders for the Foot and the Horse, in 1742, demanded arms "to be as bright as silver" (JAHR, Vol. 28, p. 55; Vol. 14, p. 84). Some sea service muskets were painted black, resulting in the two classes, Black Sea and Bright Sea muskets. When the Light Infantry and Rifle Corps were introduced, it was soon realized that a polished barrel reflecting the light was of no use to a marksman seeking to hide his position, and their weapons were frequently referred to as "brown barrelled". The process used was not very satisfactory and the socket of the bayonet—also browned—soon rubbed the muzzle bare.

In 1771-72 the Ordnance conducted a series of experiments on browning but came to no decision. One method was submitted by Lew Alley, gunmaker of Dublin. No details of the preparation were given except that it was "to be laid on the Barrells with a bit of linen rag in the same manner as a barrell is rub'd with Oyl to prevent rust, which in two days compleats the Brown of an equal shining Colour fit for Service, without any assistance of heat, or any other matter whatever that can be of prejudice to the Barrell" (SP 41/39). Most of Henry

* In 1850 Morison published *Notes explanatory of the advantages of the Pike-musket and Pike-rifle, etc.*

Nock's guns were browned and this seems to have been accepted without comment. An entirely novel idea was tried out in 1792, when a hundred barrels were subjected to a process of tinning, the invention of a Mr. Kerr. In 1812, Lt.-Gen. Lord William Bentinck drew attention to the number of barrels being worn thin by constant polishing (WO 3/204), and in the following year a Mr. Segary was paid £20 for his browning formula.

The matter came to a head in October, 1814, when the Commander-in-Chief gave his opinion that barrels should be browned and asked the Master General to state the difficulties (WO 3/210). After a report from Capt. Dundas, the Assistant Inspector of Small Arms, on the required apparatus, "an Iron Plate with a small furnace for heating the barrels on and a Boiler for Water for destroying the Action of the Acid" the Ordnance decided that it could be done. In July, 1815, a General Order was issued from the Horse Guards directing the "General adoption of the browned barrels for the Musquets of the Army". Armourers were sent from the Tower to the various depots and the necessary instructions issued to regimental armourers. The formula recommended was that used in the Tower:

Solution	Nitric Acid	$\frac{1}{2}$ ounce
	Sweet Spirit of Nitre	$\frac{1}{2}$ ounce
	Spirits of wine	1 ounce
	Blue Vitriol	2 ounce
	Tincture of Steel	1 ounce
Varnish	Spirits of Wine	1 quart
	Dragon's Blood powder	3 drams
	Shellac bruised	1 ounce

(WO 44/647)

By the reign of William IV, the flintlock had reached its final stage of development. At the end of 1833, the Ordnance took stock of its position. A comparatively small number of arms were on issue to the Army, Navy, Militia and the Volunteers in Ireland, but the storehouses were filled to overflowing. In spite of a considerable disposal of surplus India Pattern muskets—the firm of Wheeler & Adams alone had bought over 75,000 in 1831—it still had in stock 440,000 muskets of this pattern, of which only 176,000 were fit for use. Experiments on percussion arms were in progress and the evidence suggested that it would be as cheap to make new percussion weapons as to convert old ones. It was decided, therefore, not to bring the New Land muskets into general service nor to make any new arms. As a final measure the East India Company were approached to buy back the surplus muskets.

CHAPTER VIII

THE ADOPTION OF THE PERCUSSION SYSTEM

ON 11th November, 1663, Samuel Pepys wrote in his diary:

> "At noon to the Coffee-house, where, with Dr. Allen, some good discourse about physick and chymistry. And among other things, I telling him what Dribble, the German Doctor, do offer of an instrument to sink ships; he tells me that which is more strange, that something made of gold, which they call in Chymistry *Aurum Fulminans*, a grain I think he said, of it put into a silver spoon and fired, will give a blow like a musquett, and strike a hole through the silver spoon downward, without the least force upwards; and this he can make a cheaper experiment of, he says, with iron prepared."

Dr. Allen was one of many chemists who, through the seventeenth and eighteenth centuries, experimented with various fulminating compounds; but it was a Scottish clergyman who became the first man to exploit successfully the explosive powers of fulminates in firearms. Alexander John Forsyth, the son of the Rev. James Forsyth, Minister of Belhelvie, Aberdeenshire, was born in 1768. After graduation at King's College, Aberdeen, he entered the Church in 1790, and in the following year, on the death of his father, was appointed Minister at Belhelvie. Deeply interested in mechanics and chemistry he published a paper, "On certain useful Properties of the Oxygenated Muriatic Acid", in Nicholson's *Journal of Natural Philosophy* of July, 1799. It is significant that in the following month the same Journal made some comments on Edward Howard's recent discovery of a fulminating mercury in which it was observed that "the force of this powder is too great for firearms".

Howard formally announced his discovery to a meeting of the Royal Society on 13th March, 1800, and his findings were duly published in *Philosophical Transactions* of that year. Having described his method of preparing the chemical, he recounts a series of dangerous experiments with it in comparison with gunpowder. Like his predecessors, Howard directed his experiments with the aim of substituting the new fulminate for gunpowder rather than establishing its use as a detonating agent. With the permission of Lord Howe, Lieutenant-General of the Ordnance, he made some experiments at Woolwich with Col. Thomas

Blomefield, the Inspector of Artillery, and Mr. Cruickshank. As an illustration of the saving in powder which would result from the use of a fulminate as an explosive, a sea grenade $3\frac{1}{2}$ in. in diameter, normally containing 3 oz. of gunpowder, was burst with a charge of only $\frac{1}{4}$ oz. of the mercurial powder. However, he was impressed with the dangers of a substance which could be detonated by an electric shock, by friction or by the blow of a hammer, and concluded that the fulminate "from the immensity of its initial force cannot be used in firearms unless in cases when it becomes an object to destroy them".

Here was a challenge to Forsyth who, apart from his philosophical studies and experiments, was an enthusiastic sportsman with a gun. One of the great disadvantages of the flintlock was the time lag between the explosion of the powder in the priming pan and that of the main charge. The flash and puff of smoke from the pan often acted as a warning to game—some birds became adept at "ducking the flash"— and it is said that Forsyth first constructed a hood over the lock to prevent this. A better solution was obviously to find some method of igniting the charge, which was both smokeless and instantaneous. Probably as a result of reading about Howard's experiments, Forsyth began to devise some means of utilizing the new fulminate for this purpose. He soon found, as others had done before him, that the fulminates were difficult to control and did not easily act as detonators. However, by 1805, he had overcome these difficulties and had fashioned a lock which could be fitted to any firearm.

In this lock the priming pan was replaced by a round plug screwed into the barrel. A small cavity on top of this plug was connected to the touchhole of the barrel. Around the plug was pivoted a magazine, shaped rather like a scent-bottle. In what may be called the stopper end was a striker controlled by a small spiral spring and, at the other end, a container holding enough detonating powder for about twenty-five charges was connected to the plug by a hidden channel. The lock's operation was simple. The "scent-bottle" was first rotated so that the powder container was on top and a charge of powder fed by gravity into the cavity of the plug. It was then returned to its original position, which brought the striker over the primed cavity ready to be fired by the blow of the hammer (Fig. 19).

In the spring of 1806, Forsyth brought his lock to London, where he received the encouragement of Sir Joseph Banks who introduced him to Lord Moira, the Master General of the Ordnance. The latter was so enthusiastic about the invention that he obtained the sanction of the Commander-in-Chief, the Duke of York, for Forsyth to superintend the manufacture of a lock suitable for military purposes in the Tower of London. Forsyth agreed to do this on condition that his expenses would be covered and an assistant paid to look after his parochial duties. At this initial stage the question of any award was left undecided.

The popular story of what followed is well known. After difficulties with his workmen and the manufacture of a suitable powder, Forsyth succeeding in making a carbine lock and a lock for a 3 pdr. carronade (Plate 52). In the moment of his triumph, Lord Moira left office and was succeeded by a Master General who ordered Forsyth to remove "his rubbish". Unfortunately the Minute Books of the Ordnance for this period have been destroyed, so that it is difficult to arrive at a true picture of what really happened. There does survive, however, a bundle of papers, composed of various statements by Forsyth and government officials (WO 44/625), which suggests that the action of the Ordnance Office was not entirely unreasonable.

On 30th July, 1806, Forsyth was given an advance of £100 to cover his expenses and he made no complaint that this was insufficient. At

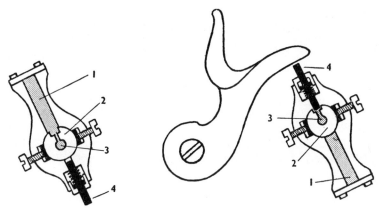

FIG. 19.—The Forsyth "scent-bottle" lock in the priming position (left) and ready to be fired (right).   (1) Fulminate.   (2) Barrel plug.   (3) Channel to touchhole.   (4) Striker.

the beginning of 1807, after the Tower gunmakers had shown no liking for the task, he was authorized to employ his own workmen and to transmit a quarterly account of wages. With the appointment of a new Master General, a further payment of £300 was granted, accompanied by a request that an account of his expenses should be made. What happened at this point is not clear. From statements made by Forsyth and his counsel Lord Brougham, it appears that an understanding had been reached with Lord Moira that, if Forsyth's lock was officially adopted, he would accept an award based on a proportion of the value of the saving in powder to the British forces.

Experiments on the locks were made at Woolwich under Col. Blomefield, and Forsyth admits that they were a failure, but asserts that they were for the purpose only of establishing the saving in powder. It is obvious, however, that the Ordnance thought otherwise, and that this was the reason for curtailing Forsyth's efforts. On 29th April, 1807, in reply to the Board's request for an account of his expenses, he informed them that he would make no claim to an award "as the Honble Board of Ordnance have not thought proper to make any use of his invention". He did, however, enclose the following bill:

	£	s.	d.
"Workmen's wages at 3 guineas a week from			
9.1. 1807 – 10.4. 1807, Rent of shop, materials etc.	58	18	6
Stipend for one year paid to assistant	145	0	0
Miscellaneous expenses	400	0	0
	£603	18	6"

The £400 "miscellaneous expenses" having already been paid, payment of the balance of £203 18s. 6d. was authorized on 1st June.

Previous to this, on 11th April, Forsyth had taken the precaution of obtaining a Patent (No. 3032) for "An Advantageous Method of Discharging or Giving Fire to Artillery and all other Firearms, Mines, Chambers, Cavities and Places in which Gunpowder or other combustible Matter is or may be put for the Purpose of Explosion". He made no claim to any particular powder and emphasized that any chemical compound easily inflammable by a blow could be used, quoting both oxymuriate of potash and fulminating mercury. But the terms of his patent so covered the method of their application that he was able to bring several successful legal actions against would-be competitors.

To market his invention Forsyth, in 1811, established a "Patent Gun Manufactory" under the name of Alexander Forsyth & Co. at 10, Piccadilly. In 1817 this was moved to 8, Leicester Street, Leicester Square, where it remained until his death.

One of his own workmen, named Vickers or Viccars, was the first to infringe the patent, and one can feel no sympathy for him or any of the other gunmakers who copied Forsyth's lock with but little alteration. But one can understand the feelings of a famous gunmaker like Joseph Manton, who, having been granted a patent for an entirely different type of lock firing a percussion pellet, found himself hauled into court, where his lock was called "a clumsy imitation" (*The Times* 14.12.1818). Forsyth afterwards complained of the high cost of these legal actions, but they must have helped to advertise his lock, for many famous personalities gave evidence and much public interest was aroused. When an injunction was sought against a rival maker called Levier, the Lord Chancellor himself heard the case and "to the great amusement of a crowded Court tried each of the guns separately, expressing an earnest hope that they were not loaded" (*The Times* 3.5.1819).

Rightly or wrongly, Forsyth's patent was upheld to cover all detonating appliances and the efforts of other inventors to improve on his lock were by necessity given little publicity. It is, therefore, difficult to decide now who was responsible for the invention of the final development in this form of ignition, the percussion cap. On 29th July, 1818, the Paris gunmaker, Prélat, patented an action which included a nipple and a hollow cock charged with a few grains of fulminate of mercury. Two years later, he filed a certificate of addition in which a copper cap containing a secret composition was substituted. In the same year another Parisian gunmaker, Deboubert, also patented a copper cap charged with fulminate of silver. Both these patents are believed, however, to have been copied from actual models made by the London gunmakers.

The man who is normally credited with the invention of the percussion cap was not a gunmaker, but an English artist, Joshua Shaw. Born at Bellingborough, Lincoln, in 1776, he was apprenticed to a sign painter and developed into an artist of some distinction. His stepfather was a plumber and glazier and no doubt through this association Shaw's first claim to fame was his invention of an improved "Glazier's Diamond", which he patented in London in 1815 (No. 3906).

In a later statement made to Henry Wilkinson (*Engines of War*, 1841, p. 78), Shaw claimed that at this date he was also experimenting with percussion caps, first a reloadable steel model, then one made of pewter, and finally a copper one. Being advised that he could not file a patent for the caps in England, he went to America and took out a patent on 19th June, 1822. The specification for this has been destroyed but there seems little doubt that it was for some kind of percussion cap. On 1st July, 1824, the Franklin Institute of Philadelphia published a report on Shaw's "improved primers". One was made of copper and, by inference, was a copper cap, and the other was in the form of a disc with the fulminate in the centre. This was laid directly on the touchhole. Another form of percussion primer was patented by Shaw when he returned to England in 1840, a screw-on cap which had a piston or plunger with a small cap on its end.

Whether Shaw was the real inventor of the percussion cap is still open to question, but he managed to convince the American Government, who awarded him the sum of 18,000 dollars in 1847. In England there were, as one writer remarked, "as many claimants to the honour of the invention as, of old, there were contending cities for the honour of having given birth to Homer".

Joseph Egg was one of those who claimed the distinction and had printed on his trade labels the proud title "Inventor of the Copper Cap".* Nevertheless his first percussion patent, dated 26th November 1822, related to a tubular magazine for percussion powder. A slightly earlier patent, No. 4648 of 12th February, 1822, by Sampson Davis, a combined percussion and flintlock, while incorporating a nipple, also does not mention a cap. The action depended on "a cavity under the jaw of the cock falling on the top of the nipple, which is primed with the percussion powder". The first British patent to mention a copper percussion cap was that of John Day of Barnstaple (No. 4861 dated

---

* In June 1820, Egg's musket lock, fired by a percussion hammer and copper cap, was tried successfully by an Ordnance Committee at Woolwich, but was rejected apparently because of the difficulties of handling the small cap.

13.11.1823). The only safe conclusion that can be drawn is that some-time after 1815 experiments were made with percussion caps but that they did not immediately oust other forms of primings. In fact, it is doubtful whether they achieved much popularity before 1824.

The reason for this lay in the choice of fulminate. We have seen that Howard first successfully produced fulminate of mercury in 1799 and that Forsyth invented a lock which would detonate any of the known fulminating powders. Forsyth seems to have favoured a mixture containing chlorate of potash, which had a strong corrosive action. The problem of properly applying fulminate of mercury, which did not have this effect on copper caps, does not seem to have been solved until 1823. On 18th September, E. Goode Wright of Hereford wrote a letter to the Editor of *The Philosophical Magazine* (Vol. LXII, p. 203) describing how he had successfully made copper caps with this type of priming (he coated the powder with gum benzoin).

The value of his discovery was acknowledged by Shaw in America in a letter to the *Franklin Journal* of 1829, and there is little doubt that it was to this new discovery that the Franklin Institute report of 1824 referred when it excused Shaw's use of corrosive fulminate with the words: "It has been the only vehicle in use till within some few months when a new discovery was made of a metallic preparation perfectly neutral". The process was taken over and brought to a manufacturing stage by the London chemist, Frederick Joyce. Col. Hawker in the third edition of his *Instructions to Young Sportsmen*, 1824, p. 469, wrote: "Since the first part of this work was printed off, a letter has been received from Mr. Joyce, chemist, 11 Old Compton Street, Soho, commenting, as he is fully justified in doing, on the injury to firearms by the oxymuriate of potash; and inclosing a specification of a new 'Anti-corrosive percussion powder'." Joyce appears in the London Directories as an "Operative Chemist" from 1823–27, but from 1828 becomes F. & E. Joyce, Percussion Powder Manufacturers. Later Joyce described himself as "inventor and sole manufacturer of the anti-corrosive gun cap".

The early copper caps of the 1820's can have inspired little confidence. In some the metal was too soft and jammed in the orifice of the nipple; in others the metal was too brittle and the unlucky sportsman could be blinded by splinters. The priming compound could vary considerably in strength, so that one cap might deliver a soft misfire and the next nearly blow the lock off. However, as manufacturing methods improved, the copper cap became a less precarious device. By 1830, Hawker, in his 6th Edition (pp. 72–75), thought it appropriate to include a special section on Copper Caps which were "now in general use as detonators", and to gracefully suggest that he had designed the first caps for Joe Manton to make.

The reader will perhaps begin to understand why the military authorities took so long in considering the introduction of the percussion system. After their expensive and abortive experiments with Forsyth's lock in 1807, the Ordnance took little interest in percussion devices until the end of the Napoleonic wars. In 1816, Thomas Manton, the London gunmaker, produced an iron tube which could be fitted into the vents of cannon and set off by an iron rod and hammer. At a special trial on a 32 pdr. gun, however, all that happened was that the tube was blown out of the vent (WO 44/498).

In the same year, the Ordnance were approached by Samuel Pauly, a Swiss, with the plans of a special mortar formed in two parts and firing an explosive bomb with a percussion fuze of oxymuriate of potash. This they dismissed out of hand as too complicated. Pauly was the inventor of many ingenious machines, including an airship (with Durs Egg), a gun with compressed air ignition, and the first breech-loader using centre-fire cartridges. None of these appears to have been offered to the Ordnance but, in 1818, he submitted a cannon lock which had a magazine containing enough fulminating powder to fire sixty charges. In August two of these locks were fitted to a 6 pdr. cannon, but they both blew up, only one registering a few successful shots (WO 44/532).

All this served to confirm the opinion that a percussion action in a high-class sporting gun might be preferable to a flintlock, but that it did not have sufficient reliability and strength for military work. The Ordnance officials were not, of course, blind to the developments being made. Sir William Congreve, Comptroller of the Royal Laboratory, began experiments in 1822 with brass tubes or quills of fulminating powder as cannon igniters. The copper cap was carefully examined in May, 1826, when a new and ingenious method of applying it by John Thomson was put forward, but the Committee, "feeling in full force the frequently repeated objection to the introduction of detonating powder in any shape", would not recommend it.

The Select Committee at Woolwich to whom all inventions were submitted was a conservative and rather cautious body of Artillery officers. While these officers were by no means as ignorant of small arms as some writers have suggested, the fact remains that they had little knowledge of practical gunmaking. Their decisions were made on a basis of trial and error and they could offer little in an advisory capacity. When, in 1830, the Board heard that France had started experiments on detonating locks and asked for a report from the Woolwich Com-mittee, that body seemed at a loss to know what to do, and could give no advice on percussion actions other than to suggest that English consuls abroad should be asked to obtain information.

With his superiors acting in such helpless fashion, a junior Ordnance official now came forward. George Lovell who has been mentioned in previous chapters, started as a clerk in the Royal Carriage Department at Woolwich in 1805. Transferred in the same year to the depot at North Yarmouth, he remained there as Clerk of the Cheque until 1816, when he was appointed Storekeeper of the Enfield arms factory. In this position he acquired considerable knowledge of the processes of firearm manufacture and factory control. He was widely read, could translate French and German technical papers, and was thus better equipped than any man before him to take charge of an arms programme, if he so wished. And Lovell did. From the beginning, he set out to re-arm the British forces with what he considered to be the best firearms in the world.

The business of criticizing any invention was not strictly within his province, but, in June, 1830, when a percussion musket by the London gunmaker Samuel Smith was under discussion, he seized the opportunity to offer some comments on the various detonating devices in use. He approved the tubes of Joseph Manton, but pointed out that they were dangerous to handle. The pellet magazine lock of Joseph Egg he disliked because of its uncertainty and the danger of explosion. Instead he advocated a back-action lock using copper caps, preferably with Syke's Patent Slider.

However, it was not until the following year, 1831, that the first moves towards the change-over from flintlock to percussion were started. Having made an adverse report on another of Egg's magazine locks—his opinion on technical matters was now automatically sought —Lovell submitted a report on "Fulminating Powders". It was a masterly effort. He suggested that three main classes of information were required before a decision could be reached. First, on the question of chemicals, he recommended that an investigation should be made by the analytical chemist, Dr. Andrew Ure. Secondly, the type of action to be chosen he considered to be within his department, and to substantiate this he produced an India Pattern musket altered to fire a percussion cap, a conversion which could be extended to all service arms at a cost of 5s. per gun. Lastly, the economic side he left to his colleague Porrett, the Chief Clerk under the Principal Storekeeper.

Then he proceeded to lay down "the essential requisites of a military weapon", strength, simplicity and cheapness. With this concept in mind, he informed the Board, he had designed a new pattern percussion musket which was nearing completion. The Master General was obviously impressed by this broad survey and on 28th September ordered the first thirty converted percussion muskets to be made for trial. He also invited Dr. Ure to prepare a report. This was completed in the following year and its author paid £70. It will be found in the early editions of Ure's *Dictionary of Arts, Manufactures and Mines* under "Fulminates". The use of fulminate of mercury mixed with a solution of mastic in spirits of turpentine is recommended.

Charles Manton, who as Master Furbisher should have been to the fore in these developments, was still engrossed with his flintlock carbine, and Lovell seems to have taken command of the percussion experiments. In October, he ordered a supply of copper caps from Joyce, and on 12th November presented his new musket for the Board's approval. It had a 39 in. barrel of ·753 in. bore and a total length with bayonet of 6 ft. 3 in. The latter was lighter and was fixed to the musket by the

Hanoverian spring catch—a hook which projected from the fore-end and clipped on to the rim of the socket. The percussion lock was a back-action type with all the mechanism behind the hammer. It had an enclosed hammer, which Lovell admitted was inspired by Nock's lock, but he had avoided the latter's cumbersome appearance by reversing the mainspring. The lock had been designed so that there were only six parts and four screws against the flintlock's ten parts and eight screws. It was also lighter than the flintlock, $10\frac{3}{4}$ oz. compared with $18\frac{1}{4}$ oz. On 29th November, 1831, the Board gave Lovell an order for 200 muskets and 100 pistols with his percussion cap conversion for trial by the Navy. The increased activities of the Coast Guard then led to an order for 2,000 pistols on 22nd February, 1832, which were also set up with converted percussion locks.

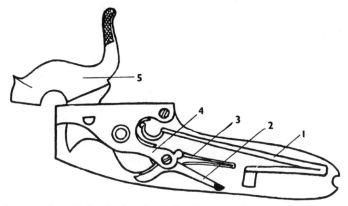

FIG. 20.—Lovell's first back-action lock with enclosed hammer. (1) Mainspring. (2) Sear. (3) Sear spring. (4) Bridle. (5) Hammer.

The naval percussion muskets were converted from new India Pattern muskets with the barrels cut down to two feet. They were, proved at the Tower by Manton, who reported so adversely on them that the Board began to have doubts that their old arms could be successfully converted. One cannot help suspecting that Manton, an exponent of the flintlock, had allowed his personal feelings to influence his actions. At any rate, it brought Lovell into open conflict with him. The guns were sent back to Enfield, where they were satisfactorily proved under Lovell's eagle eye.

No effort was spared to ensure the success of the new guns. New powder charges were calculated, $4\frac{1}{2}$ drams for the musket and 2 for the pistol. With the first batch of arms going for trial on H.M.S. *Vernon*, Lovell prepared special instructions for their use and assured the Board that "he had no doubt that locks of this kind, after their use had become familiar, would be found very superior to the present Flintlocks both in quickness and certainty of fire". The Board, by no means convinced, ordered the Select Committee at Woolwich to compare the velocity of balls fired by flintlock and percussion in a trial with six muskets; two flintlocks; two altered to percussion; and two with Baker's locks designed to fire either flint or percussion. A special iron recoiling target was provided.

The news that the Ordnance were considering percussion guns soon spread and every conceivable type of percussion action was brought to their attention; but there was a limiting factor to their choice. As Lovell said at a later date: "A multitude of inventions were offered by different individuals proposing the application of Percussion Powder in various forms, but the Department was at this early period almost bound to confine their views to some plan which would be compatible with an alteration from the flintlock—on account of the overwhelming numbers of flint arms then standing in the Armouries of the country and this very prudent consideration has all along tended to delay the final adoption of the new system" (WO 44/304).

Perhaps the most interesting of all the percussion actions submitted was Hayward's self-loading pellet lock (Plate 58). This had a tubular magazine of pellets which were fed one at a time into a hollow pan next to the touchhole by a lever connected to the toe of the hammer. It was considered by Lovell to be the best of the magazine locks and after some difficulties with the preliminary trials he suggested several minor improvements, including the brass tubular pellet holder which can be seen in the photograph. T. H. Hayward was a Winchester gunmaker and he was helped by T. W. B. Bower, the mathematics master at Winchester College. After an India Pattern musket had been successfully converted in 1832, thirty-two of the muskets were ordered for trial in October, 1833. At the same time, Lovell was told to construct some more of his back-action lock muskets (WO 44/627).

In 1834, the Board added to their approved list for trial Isaac Riviere's percussion cap musket and Joseph Manton's percussion plug lock. No description is given of the Riviere action but it was presumably the one which he patented in 1825 (No. 5175). This had a box-type, back-action lock similar to that on pocket flintlock pistols. Manton's lock* employed a conical wooden plug, through which ran a small iron pin, projecting about $\frac{1}{12}$ in. above the wood. The fulminate was inserted in the small end of the cone and was detonated by the pin. The plug was placed in a cup which replaced the nipple (Plate 57). Lovell examined and rejected two French competitors, a breechloading gun by Robert ("quite unfit for military service") and a percussion cap musket by Charoy, which had a self-loading magazine which he considered expensive and inconvenient.

Two important if rather belated decisions were also reached during the year. The long experiments on the comparison of velocities of balls from flintlock and percussion guns finished in favour of the latter, and the Committee examining the different percussion guns concluded that the percussion system was applicable to military service. It only remained to choose the action and the priming. In November,

---

* This lock was patented in 1834 (No. 6572) by Joseph's son John Augustus with whom he was then in partnership.

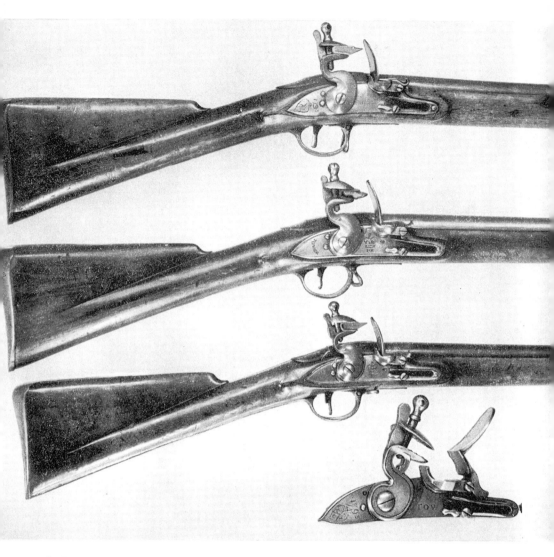

46. India Pattern arms. *Top:* One of the East India Company's muskets of 1793 commandeered by the Ordnance. (2) The Ordnance India Pattern —an exact copy. (3) India Pattern carbine. (4) Detached lock of an East India Company wall piece dated 1793.

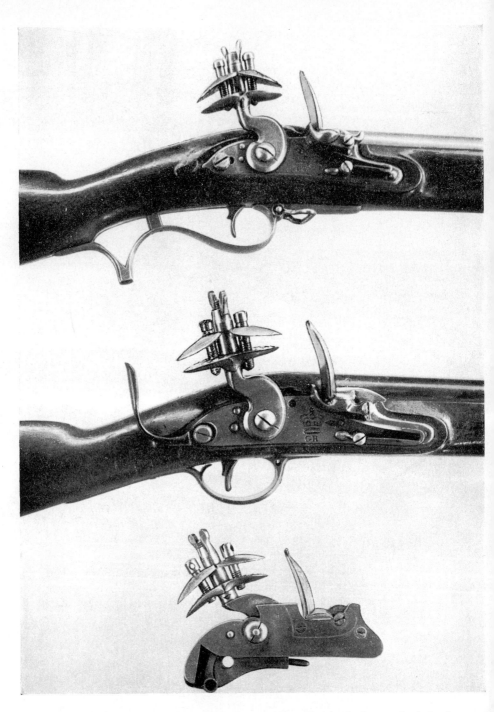

47. The Douglas flintlock. *Top:* On a Baker rifle (the lock guard missing).
Middle: On a New Land musket. *Bottom:* A detached cannon-lock.

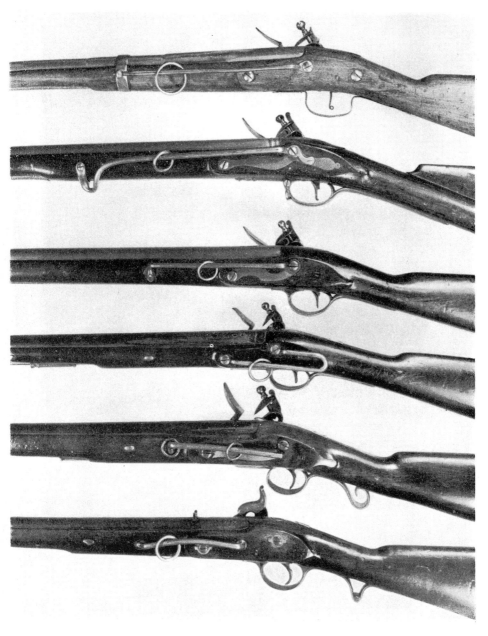

48. Cavalry carbine fittings. *Top:* William III carbine. (2) Heavy Dragoon carbine, *c.* 1770. (3) Patt. 1796 carbine (with straight rib). (4) Paget's carbine. (5) Manton's carbine. (6) Yeomanry carbine of 1844.

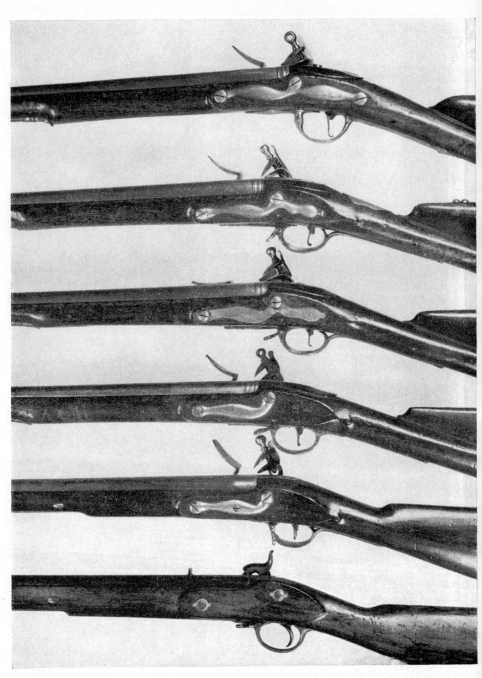

49. Side plates. *Top:* Three-screw plate on a 1720 musket. (2) Brown Bess or Long Land pattern. (3) Militia and Marine pattern 1762. (4) India pattern 1794. (5) New land pattern 1802. (6) Lovell's side cups 1842.

50. Curiosa. *Left to right:* (1 and 2) Rocket launchers fired from the shoulder. (3 and 4) Cannon igniters with detachable tubes. (5 and 6) Another style of igniter, the last with a percussion-lock.

51. Combination weapons. *Top:* East India Company pike musket. The head of the pike was detachable like a bayonet and is shown separate in the photograph. The two slots in which the butt of the pike clipped according to the required position can be seen. *Bottom:* A pike with two flintlock pistols attached, invented by Thomas Oakes, an old soldier of the 40th Regt. in 1804.

52. Forsyth's original locks made in the Tower of London; the carbine lock fitted to a Baker cavalry rifle and a detached cannon lock.

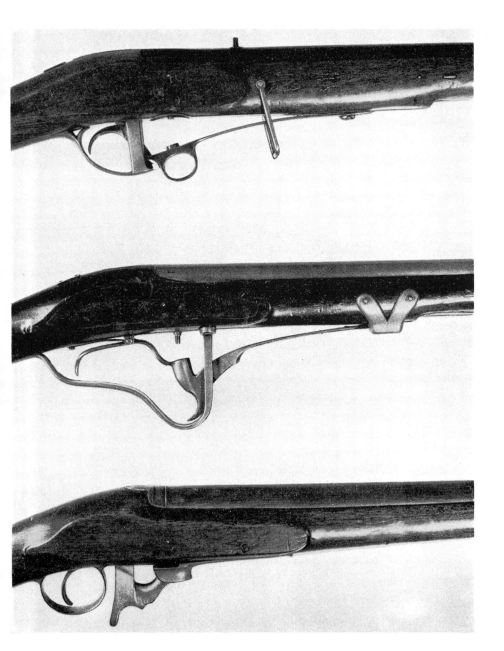

53. Under-hammer locks. *Top and Middle:* Wilkinson's experimental muskets. *Bottom:* One of Heurteloup's muskets made for the 1837 trials.

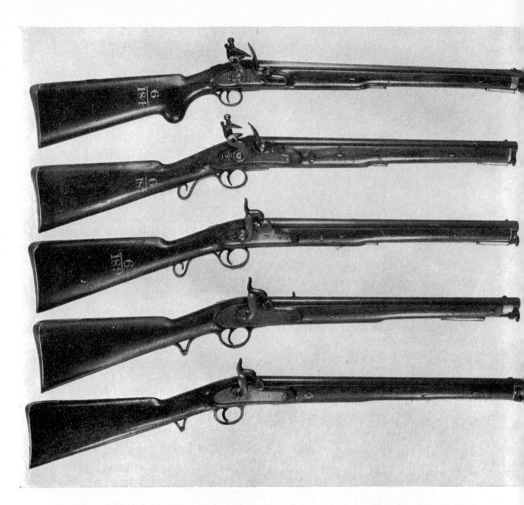

54. Evolution of the short-swivel carbine. *Top:* Baker's presentation carbine of 1822. (2) Manton's carbine, Pattern 1833. (3) Lovell's percussion conversion with a bolt to hold the hammer down. (4) Yeomanry carbine of 1844. (5) Carbine made by Robert Garden, marked XII BENGAL IRREGULAR CAVALRY.

Lovell presented the Board with a translation of a report of the percussion experiments undertaken in Baden by Capt. Ferdinand Wolf. These had commenced in 1828 and reached the conclusion in 1832 that the copper cap was the best percussion device.

The British authorities also continued to favour this form of priming. In the same month 300 more converted India Pattern muskets were ordered—250 of them were issued to the 3rd Battalion Grenadier Guards and the 1st Battalion Coldstream Guards in July, 1836. All these were conversions where a lump was brazed on the breech of the barrel, a nipple screwed on, and a connecting channel drilled to the touchhole. Several inventors thought they could improve on this by screwing the nipple on to the barrel and giving a more direct fire. In the method put forward by Eccles,* a modeller in the Inspector of Artillery's Department, the nipple was screwed on to the barrel above the touchhole position and had to be bent at an angle so that the hammer could properly strike it (Plate 57). Another idea by the gunmaker William Moore, and theoretically the simplest, was to

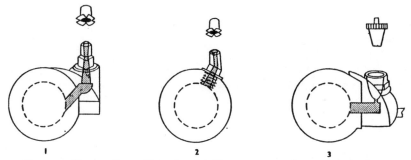

Fig. 21.—Cross-sections of barrels. (1) Common percussion cap conversion. (2) Eccles's cap conversion. (3) Manton's plug conversion. From the original drawings in the Public Record Office (WO 44/677).

screw the nipple into the touchhole and have a side-action hammer (Plate 55). A Baker rifle was also adapted to this type of lock by Col. Miller of the Rifle Brigade.

The most revolutionary plan was to place the nipple under the barrel. This had the advantage of shielding the soldier's eyes from any danger of the cap splitting. In the view of the Woolwich Committee, however, the cap would be liable to fall off and the action of the mainspring was considered weak. First submitted by Col. Whitelock, Aide-de-Camp to the King of Sweden, in November, 1835, it was the only one of the three direct actions to be rejected. It is interesting to note that, in 1840, Henry Wilkinson submitted an almost identical gun which he had patented (No. 8119 of 1839). Although the Committee drew attention to the Whitelock report the gun was nevertheless subjected to a 1,000-round trial before it, too, was rejected (WO 44/646). Wilkinson describes in his *Engines of War*, 1841, p. 80, how he sent one

* Samuel Eccles, the Modeller, became Foreman of the Royal Brass Foundry at Woolwich, retiring in 1855. His name appears on cannon cast there in the 1850s.

of these muskets to the Emperor of Russia, who reciprocated with a splendid diamond ring.

The percussion cap itself was still a matter of concern and Lovell persuaded the Royal Laboratory to undertake experiments on their manufacture, an important consideration in view of the enormous quantity which would be required. He examined several types of caps, made of copper, iron and mixed metals, offered by Walker of Birmingham and, in September, 1835, placed an order for 10,000 of the improved copper variety. Walker's offer to sell the secret of his composition, together with a machine capable of priming 50,000 caps an hour, was refused. Lovell quite obviously believed that he would discover these secrets himself before long. The main cap contractor, Frederick Joyce, made no secret of his formula. In March, 1835, Lovell ordered from him 10,000 caps primed with equal portions of Potassium Chlorate and Sulphurate of Antimony moistened in Lac Varnish. Another 70,000 at 6s. per 100 were ordered in December. Lovell also put into production an improved nipple (the channel shaped like an hour-glass) which was illustrated in William Greener's *The Gun*, London, 1835, p. 131. To make these nipples, two drilling machines, which could be operated by boys, were purchased from Evans & Son of 114, Wardour Street, London.

At the end of the year, the Committee on Percussion Arms at Woolwich were confronted with the voluminous reports of the trials made by the Hanoverian Army in 1833–34. Their own efforts had been equally as thorough and were nearing conclusion. The following muskets had been tested, up to 6,000 rounds being fired through each:

	Type	*Weight*	
		lb.	oz.
Common Percussion	Cap	9	8½
Lovells Percussion	Cap	9	11¾
Lovells Improved Percussion	Cap	9	11¾
Moore's Percussion	Tube	10	1¼
Hayward's Percussion	Pellet Magazine	9	15
Hayward's Improved Percussion	Pellet Magazine	9	14½
Riviere's Percussion	Cap	10	0
Manton's Percussion	Plug	9	13½
Charoy's Percussion	Cap Magazine	9	6¼
Eccles' Percussion	Cap	9	15
Moore's Percussion	Cap	10	5
Light Infantry Pattern	Flintlock	10	2½
Lovell's Improved L.I.Patt	Flintlock	10	0½

These preliminary trials revealed several weaknesses; the mainspring of Riviere's lock was liable to breakage; Hayward's magazine constantly misfired or broke; and four of the hammers of Lovell's muskets were fractured. He quickly strengthened this part and his was one of the four guns chosen for the final regimental trials. The others were the Common Percussion Cap, Manton's Plug and Eccles's Cap muskets. In March, 1836, twenty muskets of each type, divided into five sets of four, were got ready for distribution together with sets of instructions and lists of questions to be answered. They were issued to the 52nd Regt. in Gibraltar, the 80th Regt. in Chatham, the 85th Regt., which took them to Canada, and the 12th and 33rd Regts. in Dublin. A further set was later issued to the Royal Marines, a report being received from a battalion of that corps stationed on the north coast of Spain.

As in most trials of this nature, the reports, when received, were in parts conflicting. The Marines, for instance, thought Manton's plugs were easier to handle and more effective, but the other regiments considered that they were too easily affected by moisture. The verdict

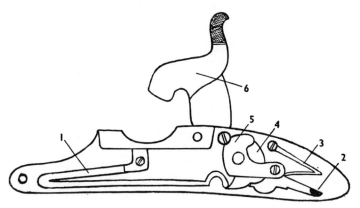

FIG. 22.—The Common conversion percussion lock (Pattern 1839).
(1) Mainspring.   (2) Sear.   (3) Sear spring.   (4) Tumbler.   (5) Bridle.
(6) Hammer.

was plainly in favour of the converted musket firing a percussion cap, although admiration was expressed for the quality of Lovell's new arm. The criticism against the latter centred on its lock, which, being enclosed, was thought likely to induce rust and swelling of the stock in wet weather. The 80th Regt. suggested that this "could be obviated by the hammer being fixed on the outside of the lockplate" (WO 44/677). Very reluctantly, it can be imagined, Lovell redesigned his back-action lock without the enclosed hammer (Fig. 23).

The Navy, as usual the least discriminating, virtually adopted the converted percussion cap arms in June, 1836, ordering 2,000 muskets in November. The Ordnance were still not entirely convinced, however, that some new invention would not materialize. At the end of the year another group of officers, the Pall Mall Committee, were ordered to make a final examination of the subject, before a gun was chosen for the Army.

The most important gun examined by them was Baron Heurteloup's famous *Koptipteur* gun. Charles Louis Stanislaus Heurteloup (1793–1864) was a distinguished French urologist. In 1834, while resident in London, he took out a British patent, No. 6611, for a self-priming percussion gun, which had a magazine running through its butt containing a long soft metal tube of priming. This was automatically fed on to the nipple as the action was cocked. When the hammer fell, it cut off a small part and detonated it—the cutting and striking action which gave the gun its name. In 1836, he published in Paris a *Mémoire sur les Fusils de Guerre*, in which he described an improved model of his gun with an under-hammer action. He brought this to the notice of Capt. J. W. Chalmers, the Secretary of the Percussion Committee, and after a preliminary trial in which 200 shots were fired without any fault, twelve muskets were ordered by the Ordnance (JAAS Vol. III, pp. 59–81).

In the meantime, George Lovell was engaged on a variety of projects. As the percussion trials entered their final stages he was entrusted with the design of a completely new percussion rifle which will be described in the next chapter. He also turned his attention to the carbine. Thirty of Charles Manton's carbines converted to percussion, which had been out on trial (five each had been issued to the 2nd, 3rd, 4th, and 6th Dragoon Guards, the 8th Hussars and the 14th Light Dragoons) came back in July, 1836, to be fitted "with a bolt to the cock when down" (Plate 54). This was to secure the cap in position when the carbine was slung. Lovell now designed a carbine of his own with his back-action lock "bolted to the bearer". He lengthened the barrel to 2 ft. 2 in. and retained the swivel rammer. Otherwise it was a much plainer weapon than Manton's, without the scroll guard. Known as the Victoria carbine, it began its probationary period without meeting any serious criticism.

But a decision on the musket was still awaited—late in 1836 a musket with a sword bayonet made a brief appearance—and Lovell resolved on a measure which to some extent forced the issue. In February, 1837, he suggested that the musket size ball of $14\frac{1}{2}$ to the lb. should become the standard ball for all weapons. The Duke of Wellington had apparently considered this in 1821–22, but had been frustrated by the great variety of weapons in use. He proposed the following weapons:

(1)	Line Musket	3 ft. 3 in. barrel	·753 in. calibre
(2)	Rifle	2 ft. 6 in. barrel	·704 in. calibre
(3)	Carbine	2 ft. 2 in. barrel	·733 in. calibre

In effect the bore of the barrel and consequently the windage were adjusted according to the accuracy required. The pistol, "an ineffectual weapon", was to be discarded. The Master General, formerly an Inspector of Cavalry, agreed on the "worse than uselessness of the pistol" and gave his ready support. In the following month, Lovell sent him specimens of the proposed musket bore arms with estimates of their cost, 67s. for the rifle, 48s. 6d. for the carbine and 49s. 6d. for the musket, for which he had also designed an alternative side lock. On 10th July, 1837, the standardization of the bore was approved by the Commander-in-Chief and the Board. Soon afterwards, a set of the three firearms was presented to the Danish Government. Nevertheless Lovell's musket was still not officially adopted.

Twelve of them had, however, been made for trial against Heurteloup's *Koptipteurs* and this was to be the final test. The trial took place at Woolwich and Chatham under the direction of Lieut. G. Black of the 80th Regt. Although the results were not published, Lovell soon afterwards declared that his musket with a back-action lock for copper caps had "maintained its superiority over certainly one of the most ingenious contrivances which has yet been offered". Late in 1837, satisfactory reports were received from Col. Chesney of percussion arms taken on his Euphrates Expedition. In January, 1838, 800 New Land muskets converted to percussion were ordered for issue to a battalion of Guards for climatic tests in Canada, and 700 of Lovell's carbines were put into production. It was obvious that a decision could not be delayed much longer. The Pall Mall Committee made a final report in March, which settled the adoption of the copper cap and gave preference to Lovell's musket, although, as Lovell acidly remarked, "some members appear to have indulged in the vague imagination that some (not defined) more perfect method might be hit upon at a further time".

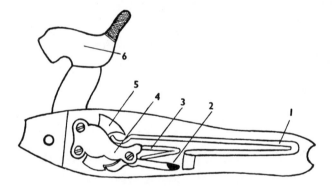

Fig. 23.—Lovell's second back-action lock (Pattern 1838).
(1) Mainspring. (2) Sear. (3) Sear spring. (4) Bridle.
(5) Tumbler. (6) Hammer.

In October, 1838, a sudden rumour that the percussion arms in France had met with a serious failure sent Lovell hurrying to the Royal Manufactory at Châtelleraut. Learning that the rumour was incorrect, he made a thorough examination of the factory, its methods, and the various arms under production. He was interested in a machine for making gun stocks and mentioned in his reports that the muskets of Charoy (magazine primer), Brunel (percussion cap on cartridge) and Heurteloup were still undergoing tests. He visited the Musée d'Artillerie in Paris to examine some experimental arms and then went on to Liège, where he reported that 4,000 Heurteloup guns were being made, being careful to emphasize that they did not function very well (WO 44/520).

While Lovell was away the Principal Storekeeper drew the Board's attention to the low state of arms—109,000 muskets compared with 722,000 in 1829. This startling reduction in the stock of arms was due mainly to the large issues of "extra service" muskets which had been made to allies, colonies and friendly monarchs. The Storekeeper's report of 4th October detailed these withdrawals:

1829–37	West Indies	10,165
1829–37	Gibraltar and Corfu	1,969
1830	French Government	88,960
1831–33	Fernando Po, Sierra Leone and Gambia	3,240
1831–36	Ceylon	750
1834	Hanover	2,000
1834	Pasha of Egypt	2,000
1834–38	Spain	341,600
1835–36	Cape of Good Hope	5,800
1835	Shah of Persia	2,000
1838	Canada	30,000
		488,484

As an emergency measure to replace these losses it was agreed to set up 30,000 India Pattern flintlock muskets from materials in store "not intended for the British Army, for which Percussion Arms will be gradually prepared" (WO 44/677). There was still some hesitation over the percussion arms—the Commander-in-Chief now expressed doubts over the reduction of the powder charge from 6 to $4\frac{1}{2}$ drams—but the Board decided to go ahead with their introduction. On 25th March, 1839, 2,000 of Lovell's muskets (Pattern 1838) were ordered to be set up by London and Birmingham gunmakers, and on 17th May, influenced by Lovell, the Board decided to use the materials in store not for flintlocks but for conversion to percussion muskets (Pattern 1839), for Regiments of the Line.

On 2nd March, 1840, Charles Manton, the Master Furbisher, who had been bothering the Board with his erratic behaviour resigned. George Lovell, who had guided the Ordnance in its somewhat tortuous path from flintlock to percussion and had re-designed nearly all the arms of the British service, was now rewarded with the post of Inspector of Small Arms in charge of all production.

But what of the man who had started it all? Alexander Forsyth was still alive and still Minister at Belhelvie, but he was over seventy and needed financial assistance. Encouraged by friends and the support of the press, he began, in 1840, a campaign for some award for his original invention. In a petition, which eventually appeared as a printed Parliamentary Supplement to the Votes and Proceedings (15.7.1840), he gave his version of the events of 1806–7. It included the apparently inaccurate statement that he had had to pay his assistant out of his own pocket. The Ordnance took the view that their adoption of the percussion cap had nothing to do with Forsyth's experiments in the Tower. The only person to benefit from those had been Forsyth himself. However, they submitted all the papers to the Treasury.

On 21st April, 1842, C. M. Trevelyan the Secretary, replied "My Lords are not satisfied from the papers before them whether the Percussion Lock now introduced into Her Majesty's Service is the invention of Dr. Forsyth or whether it is not rather a Lock of which he furnished the idea but which subsequent experience had rendered available for the Public Service". A "moderate donation" of £200 was, therefore, given to Forsyth. This, however, only infuriated his supporters and in the face of a public outcry the Ordnance and the Treasury were forced to accede that this compensation was inadequate. A further sum of £1,000 was awarded but, by the time Treasury sanction had been obtained in September, 1843, Forsyth had died and the money was divided among surviving relatives (WO 44/625).

CHAPTER IX

THE BRUNSWICK RIFLE

IN 1808, Henry Beaufoy ("A Corporal of Riflemen") published his *Scloppetaria*, a book which has been quoted many times because it contains the famous reference to oval bored rifles, which are dismissed as "a very old invention, though quite obsolete in our time". Although this was to prove a decidedly inaccurate forecast, Beaufoy makes the point that the Baker rifle, with a small twist to its rifling, was accurate at short ranges only. He asserts that other gunmakers (Smith and Squires are mentioned) found that "owing to the smallness of the twist, the rotatory motion communicated to the ball, in its passage through the spiral, although sufficiently strong to answer the purpose for a little way, yet was lost when the distance was increased". Rifles made by them for Volunteer Corps, therefore, normally had grooves making three-quarters of a turn in the length of the barrel. The military rifle maker had to strike a happy medium between a twist which would give the greatest accuracy and one which would not foul or strip under battle conditions. It was a problem which seemed to have no definite answer. To use the words of that great eighteenth-century mathematician, Benjamin Robins: "The degree of spirality, the number of threads, or the depth of the channels, is not regulated by any invariable rule, but differs according to the country where the work is performed and the caprice of the artificer."

One of the reasons given by Baker for the choice of his rifling, which had only a quarter turn in thirty inches, was that "the barrel was less liable to foul from frequent firing, than the whole, three-quarters, or half-turns". Certainly there is very little evidence that the Baker rifle caused much trouble in this direction during its thirty-five years' service, but to some extent accuracy had been sacrificed, and this became particularly noticeable in some of the rifles made in Birmingham during the stress of the Napoleonic War.

In 1828, complaints about this were made to the Ordnance who were then engaged in making rifles at Enfield, and the whole matter of whether the existing rifle was good enough was raised. George Lovell was directed to make three rifles "in exact accordance with the Pattern American Rifle and three upon the same principle but with every improvement it will admit of. Also six belts and pouches corresponding with those sent him." The American pattern was presumably Hall's breechloading model of 1819 and, knowing Lovell with his fetish for strength and simplicity, we can assume that he had no love for this weapon with its tip-up breech, resembling that of Egg's carbine of 1786.

Among his many qualifications, however, Lovell included the ability of a marksman. He showed an early interest in rifles when he persuaded the Board in 1826 to buy the rifling machinery of Joseph Manton for £15. Originally made for a rifled cannon to the order of the Duke of Richmond, Lovell found that it could be adapted for small arms. In spite of his preoccupation with the introduction of percussion, he began to make a study of the rifle problem as well. In his original report on detonators in June, 1830, he informed the Board that the Baker rifle was inefficient at long ranges and suggested one with a back action lock and a chambered breech. His advice was apparently ignored and in the following year another American rifle was purchased for £5 12s. 8d. and a copy made.

At the same time a Hanoverian rifled percussion musket was sent to Lovell for examination. About the only part of this gun which he approved was the spring fastening for the bayonet, which he incorporated in many of his own weapons; but he was intrigued, and his attention turned to the experiments which were being made in Germany. In 1832, hearing that the Bavarian army had adopted a new rifle, he persuaded a friend, a Captain in the Bavarian Artillery, to obtain one. It was carefully examined the following year but again only a minor point was of interest—the manner in which the cap was held on to the nipple. In July, 1834, the Paymaster of Military Pensioners in Hanover reported that the Hanoverian Army had tried a smooth-barrelled Light Infantry Musket with an oval bore which had proved far superior to all others for facility of loading and precision of fire. One of these rifles was imported and, during the autumn of 1835, was subjected to a trial against the Baker.

This brought up the old bogy that the Baker could not be fired with its sword or hand bayonet fixed, and Lovell was quick to note that, while this could be remedied, the stock of rifles was low and those in use worn out. There was only one answer to this. On 5th February, 1836, 2,000 new rifles were ordered by the Board and Lovell was instructed to produce a suitable pattern. It is quite obvious that the Hanoverian oval bored rifle had failed to impress him, for the first model he produced was rifled in the usual way, but with eleven grooves instead of seven. The twist of this rifling was increased to a three-quarter turn in the thirty inches of the barrel. This, as he put it, was to give more rotation but less friction. The stock was not as straight as the Baker, in order to give a better aim, and the furniture was of iron, blued or case hardened, to avoid the glitter of brass. Other features were a back-action percussion lock, a fixed backsight for 200 yards with a folding leaf for 300 yards, and a sword bayonet instead of the "present light Hand Bayonet" (Plate 59). This bayonet had a similar grip to the Baker hand bayonet, with a wide double edged blade 17 in. long. It was attached to a round lug near the muzzle.

This rifle was quickly put to the test. Officers of the Rifle Brigade were then invited to comment, but they seemed mainly concerned with the bayonet controversy. Lt.-Col. Eeles agreed that the new rifle should have a sword attached to the barrel "in the same manner that the Swords were fixed during the time of the War". In May, 1836, Lovell was, in fact, instructed to prepare an experimental rifle with a sword bayonet, probably like that illustrated on Plate 59. The bayonet which fits this gun (it is in an unrifled state) has a blade 25 in. long and a knuckle bar. On the other hand another Rifle Brigade officer, Lt.-Col. Brown, advised a long light bayonet instead of the short sword formerly supplied to the Rifle Corps, recollecting that "the use of them was discontinued owing to the soldiers using them for billhooks etc." (WO 44 /677).

In the meantime, a Mr. Seabright, acting on behalf of the Duke of Brunswick, had submitted a rifle which was stated to have been developed by his Field Adjutant, Capt. Berners. It had a barrel 3 ft. $3\frac{1}{2}$ in. long with two wide round grooves making a complete turn. Lovell tried it out in June against his eleven-grooved rifle and, although it was very similar to the Hanoverian rifle of 1835, he was immediately impressed. "Certain it is", he reported, "that the shooting of this Rifle in my hands has been very excellent and I would therefore propose to make further inquiries into the principle upon which it is constructed." The only objection he found was the difficulty of placing the belted ball in its proper position on the muzzle in loading.

Maj. Dundas and the Woolwich Committee were not so enthusiastic. They agreed that "it shot as well after 50 rounds had been fired from it as at the commencement of the Day's practice without it having been once wiped out". But they pointed out that a cartridge could not be used, and concluded: "This rifle is infinitely more correct in its firing at long ranges than the common rifle but from the ball having less initial velocity, it requires a complication of sights which together with its great weight [10 lb. 7 oz.] and less facility in loading would render it very unmanageable for the use of troops in the field" (WO 44 /520).

Lovell, however, exhibiting that trait of stubbornness which was so characteristic, refused to be deterred. He told the Board that he had had second thoughts about the rifling of his new pattern rifle. One he had made with the two grooves in the style of the Brunswick had proved superior to the eleven-grooved model. As the general design of the rifle had been agreed with the Rifle Brigade and orders had been placed for materials, the question of rifling was now urgent. During November and December, six of Lovell's first model two groove rifles (Plate 59) were given a searching test by a Committee of Officers under Maj.-Gen Millar, Director General of Artillery.

This rifle was similar in appearance to the original eleven grooved model but it now incorporated the Brunswick rifling made to a calibre of ·654 in, with the twist increased to a complete turn. Two of the faults to which the Committee had objected in the Brunswick specimen had been remedied. Where the rifling left the muzzle, Lovell made two semi-circular notches into which the belt of the ball fitted, a considerable help to loading. The total weight was also reduced to approximately 9 lb. The bayonet had a more substantial handle and the blade was lengthened to 22 in. The round lug on the barrel was replaced by the old flat bar with its notch towards the muzzle. It should be noted, incidentally, that Lovell moved this bayonet bar back from the muzzle so that with the bayonet fixed its guard was not in front of the muzzle— the main fault of the Baker.

On Boxing Day, 1836, Millar reported that the rifle had four great advantages over its rivals:

(1) It was as accurate as the others at short ranges and superior at longer ranges.
(2) There was no difficulty in handling or loading it.
(3) It shot correctly for a longer period without cleaning.
(4) The greater smoothness of the barrel made it less likely to wear away than those with projecting bearings or lands.

The best effect was obtained by using a loose ball in a greased linen patch and it was suggested that two thirds of the ammunition should consist of this kind, with the powder charge of $2\frac{1}{4}$ drams contained in blank cartridges. The remainder should be normal cartridges with balls of 17 to the lb. for use in the line when rapid firing was necessary. Under ideal conditions high rates of fire—for a rifle—had been recorded; with the belted ball 10 rounds in $7\frac{1}{2}$ minutes, and with the cartridge 10 rounds in $4\frac{1}{2}$ minutes. This compared with 10 rounds in $3\frac{1}{2}$ minutes, the average with a smoothbore musket.

In January, 1837, the Adjutant General, Maj.-Gen. Sir John MacDonald, approved of the suggestions made, and the 2,000 rifles in course of preparation were ordered to be made accordingly. Lovell had already made one slight alteration before this by changing the furniture from iron to brass. On 3rd February, however, he put forward his plea for the standardization of the ball for military use. Under these proposals the bore of the rifle would be increased to ·704 in. The Board in conjunction with the Commander-in-Chief formally agreed to this policy on 4th August. Several of these musket bore rifles were set up straight away as patterns. The one illustrated on Plate 59, made at Enfield, has an official wax seal recessed in its butt and is engraved on the trigger guard "PAT. OF 1837 No. 3".

The first bulk order for the setting up of 1,000 rifles at Enfield was given on 25th October, 1837. In January of the following year, it became apparent that 600 of these would be required urgently for Col. Brown's Battalion of the Rifle Brigade and that the Enfield factory would not be able to supply them in time. The whole of the order was, therefore, put out to the trade in London at a charge of 38s. per rifle. The first Brunswick rifles to be made were set up by the following gunmakers:

Thomas Potts	212	Wm. Heptinstall	55
Barnett & Co.	212	Reynolds & Son	55
Lacy & Reynolds	210	Yeomans & Son	55
E. J. Baker	146	Thomas Leigh	55
William Parker	80	W. Mills & Son	55
R. E. Pritchett	80	W. T. Bond	55
Thomas Ashton	80		
			1,350

It was ironical that these gunmakers should at the same time be fulfilling the last orders for the old flintlock rifles.

With the pattern of the rifle settled, there came next the question of accessories. Lovell submitted a set of implements in September, but Charles Manton won a minor triumph by getting the Rifle Brigade officers to approve a set of his own design. This consisted of a ball drawer, a brass jag and a combination tri-armed nipple key, which included a turnscrew, a ramrod lever and a pricker (Plate 74). If should be explained that the ramrod had a flat pommel and a hole for the lever at one end, and a brass tip with female thread for the jag at the other.

The method of carrying these implements and also the linen patches had now to be decided. When Lovell designed the butt box (the first models have a cover about five inches long) he apparently intended it for greased patches and a piece of rag for wiping the barrel. In January, 1839, however, Maj. Boileau submitted a design for a larger box which had two compartments; a large rectangular cavity with a turn catch or button to hold the implements (but not the nipple key) and a smaller round one for the patches or grease. Although Lovell objected, this larger trap, six inches long, was adopted.

Lovell had brought into production three entirely new standard weapons, a carbine, a musket and a rifle. While undertaking a host of other duties, he had been responsible for practically the whole of their design and he was naturally proud of his achievement. Learning that his carbine had been called the Victoria carbine but that his musket had been designated Lovell's Pattern, he wrote, in March, 1839, to ask that the rifle might be named "Lovell's two-grooved Percussion Rifle". He went on: "I am satisfied that my system is the best yet. . . . My carbine has been named after the Queen, which gallantry and loyalty will not allow me to find fault with—but I should like to have credit for the Musquet and Rifle". The Master General replied that as the rifle was a modification of one sent by the Duke of Brunswick, it should be called "Lovell's improved Brunswick Rifle". This was hardly a generous action especially as, in 1841, when it was suggested in some quarters that a presentation should be made to Capt. Berners, the Master General then stated that the rifle was developed from the Hanoverian model.

In his endeavours to improve the accuracy of his rifle, Lovell found that, with the normal casting of the lead ball and particularly the belted shape, there was a perceptible variance in the weight due to faulty casting, impurities and air bubbles. In October, 1837, he proposed that the rifle balls should be made by the compressing machine of David Napier, an engineer, which produced a smoother finish and a more solid result. Made in this fashion they weighed 559 grams or 12½ to the lb. Extensive tests were carried out between cast and compressed balls and, in March, 1839, a Committee came to the decision that, while compressed balls made little difference in a musket, there was an advantage to their use with rifles. An agreement was reached to purchase Napier's machine for £1,000, subject to twelve months maintenance and a further payment of £500 if satisfactory. The latter was duly authorized on 18th April, 1842 (WO 44/677).

On the subject of bullets it is interesting to note that, in February, 1841, an explosive or fulminating ball for rifles was offered by Mr. McKirdy, but the Committee drew attention to the fact that it was similar to the shell invented by Capt. Norton which, "altho' the Committee have acknowledged, they have not considered of sufficient importance to recommend for adoption into the Service". Capt. Norton was the most prolific of inventors and from 1823 onwards he submitted to the Ordnance a constant stream of projectiles of all types including many of the detonating variety. He has been flattered, perhaps, by the praises of some authors, for none of his efforts seemed to win the approval of the various Committees at Woolwich. In 1839 he submitted, for the rifle, a highly polished ball and one which was covered with a linen thread web which was said to be elastic and would not crease or fold (the fault of calico and linen patches). Neither was adopted.

A variant of the infantry rifle was introduced in 1840. When the musket bore was adopted as standard for all arms, Lovell had to design a new Sergeant's musket. He proposed a smoothbore musket for Sergeants of the Line regiments and, for Sergeants of the Guards, a gun with the same barrel as the rifle, which could take a common cartridge. He decided this after reading in the *Moniteur Parisien* that the French had adopted rifles for their N.C.O.s. The "Musket, Serjeant's, rifled, for Foot Guards (two-grooved barrel)", as it was officially named, was very similar in appearance to the infantry rifle except that it had a 2 ft. 9 in. barrel for use with a socket bayonet. To maintain the proper sighting, the bayonet stud was fixed underneath the muzzle.

Two hundred and fifty of these rifles were ordered in March, 1840, for the three regiments of the Guards—apparently the only order. In February, 1843, however, fifty more were ordered to be set up for service in the Cape of Good Hope. Certain unspecified alterations were to be made. On the assumption that these rifles were intended for the

Cape Mounted Rifles, the rifle illustrated on Plate 60 would appear to be of this type, although it is actually dated 1847. The only alteration consists of the addition of a side bar and ring.

The ammunition used in the rifled muskets was the same as that for the rifles. A blank cartridge with a charge of $2\frac{1}{2}$ drams of rifle powder was packed in a dark green paper and a loose belted ball weighing $12\frac{1}{2}$ to the lb. was tied up in a calico patch with a black band round it to indicate the position of the belt. A proportion of tallow was also issued for greasing the ball. The percussion caps were carried in a tin magazine placed in the cartridge box, those for immediate use being kept in a pocket attached to the ball-bag of the Rifleman's accoutrements. The following implements were also issued to the riflemen:

> One three-arm nipple wrench with turnscrew and pricker.
> One ball drawer and a brass jag carried in the butt-trap.

For use where no Sergeant Armourer was available, Sergeants and Corporals of the Rifle Regiments were furnished with a spring cramp for the locks, and three spare nipples.

At this point what may be termed the "heavies" can be discussed. The main advantage of the two-groove rifling was its accuracy at long ranges, an attribute which was of prime importance in two classes of arms: wall guns; and what the Admiralty termed "guns for the tops". We have seen that the first guns made for the latter purpose, the seven-barrelled guns, were originally rifled and, although they were subsequently made with smoothbores, it remained the opinion of many naval authorities that a good rifle was better than a multi-barrelled arm. In 1829, Sir Howard Douglas, the naval gunnery expert, wrote: "The best method of opposing the enemy's top-men is to have a few expert marksmen similarly posted."

In January, 1836, the Admiralty informed the Ordnance that they would like a suitable percussion gun "for a certain number of good Marksmen in the Tops of Men of War". They emphasized that the weight was of little object compared with the range and weight of the ball, and that bayonets were not essential. Lovell at first made up some converted muskets and at the end of the year was told to select twenty of the old seven-barrelled guns in store and prepare them for service, presumably for a trial. While the Navy was leisurely considering this matter, Lovell made the acquaintance of some large rifles. When he was in France, in 1838, making inquiries about the percussion plans, he heard that the French were experimenting with rifles with the Delvigne breech, which were to be issued to twenty picked men in each regiment. Also he was informed that a large rifle, with a ball of $1\frac{3}{4}$ oz., was under trial in North Africa against the Arabs, who had been picking off French soldiers with their matchlocks at long ranges. He managed to bring back two of these rifles.

The lightest of them, the infantry pattern, had eight grooves with a half turn, and a Delvigne breech. The latter was simply a chamber, on the shoulders of which the ball was expanded by a blow from the rammer. This meant that a ball could be easily loaded, but would fit tightly to the rifling on ejection. With this rifle was used Brunel's pattern cartridge with a wooden sabot and a greased woollen patch. The heavy rifle—it weighed 13 lb. 6 oz.—was a larger edition with a barrel 2 ft. $9\frac{3}{4}$ in., rifled with twelve grooves making a third of a turn and firing a ball of 10 to the lb.

Lovell was given permission to make a rifle similar in size to the heavy French one but with two-groove rifling, and also a copy of a French breechloading gun with the same grooves. This breechloading gun (Plates 62 and 64) is identical to the French breechloader, Model 1831, except for the rifling and shorter barrel. In the subsequent trials, early in 1840, it failed because of the excessive fouling of the breech. Lovell's muzzleloader was slightly different to the French equivalent. The barrel was 2 ft. $8\frac{1}{2}$ in. long and although of the same bore, approximately ·79 in., its two-groove rifling made a complete turn. The total weight was just over 12 lb. The theory that the increased twist would give greater accuracy was borne out in practice. At a distance of 300 yards the English rifle hit the 6-ft. square target 17 times out of 20, compared with the French rifle's 12 hits.

The Admiralty's request for a gun for the tops was now remembered. An infantry rifle and the new heavy rifle were sent to Whitehall for inspection. Both weapons were approved and the following distribution suggested:

Heavy Rifle   10 to Line of Battle Ships
                  6 to Frigates and Sloops

Infantry Rifle   20 to Line of Battle Ships
                  10 to Frigates
                  6 to Sloops

It is not clear whether the Navy's intention to use the infantry rifle was carried into effect, but on 27th July one hundred of the heavy rifles were ordered. With the exception of some parts—wood screws by J. S. Nettlefold, brasswork by W. S. Jennings and small iron parts by Joseph Ashton—the manufacture of these rifles was carried out entirely at Enfield.

They are very similar in appearance to the lighter infantry model with Lovell's back-action lock, but there is no provision for a bayonet. A large three-leaved rear sight is prominent on the barrel. As far as I can establish from the records, only the original batch of one hundred was made and the locks and barrels of all specimens which I have examined, are marked ENFIELD 1840. These rifles were allocated as follows:

Master General   1
Portsmouth   34

Devonport	38
Chatham	18
Royal Laboratory	1
H.M.S. *Excellent*	6
Insp. of Artillery	1
Storekeeper	
(as pattern)	1
	100

The six rifles sent to H.M.S. *Excellent* were for the purposes of a full trial on board ship. This was conducted by Capt. Sir Thomas Hastings, who reported that, although they were far superior at long ranges, there was some difficulty in loading, and at short distances the common musket was preferable because of its high rate of fire. He recommended that the sights should be marked for distances of 200, 300, 400 and 470 yards. A revised allocation of the rifles was made:

12 to Ships of the Line
10 ,, ,, ,, ,, 4th class
8 ,, ,, ,, ,, 5th class
6 ,, ,, ,, ,, 6th Class

(WO 44/520)

The Navy rifle was loaded in similar fashion to the infantry rifle except that the blank cartridge contained $3\frac{1}{2}$ drams of rifle powder. The belted balls, weighing nearly 8 to the lb., were tied up in calico patches with a black band showing the belt. One hundred and fifty rounds were issued to each rifle. A three-arm nipple wrench and a ball drawer and brass jag were supplied with each rifle. As the balls were not made by compression, a suitable bullet mould was issued, one to every six rifles. When the rifle was not in use a plug-rod covered with greased wool was put into the barrel to preserve the interior from rust.

Several experimental large-bore rifles were made at this period. In August, 1841, the Master General ordered one "of a calibre the same as the two ounced Rifle but six Inches longer in the Barrel and to weigh 15 pounds to be made with a view to its trial as a Wall piece". I have not traced this particular gun, but in the Tower there is a wall piece on a swivel mounting which has a barrel 4 ft. $1\frac{1}{2}$ in. long with a bore of approx. 1 in. rifled with two grooves. The lock is Lovell's enclosed back-action pattern and it is attached to the barrel tang and so inset into the stock that only the hammer protrudes.

Another rifle in the Tower is a mystery. With a barrel the same length as the Navy rifle, it weighs nearly 15 lb. Although it is obviously of the Brunswick family and of English manufacture—the lock is undoubtedly Lovell's—it bears no marks and it is rifled with *four* grooves, the muzzle being notched for a double-belted ball of approx. 10 bore. I found this rifle some years ago at the Royal Arsenal, Wool-

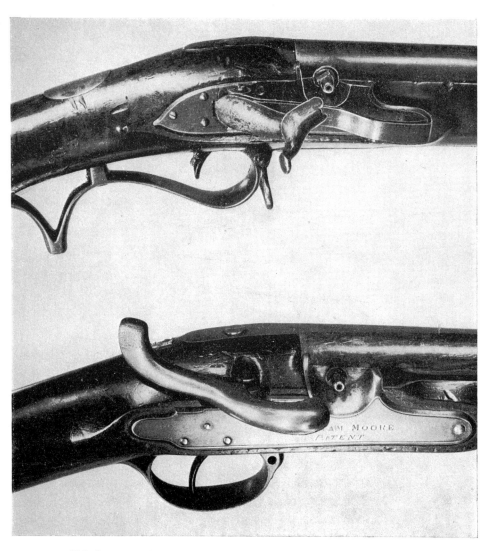

55. Side-hammer locks. *Top:* Baker rifle converted by Colonel Miller.
Bottom: William Moore's Patent lock.

56. Tube locks. *Top:* By Joseph Manton. *Bottom:* By William Moore. Both locks have a flash protector fastened on the side of the hammer.

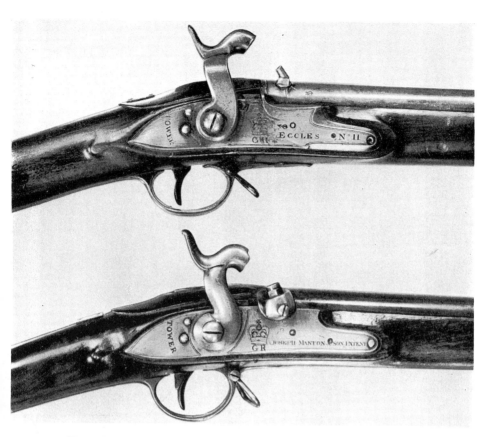

57. Two of the muskets which took part in the final percussion trials. *Top:* Eccles's conversion. *Bottom:* Joseph Manton's plug lock.

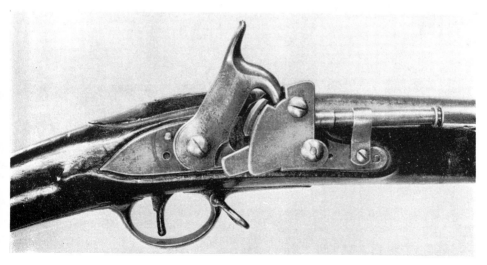

58. Hayward's self-loading pellet lock. The improved model in the fired position.

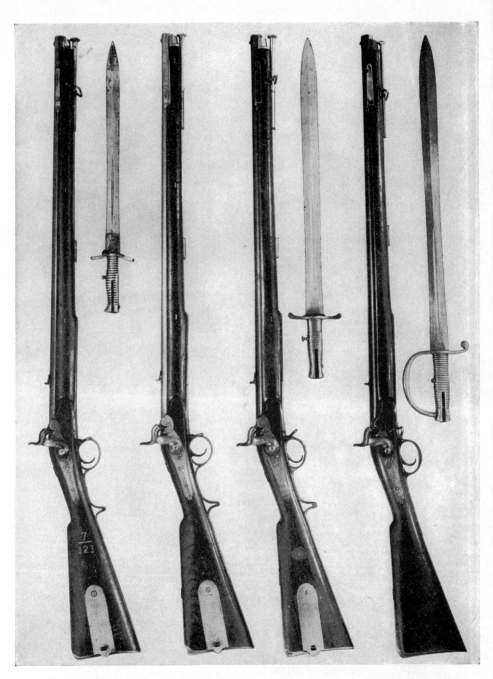

59. Evolution of the Brunswick Rifle. *Left to right:* (1) Lovell's first rifle with eleven-groove rifling, 1836. (2) Lovell's second rifle with iron mounts and two-groove rifling, 1836. (3) Sealed pattern rifle of 1837. (4) Experimental smoothbore model, dated 1841, with large sword bayonet.

60. Variations of the Brunswick Rifle. *Left to right:* (1) With back-action
lock and large butt box. (2) Musket, rifled for Sergeants of Foot Guards
with 2 ft. 9 in. barrel and socket bayonet. This specimen has been converted for cavalry, a side bar and ring not visible in the photograph being
fitted. (3) Heavy Navy rifle of 1840. (4) Four-groove experimental rifle.

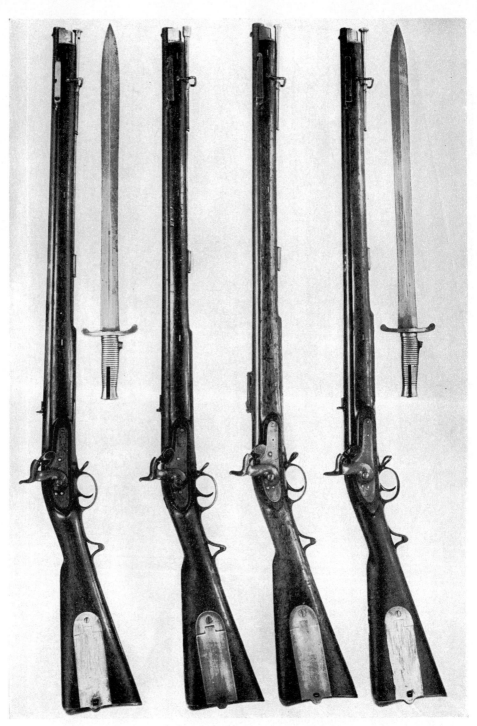

61. Side-action Brunswicks. *Left to right:* (1) Model of 1847 with improved bayonet fastening. Note the notch half-way along the bar. (2) Privately rifle made by Charles Lancaster with patent breech. (3) Three-groove rifle made by Potts and Hunt, sighted up to 800 yds. (4) Tower Brunswick dated 1864.

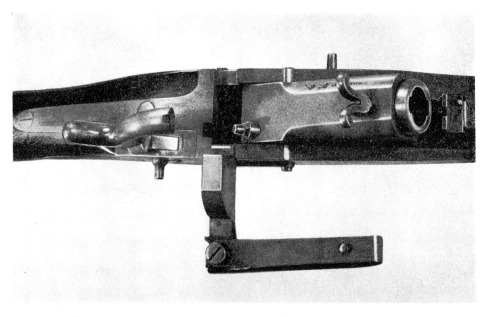

62. Close-up of the breech of the breechloading wall piece with two-groove rifling.

63. The muzzles of the Brunswick and the Jacob rifles compared.

64. The Brunswick wall pieces. *Top:* The heavy muzzleloader. *Middle:* Lovell's 1840 copy of the French breechloader. *Bottom:* The sealed pattern Brunswick compared for size.

wich, where it had presumably been left following some unrecorded trial.

To return to the infantry rifle, two more alterations were to be made. In August, 1841, Lovell discarded his back-action lock in favour of a lighter lock with a side action, which could be fitted to all the standard firearms. The new lock was fitted to 4,000 rifles ordered on 31st October, 1845, the list of priced parts issued in November describing them as "Locks, established patt. for all arms—7/–". Half of the rifles were made at Enfield and the other half by the London gun-makers, who were paid 32s. for setting up and 12s. for "sighting, swording and browning".

The Enfield factory, it will be noted, was still not capable of handling a complete order, and some light is thrown on the state of its machinery by Lovell's report of 24th November, 1845. He informed the Board that the rifling at Enfield was done "by means of steel spiral rods filed out by hand, each degree of twist being given by its peculiar Rod, and the formation of these rods being dependant upon the dexterity of one particular Artificer who is growing old and his sight failing". As a result of this, a rifling machine was bought from Evans & Sons of Wardour Street for £110, "in which the spiral being given by an inclined plane, acting upon a Rack or double toothed pinion, any twist may be given to the groove by simple adjustment".

The Brunswick was now barely ten years old, but already there were signs of dissatisfaction with its performance. On 23rd March, 1846, Lovell was authorized to buy from Liège a rifle "of a peculiar construction" called the *Carabine à Broche* "that had lately been brought into favourable notice on the Continent from its very great accuracy at extraordinary ranges". An English contender appeared in the field of long-range rifle makers—Charles Lancaster of 151, New Bond Street. He was given an order to make 24 rifles with patent breeches designed to fire up to 1,200 yards, the length of the barrel and all the parts to be in exact conformity with the Brunswick. At the end of the year, successful preliminary trials of the rifles were made at Woolwich. The rifle illustrated on Plate 61 may be one of these. It is identical with the standard rifle, but the lock bears only the signature C. LANCASTER. A standard barrel made by the Birmingham contractor, Ezra Millward, with two-groove rifling has been fitted with a cup-shaped breech. The rammer has an unusually shaped head meant for a conical shaped bullet and this may have been added in July, 1854, when for a short while experiments with this kind of bullet were made with Brunswick rifles.

The London gunmakers, Lacy & Reynolds, introduced the last change in October, 1847, when they submitted a rifle with an improved spring fastening for the sword bayonet. The rifle on Plate 61, dated 1847, has this fitting. It is easily recognizable, the notch on the bayonet bar being half-way along instead of near the muzzle. Conversely the release button on the bayonet handle is close to the cross guard instead of being in the middle. This stronger fitting—the Brunswick bayonet was after all a heavy weapon weighing nearly two pounds—was approved for general adoption by the Commander-in-Chief in June, 1848.

During 1850 a further batch of 4,000 rifles was put under construction but by then a new conception of rifle was under preparation and in the following May the Board agreed that the Brunswick would probably be superseded by the Minié. On 20th October, 1852, the stock of Brunswick rifles was reported to be:

Brunswick Rifles	In store	at home	3,883
		abroad	823
	With troops	at home	2,012
		abroad	4,812
			11,530

Belted Ball Cartridges In store	at home	1,270,544
	abroad	2,347,213
		3,617,757

Of these 1,312 were engaged in the fighting at the Cape and 624 were with the Canadian Rifle Regiment. With the end of the Brunswick in sight, it was decided to complete only those rifles for which there were materials in store.

In January, 1853, the Rifle Corps were told to hand in their Brunswicks in exchange for the Minié or Patt. 1851 rifled musket. The following year the old rifles were issued to appropriate Militia regiments. Some of these regiments had their rifles made privately, not always in strict conformity with the Government pattern. The London gunmakers Potts & Hunt seem to have been mainly responsible for these privately made arms. A rifle in the Tower with normal two-groove rifling made by them bears the regimental markings of the Ayrshire Militia. Another rifle by the same makers (shown on Plate 61) looking exactly like a Brunswick has *three*-groove rifling.

In connection with the privately made rifles of the Crimean War period can be mentioned the Jacob rifle, which was indirectly inspired by the Brunswick. On 4th March, 1854, John Jacob, then a Major commanding the Scinde Irregular Horse, sent "Memoranda on Rifle Muskets for the Army" to the Military Board of the East India Company in Bombay. He published this in his *Record Books of the Scinde Irregular Horse*, London, 1856, and in his booklet on *Rifle Practice*, London, 1855. In the latter he describes how, on a specially constructed range at Jacobabad, he had conducted a series of trials over ten years "on a scale probably almost unequalled even by public bodies elsewhere". Early in the trials he found that the two-grooved Brunswick had defects which rendered it "quite unfit for the Army". First of all he produced a four-grooved single barrel rifle for use with a double-belted ball. On referring this to the Indian Government, however, he was informed "that the two-grooved rifle, which was thought good enough for the Royal Army was good enough for the soldier in India".

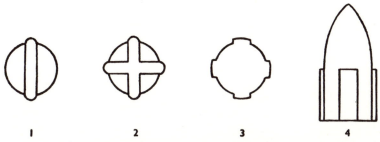

FIG. 24.—(1) Brunswick belted ball. (2) Double belted ball. (3) Jacob's shell (base). (4) Jacob's shell (side).

One of Jacob's difficulties was that he had to have all his rifles made in England. Consequently he did not see the rifle submitted to the East India Company in London until after its rejection. Undismayed, however, he continued his experiments. Next came a conical bullet with four studs to fit the grooves of his rifle, which could be fitted with a copper percussion tube to constitute "the most formidable missile ever invented by man". His first four-groove military rifle had a single barrel 30 in. long of 24 gauge, weighed $9\frac{3}{4}$ lb. and, with a powder charge of 2 drams, was effective up to 1,200 yards. It was also armed with a sword bayonet "of peculiar form not easy to describe in words". This was the rifle he recommended in his *Memoranda* of 1854.

Each year, however, Jacob altered his "ideal" rifle and bullet. In various calibres and size barrels they were made by John Manton, Witton and Daw, and Swinburn & Son. By 1856 he had become converted to double-barrelled rifles, and he and some fellow officers achieved spectacular results with the explosive shells blowing up ammunition carts at long ranges. Finally, in 1858, just before his death, he raised the 1st Regt. of Jacob's Rifles, and in the 4th Edition of his booklet, he gave the specification of his army rifle: double 24 in. barrels of 32 bore, the four grooves making four-fifths of a turn, with "four points to be inserted inside the barrel near the breech for tearing open a blank cartridge when rammed down whole".

The Jacob rifle illustrated on Plate 67 conforms to these measurements, although there is no evidence of the cartridge points. It was made for Jacob's Rifles by Swinburn & Son in 1861. In that year the regiment was re-designated the 30th Regt. of Bombay Native Infantry; but it was allowed to retain its original title and the words JACOBS RIFLES are engraved on the butt-box of the rifle. Folding leaf sights are provided for ranges from 100 to 300 yards, and from there up to 2,000 yards a long vertical sight with a sliding bar is used. When not in use, this sight folds down along the barrels and is protected by the shoulders of the barrel band. The photograph also shows the sword bayonet with its elaborate hilt and blade, 30 in. long.

The Brunswick was revived in 1864, when some were made for the East India Government. One of these is illustrated (Plate 61). The butt is impressed with the wax seal of the Small Arms Factory, Enfield, and the India Office Store Department, and bears the following inscription: BRUNSWICK RIFLE FOR E. I. GOVT. WITH 53 LOCK VIDE LETTER FROM DIR. GNL. OF STORES APRIL 1864 TAKEN FROM SUPPLY SEALED 30.7.1864. The bayonet which has the improved catch is similarly inscribed. Privately made Brunswicks have been noted with dates in the 1870's.

In spite of this apparent popularity, the Brunswick rifle received more unfavourable criticism than any other British arm. During the Enfield trials of 1852 the disparaging comment was made: "The loading of this rifle is so difficult that it is wonderful how the rifle regiments can have continued to use it so long. The force required to ram down the ball being so great as to render a man's hand much too unsteady for accurate shooting". It is all very strange when one considers the careful trials which led to its adoption.

CHAPTER X

LOVELL'S PERCUSSION ARMS

LOVELL'S first year of office as Inspector of Small Arms in 1840 was a busy one. His duties now included the direction of the Government factory at Enfield, the supervision of work in the Ordnance small-arm workshops in London and Birmingham, and the control of orders to the various contractors. All this had to be arranged so that a satisfactory supply of arms was produced without endangering the flow of work to his own factories, the productive power of which was still an uncertain factor. Apart from such matters of administration, all questions of a technical nature were, in the first place, referred to him.

His first task was the design of the Sergeant's musket. Until the introduction of the standard musket bore, the arms carried by Sergeants of the Line were of carbine bore which the Army called "Fusils" and the Ordnance "Carbines for Serjeants". A new gun and a new name were now required. As already described, Lovell designed a rifle with a 2 ft. 9 in. barrel for Sergeants of the Guards which bore the name "Muskets, Sergeants, rifled, for Foot Guards, (two-grooved barrel)". For Sergeants of the Line, he made a gun with a smooth-bore barrel of the same length (Plate 69). Although it was similar in appearance to the Patt. 1839 musket and the same converted side lock was used, the calibre adopted was that of the Victoria carbine, ·733". Used with the common cartridge it was meant to give greater accuracy "as the Serjeant being occupied with his other duties did not fire as often as the Soldier". The Sergeant's ammunition was also restricted to twenty rounds (WO 3/293).

These were not the first Sergeant's arms designed by Lovell, as, in August, 1835, he had prepared two double-barrelled carbines with percussion locks "upon a principle considered to be applicable to the service of the Police Force in Ireland". These were fitted with his enclosed back-action lock. Although this model does not seem to have found favour with the constabulary, in January, 1838, fifty double-barrelled carbines of "Mr. Lovell's last pattern" were ordered for Sergeants of the Guards under orders for Canada. Again these met with unfavourable reports and, in February, 1840, they were withdrawn, the two-groove rifled muskets taking their place.

Double-barrelled carbines seem to have held a fascination for some Masters General and it is difficult to keep track of all the different patterns made. Lovell's first efforts were quickly followed by two carbines made by Wilkinson the gunmaker to the order of Sir Richard Hussey Vivian, Master General from 1835–41. These were also sent to Ireland in January, 1836. They were plain weapons with conventional back-action locks and patent breeches and were armed with a curious bayonet. This had a brass hilt, a flat guard and a dagger blade 14 in. long, and was fitted to a bar underneath the muzzle. The carbine illustrated on Plate 68, which is of 17 bore, appears to be one of these, but evidently another design was submitted later for, in July, 1839, the Inspector General of Constabulary in Ireland wrote to say that the double-barrelled carbine of musket bore submitted for his approval was too heavy. He suggested a carbine made by the Birmingham makers, Tipping & Lawden, to his design, which was two pounds lighter. The bayonet of this carbine, its blade lengthened to 17 in., was fitted on the side of the barrel as loading had been found difficult with it in its former position. Two hundred and fifty of these carbines were ordered, the original price of £4 17s. being increased in August to £5. The one illustrated (Plate 68) is marked TIPPING & LAWDEN but other specimens in the Tower Armouries, almost identical, are marked TOWER and dated 1839, 1840 and 1845, indicating that repeat orders were put through the normal channels of supply.

On 15th November, 1841, another Birmingham gunmaker, Richard Cutler, received an order for twenty-five double-barrelled carbines for the same service. If the one shown on Plate 68 is one of these, then a reversion to the heavier bore seems to have taken place, for it is a musket bore gun with bolted side locks and a butt box. The locks are signed CUTLER & SON and it is fitted with the Tipping & Lawden type of scroll guard and bayonet.

Lovell showed little interest in these police carbines, but when, in February, 1840, the Irish authorities asked for a pistol and a single-barrelled carbine to be made by the Ordnance, and sent over what they considered to be suitable patterns, he quickly put his foot down. As one might expect, a carbine of his own design was adopted in preference to the Irish one. The sealed pattern of Lovell's Constabulary carbine is illustrated (Plate 69). It is made from the usual converted flintlock materials with a barrel length of 2 ft. 2 in. and, like most of these carbines, it has the lower sling swivel screwed into the butt instead of being attached to the trigger guard. Two thousand of these were made "with a spring in the Bayonet to hold it in the scabbard". The purpose of this spring catch, which clips into the inside of the scabbard locket, was to prevent the bayonet from being snatched out of its sheath and turned on the constable.

Another double-barrelled carbine of this period, and often confused with the police issue, was the carbine for the Cape Mounted Rifle Corps. Paradoxically, it is not rifled but it is easily distinguished by its swivelled rammer and a side rib and ring. It will be remembered that Lovell made a double-barrelled carbine for the Corps in 1823. In October, 1835, he was asked to construct another of these carbines from a description furnished by one of the corps' officers, Capt. Aitcheson. A percussion lock was used, but whether it was Lovell's back-action model is not known. The pattern carbine was approved in January, 1836, and 247 were subsequently made.

Manufacture of a further 250, not necessarily of the same pattern, was started in 1840. This time full details of the costs and contractors are given in the minute books. All the work was done by Birmingham men except for the back-action locks, at 15s. a pair, which were supplied by Joseph Brazier of Wednesbury. The barrels, at 35s. each, were made by Henry & John Clive, John Clive, Ezra & William Millward and Joseph Turner; the iron work by Joseph Ashton, the brass work by William Jennings, and as usual the wood screws by J. S. Nettlefold. The setting-up, allocated to the Birmingham men because of their previous experience of this type of arm, was shared by Richard Hollis & Son, Tipping & Lawden, Thomas Tucker, Phillips & Son and Wheeler & Son at a price of 63s. for each carbine.

But it was an unlucky series of arms. After considerable delays in production—they were "not favourites with the Artisans in consequence of their requiring great niceness in their construction"—nearly the whole of the stock was destroyed in the fire at the Tower, in 1841.

A late revival of the flintlock arm occurred in October, 1840, when 200 carbines were ordered for the Revenue Police, the barrels in store for this service being found only suitable for the flintlock. The majority of these Victorian flintlocks are distinguishable, not only by the VR cypher engraved on them, but by the shape of the tail of the lock which is rounded instead of pointed. It is not known when the last issue of flintlocks took place. In 1846, for instance, there was an issue of flintlock carbines for the warders of Millbank Prison in exchange for their old blunderbusses.

The Militia of North America, making heavy demands in the same year for arms which could not be met by the supply of percussion arms, were temporarily armed with flintlocks taken from their depots. The following stock was reported:

	Land	Sea
Quebec	15,220	429
Montreal	13,157	92
Île aux Noix	128	—
Kingston	11,814	656
Toronto	6,015	515
Halifax	7,640	346
Annapolis	320	—
Prince Edward Island	170	—
New Brunswick	9,805	3,996

During 1840–41 Lovell also faced some criticism of his own musket and carbine. Early in 1840, six light infantry muskets were fitted with barrels with "chambered plug" breeches and tested against six similar muskets belonging to the East India Company. In May, 800 of Lovell's pattern musket were ordered to be made with this breech, apparently one of Wilkinson's invention. Needless to say, Lovell did not take kindly to this modification of his gun. However, he was himself forced to make some alterations. After complaints from the 2nd Battalion of Foot Guards, who were armed with his musket, he strengthened the tumbler nail of his lock and reduced the strength of the mainspring. This large back-action lock was never a satisfactory action and, in March, 1841, when Wheeler & Son of Birmingham received a contract to make 600 of Lovell's muskets, the small lock used on the rifle and Victoria carbine was fitted instead (Plate 70).

The main trouble developed with the carbine. It had been put into service with the forces in Canada and, as a result of their experiences, Lovell made several modifications which were approved by the Commander-in-Chief on 12th September, 1839. The safety bolt on the lock which had caused more nuisance than it was worth, was removed. The swivel attachment on the barrel was strengthened and the swivel itself made of tempered steel instead of case-hardened iron. The ramrod could now be made to "tell" or strike on the face of the breech-plug instead of bearing with its head on the swivel. The last alteration was a concession to the cavalry drill in which the rammer was slammed down the barrel in a loading motion—a pleasing movement from the drill point of view but with dire consequences to the inside of the barrel. The short swivel which had been introduced by Manton in 1833 (the East India Company had adopted it in 1819) was not really suited for this treatment. On the other hand it was better than the long swivel previously in use.

For some time Lovell could not understand why the swivels kept breaking—he was driven at one point to suggest separate rammers after the fashion of the French, Austrian and Prussian cavalry—but finally there occurred the amusing episode when, on a visit to Birmingham, he went to the cavalry barracks there and stood aghast on the parade ground at the sight of what the troops were doing to his carbines. Returning to London he complained bitterly to the Commander-in-Chief of the "viciousness' of the cavalry exercise. Lord Hill very tactfully agreed that the solution was a "more gentle use of the Rammer", and directed the attention of the Inspector General of Cavalry to this point (WO 3/293).

It was unfortunate for the latter gentleman that not long after this, in November, 1841, he should choose to submit a copper protecting cap for percussion nipples. Lovell did not take very long to prove that this copper snap-cap would not withstand repeated blows from the hammer, and to secure the adoption of a very similar cap of his own design made of malleable cast-iron. The issue of these snap-caps was discontinued in 1851 after Lovell proved that a well-made nipple could endure 7,000 blows without deterioration (WO 3 /326, 29.9.1855).* Another accessory introduced by him was a muzzle stopper in 1843.

There was an addition to the ranks of Lovell's percussion arms in March, 1841—a carbine for the Royal Sappers and Miners. As far as possible, all Lovell's firearms now conformed to a simple standard pattern and the Sappers' carbine is only distinguished by the length of its barrel, 2 ft. 6 in., and its peculiar bayonet. The first pattern bayonet was a wicked-looking weapon with a saw-backed blade just over two feet long and a complicated hilt. The carbine which accompanies this bayonet in the illustration (Plate 65) is dated 1841 and is engraved on the butt tang FOR SAPPERS FUSILS.

Manufacture of the carbine commenced in June, 1842 (1,354 were ordered) but the bayonet soon caused trouble. The elaborate hilt was difficult to make, and the opinion was held in some quarters, to use the words of the Master General, that "the Saw Bayonet is not a proper weapon to be used in Civilized Warfare". In vain a Select Committee pointed out that the saw edge was intended for "Palisadoes and Barriers". A plain-bladed bayonet with a simpler socket hilt was substituted in January, 1843 (Plate 65).

This Select Committee was appointed to consider the question of bayonets for the two regiments under the jurisdiction of the Board of Ordnance, the Royal Sappers and Miners, and the Royal Artillery. The Artillery carbine, introduced in September, 1841, was like the Sappers', but the two corps' duties being different, the Sappers' bayonet was not suitable for artillerymen. After much earnest discussion, the Committee recommended that the gunner on Garrison service should have the ordinary infantry bayonet, but when employed with Field Batteries should carry a sword with a steel scabbard. The existing cross belts for bayonets were to be superseded by a waist belt with a frog to take either bayonet or sword.

The reader may, perhaps, have become somewhat confused with the number of new firearms, as many army officers and Ordnance officials were at the time. On 7th May, 1841, it was thought necessary to print *A Statement respecting the New Series of Military and Naval Percussion Arms and their appropriate Ammunition etc.* This was also published in the *United Services Journal*, No. 157, December, 1841. For the sake of clarity it is worth repeating the main points here. Arms listed were:

MILITARY PERCUSSION ARMS

Musket, Rank and File, for Foot Guards, Lovell's pattern of 1838.
Musket, Rank and File, for Regiments of the Line, pattern of 1839.
Musket, Serjeants, rifled, for Foot Guards, (two-grooved barrel).
Musket, Serjeants, plain, for Regiments of the Line.
Rifle, Lovell's improved Brunswick pattern, (two-grooved barrel) with sword bayonet.
Carbine, light, for Royal Sappers and Miners, with sword bayonet, saw backed.

* The practice of snapping cocks on nipples was later stopped and the snap-cap reintroduced.

Carbine, Victoria pattern, with swivel rammer for Heavy and Light
Cavalry.
Carbine, double-barrelled, (not rifled), with swivel rammer for the
Cape Mounted Rifle Corps.

NAVAL PERCUSSION ARMS

Musket Sea Service
Pistol Sea Service
Rifle, Heavy Navy Pattern

The Statement also contained valuable information about ammunition and accessories. The calibre of all percussion arms was "so far
approximated that they all receive the musket ball and therefore may
be described as of the musket bore". The ammunition for musket and
carbine was made up like that for flintlock arms—blank cartridge in
blue paper and ball cartridge in white. The several charges of powder
were:

Musket ball cartridge	$4\frac{1}{2}$ drams
Carbine ball cartridge	$2\frac{1}{2}$ drams
Blank cartridge	$3\frac{1}{2}$ drams

The same nipple and percussion cap were used for all arms, the
proportion of caps being five to every four cartridges. The problem of
carrying the caps had caused some anxiety. At first various magazines
of the type used for sporting guns had been tried. One designed by
Lt. Margary, a brass holder which could be worn round the neck, was
given a trial by the 2nd Dragoons. Three hundred and twenty were
made by Thomas Lingen of Birmingham at 4s. each but they were
rejected as useless in 1844. Another percussion cap carrier made by
F. Willett of Hatton Garden was also examined by the Select Committee
and failed to win approval (WO 44/636). All these gadgets were not
strong enough to stand up to rough military usage. Eventually all
regiments of cavalry and infantry, except rifle corps, were furnished
with a leather pouch and a tin magazine for the caps. The latter was
carried in the cartridge box and held the main supply, but caps intended
for immediate use were carried in the pouch, which was made of waterproof patent leather. In infantry regiments the pouch was attached to
the coat on the right side by means of a ring, and in cavalry it was
attached to the waist belt. The regulations on this subject which were
published by Circular Memorandum in 1840, and appeared in Queen's
Regulations 1844, were never strictly adhered to. (See JAHR, Vol.
XVIII Notes, pp. 47,114,184).

Implements for the musket and carbine, the three-arm nipple
wrench with a turnscrew, pricker and worm, and a spring cramp were
issued only to sergeants and corporals making a proportion of eight of
each to the company, together with twenty-four spare nipples. The
Ordnance always discouraged the soldier from taking his lock to pieces,

this being considered the armourer's job, and the implements were for emergency use only.

The Sea Service section of the Statement contains one different type of ammunition from those in use by the military. This was the pistol cartridge which had a charge of 2 drams and a ball of 34 bore. Implements for the Navy were issued in a different way, one nipple wrench to every eighteen muskets and one to every eighteen pistols. There was one spare nipple to every six muskets and every six pistols. Spring clamps were issued on a basis of two to each ship.

No sooner had this comprehensive statement reached the hands of the troops than Lovell began making changes. The one weak spot of his musket had always been the back-action lock, and now Lovell, its staunch supporter for many years, decided to scrap it. He designed a new musket with a lighter side-action lock* which could be used for every arm in the Service except the pistol. The advantages of this were obvious. Other new features of the musket were a new barrel with the nipple seat welded instead of brazed on, screws of a standard size and thread, an improved stock and the fitting of two small cups in place of the side piece (Plates 49 and 70).

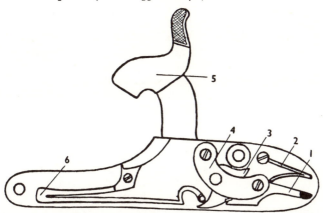

Fig. 25.—Lovell's side-action lock (Pattern 1842). (1) Sear. (2) Sear spring. (3) Tumbler. (4) Bridle. (5) Hammer. (6) Mainspring.

The pattern of the new Line musket was approved and sealed on 27th October, 1841. Three days later, however, a disastrous fire ravaged the Tower of London and 280,000 stand of arms, including most of the new percussion arms, were lost. The Small Arms workshops were destroyed but, on 5th November, Lovell reported that he had started work again in the buildings on the wharf. Although many flintlock arms were lost, it was the destruction of the percussion arms that was most serious. However, new orders were dispatched and the production of the new Line muskets began the following year, thus giving it its classification of Pattern 1842.

* It was modified in 1845 when Lovell replaced the square tumbler peg with an oval one.

The price make-up of this musket was given by Lovell in 1849 as follows:

	s.	d.		£	s.	d.
Barrel	12	0	Cock in stamped state			2½
Lock	7	0	Breech & side nails (3)			1
Bayonet	2	10	Nipple			5
Rammer		9	Wood screws (5)			2
Rough stock	3	0	Back sight			2½
Jointing & percussioning		3½	Bayonet spring			5½
Hardening tumblers, etc.		1½	Rammer spring			2½
Jegging barrels & filing	1	0	Pair of swivels			4
3 Bolts		1¼	Trigger			¾
Brasswork & two side cups	1	2	Setting up	1	6	3

Total   £2 16 8

(*Report of Select Committee of House of Commons*, 1849, p. 303)

In March, 1842, Lovell was able to report that 800 percussion arms were being made each week and that he hoped to increase this figure to 1,200. His policy of standardization was paying dividends. Regiments were now allowed to hand in their flintlocks to be exchanged for percussion arms, even if they had not been kept the regulation period of twelve years. For the information of these troops Lovell published with official approval, in 1842, his *Suggestions for the Cleaning and Management of Percussion Arms*. On 4th June, it was promulgated as a General Order to the Army (No. 559), a copy being distributed to each troop, Regimental Field Officer, Adjutant, Sergeant-Major and Armourer Sergeant.

In fact, 1842 was probably Lovell's most successful year. He had reorganized the Ordnance factories; firearms recognized as his design were being widely used and praised. One of the officers concerned in the field trials of Lovell's musket, Col. Arbuthnot of the 72nd Highlanders, affirmed that 300 of his muskets were the equal of 500 flintlocks. What is more, his most serious rival, Baron Heurteloup, was finally vanquished. The *Koptipteur*, in an improved model, was revived in 1841, assisted by a pamphlet *The Koptipteur and Copper Cap Muskets compared etc.* and much correspondence in *The Times*, which referred to the guns' trials in Russia. Lovell now realized that his whole project was in danger and he made a highly critical attack on the gun and dismissed the claims of the pamphlet as a mere "puff". In 1842, thirty strips of Heurteloup's priming were subjected to a severe series of heat and moisture tests from which they emerged oxydized and brittle. Having exposed the weak point of the *Koptipteur*, the Ordnance took no further interest in it. The percussion primers of Westley Richards, made of pasteboard covered with tin-foil with the fulminate in the centre, were also rejected at this time, notwithstanding the fact that they appealed to the Navy as they caused less damage to sailors' bare feet when dropped on the deck than did the copper caps.

The year was also noteworthy because Lovell introduced two new pistols. Although the pistol had been abolished as a cavalry arm in 1838, the Lancers had been allowed to retain one each, and each cavalry regiment was given an issue of thirteen pistols for the use of Sergeant Majors and Trumpeters (see also *Queen's Regulations*, 1844). The musket bore pistol designed by Lovell for this purpose was a rather ugly-looking job with a short butt, a side lock and a 9 in. barrel with a swivel rammer (Plate 71). Lovell had, of course, little scope in designing his pistols. Nearly all his Sea Service pistols had to be made from converted flintlock materials, and the result was at least a dozen varieties with different locks, swivels, butt caps and furniture. Those intended for the Navy or the Coast Guard were fitted with a belt hook at the side. With this appendage removed,* these 6 in. barrel pistols were issued to police and Land Transport Corps and in 1852–53 to forces in Victoria, New South Wales and Van Diemens Land.

The other pistol, the most unusual of all the percussion series, was specially made for the Irish Constabulary "when serving in plain clothes on special duty" (Plate 71). It was a pocket pistol of the box-lock type with the frame of the action integral with the barrel. It had a total length of 9½ in., the barrel of 17 bore being only 4½ in. long. Five hundred of the pistols with leather cases were ordered in December, 1847, and they were made the following year by Hollis Bros. for 22s. each. Those I have examined are marked on the side TOWER 1848 and are stamped on the barrel with Irish registration marks.

On 10th March, 1843, Lovell's son Francis, who had been acting as clerk, was appointed Assistant Inspector of Small Arms in order to help his father, whose duties kept him on the move between Enfield, the Tower and Birmingham. In solemn fashion Lovell pledged himself to complete the task of arming the British forces with percussion weapons. Just after this, Victoria carbines with back-action locks were received back after undergoing severe service. These he decided to fit with the new side lock and to make the barrels of plain iron instead of twisted stubs, welded by a new process of rolling; and he told the Board this measure would "bring all military arms as much as possible into one system of construction".

He also introduced a new Cadet's carbine, "formed upon the same model but smaller in all its dimensions than the Musquet lately adopted for Royal Artillery" (Plate 65). It had a 2 ft. 3 in. barrel of carbine bore and the only point of interest is an oblong escutcheon. The model was approved in December, 1843, and 180 were made in 1844. In January, 1847, another 200 flintlock carbines in use by cadets were returned and converted to the new style.

At the same time there was an urgent call for a carbine for Yeomanry Cavalry. Lovell was directed to supply a carbine with a 20 in. barrel, and at first Elliott's carbines with flintlocks were cut down to this size.

* The belt hook was not removed from completed guns; it was simply omitted from the parts issued to the gunmakers setting up this new range of Land Service pistols.

Manton's carbines, however, had been made with this length barrel and, in 1844, 5,000 of the materials in hand for this pattern were converted to percussion (Plate 54). In October, 1845, carbines required for the Yeomanry were estimated to be 13,827 of which 5,964 had been issued. The demand continued until 1847 when, with Manton's materials apparently exhausted, it was decided to bring into service the old Paget carbine with a 16 in. barrel. At first completed flintlocks were converted and then flintlock materials were percussioned and set up as new. These carbines were described variously as "Paget's altered pattern percussion carbine" and "the altered Paget 6th Carbine".

It will be seen that Lovell did not always have a free hand and did not have unlimited supplies available. Many of his decisions were governed by this knowledge. But the gunmakers, sportsmen, engineers and eccentrics who now besieged the Ordnance with their inventions could not appreciate this. The final arbiter on all these matters was the Master General but he relied on the reports of the Select Committee of Officers at Woolwich. As I have said before, this Committee was somewhat unjustly accused of knowing little about small arms—army officers were apt to refer scornfully to the fact that *Naval* officers were often present—and it was considered by many that the real decisions were made by Lovell. It was upon his head, therefore, that rejected inventors heaped their vilifications.

William Greener, the gunmaker, and Col. Peter Hawker were two who suffered what they regarded as humiliation from the Select Committee and did not forget it. As they were both successful authors, they replied in kind. Hawker in his *Instructions to Young Sportsmen, etc.*, 9th Edit., 1844, p. 349, demanded the reform of the department and asked "what can the gentlemen of this committee, whose profession is fortification, the use of cannon etc. be supposed to know about *small arms*, more than other amateurs or non-professionals?" He suspected that they relied on their assistant or inspector "who must, of course, have but a superficial knowledge of arms. . . ." In his diary, Hawker refers witheringly to Lovell and his "nonsense". Greener indulged in more rhetorical language. "Shame, I say, on England, that her artizans [*sic*], and her scientific, to succeed, must submit to be the football of some upstart pretender to the knowledge of that divine bestowed qualification, which only exists in true genius" (*The Science of Gunnery*, 1841, p. 306). He went on to describe Lovell's Brunswick rifle as "an abortion".

Hard words, but Lovell could be just as outspoken. On a musket submitted by Capt. Hare in 1833 he commented: "The Captain appears to have lost sight of the main requisites of a soldier's musket in his desire to effect an object of very doubtful advantage." On Hawker's under-hammer musket—it was an improvement on Wilkinson's —he wrote, in 1842: "These very ingenious fancies tho' agreeable to Sportsmen, offend against all the requirements of Military supply."

In reading the masses of correspondence with the persuasive, often impassioned, pleas of the inventor on the one hand and the cold comments of the Ordnance officers, be it the Committee, the Master General or Lovell, on the other, one cannot help feeling on occasion that all their judgements were not entirely unbiased or dispassionate. Not that they were to be blamed on some occasions. Here, for instance, is the opening sentence of the submission made by M. A. Dillon of Dublin in 1848 with all the glorious blarney of his race:

"Premising that there is neither legerdemain nor mystery, nor difficulty nor expense of any kind or description whatsoever, attending the seemingly paradoxical feats which I propose to accomplish and that I shall undertake to satisfy your Lordship's intellect in ten minutes that the most neglected and simplest agents are often the most powerful—and that *the terrific simplicity* of the plans which it has been my lot to discover, render their instantaneous adoption requisite."

and there were pages of this stuff leaving the reader no wiser at the end.

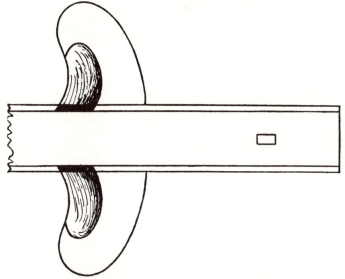

FIG. 26.—Deshogues's muzzle-brake. From the original drawing in the Public Record Office (WO 44/624).

Some inventions were dismissed with the scantest of terms. There was the case of M. Deshogues who worked in the Arsenal at St. Helier in the Channel Islands and in 1843 wrote to the Ordnance offering to increase the range of a musket to 750 yards. Vastly intrigued, the Committee interviewed him, only to be told that the basis of his idea was to double the charge. However, Deshogues proposed to lessen the recoil by cutting two slots at the muzzle end of the barrel and soldering to each a cup-like projection, "une oreille au champignon", to catch some of the "rush of fluid" and counteract the recoil. This idea, the first muzzle brake, was labelled without trial as "visionary and useless".

In other instances, however, the Committee went to endless trouble. In 1843, 100 Sea Service muskets were electro-plated with copper and 100 with zinc by Elkington & Company's patent process to see if this coating was better than browning. They were subjected to various trials on different ships and it was not until 1847 that they were finally rejected by Lovell. Another suggestion was that cartridges should be encased in sheep-gut instead of paper to make them waterproof. While some samples were being carefully tested in different temperatures of water, the appropriate Commissary Department was told to procure a statistical report on the sheep population of Great Britain and its ability to produce enough gut to keep an army supplied in war.

In all these deliberations one has to admire the resolution of George Lovell to carry out what he believed to be the correct decision against all criticism from his superiors. This was never better demonstrated than by his brushes with the Duke of Wellington, as Commander-in-Chief. Lovell first crossed his path in 1844, when the Ordnance decided to alter the method of fixing the bayonet on the musket. Up to 1814, the majority of arms had plain socket bayonets with no spring fastening, but with the New Land Series a short straight spring was fitted on the bayonet socket. In 1838, after trials against a bayonet of Baron de Berenger, Lovell adopted the Hanoverian method for all his percussion arms—a spring hook under the muzzle which clipped on to a ring or reinforcement round the edge of the bayonet socket. As this method still proved unsatisfactory, four special bayonet fittings were subjected to a severe trial by the Woolwich Committee. Their findings were communicated to the Duke for his decision. With the best of intentions the latter chose a bayonet with a locking ring on the French principle. Lovell, who was now consulted, reminded the Board that this idea had already been tried in 1794 by the 43rd and the 52nd Regts. and had

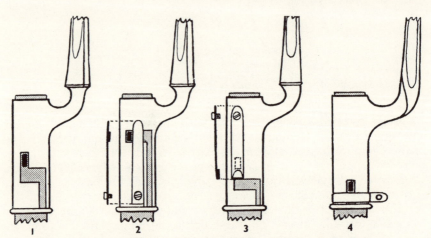

Fig. 27.—Bayonet fittings.   (1) Common socket.   (2) East India Company spring.   (3) New Land pattern spring.   (4) Nock's locking ring.

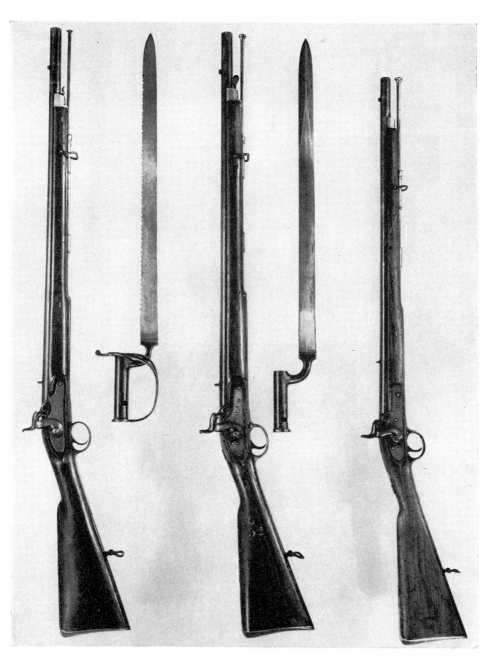

65. *Left to right:* (1) Sappers and Miners' carbine dated 1841, with the first pattern sword bayonet. (2) Another S & M carbine dated 1847, with the second sword bayonet. The Artillery carbine was similar. (3) Cadet's carbine 1844.

66. Double-barrelled Cape carbines. *Left to right:* (1) Four-groove rifled carbine of 1854. (2) Smooth-bore percussion carbine by Barnett marked CAPE CAVALRY. (3) Smooth-bore flintlock carbine of 1822.

67. Double-barrelled India carbines. *Left to right:* (1) Jacob's rifle with sword bayonet, by Swinburn & Son, 1861, marked JACOBS RIFLES. (2) Smooth-bore carbine by Swinburn & Son, 1860, marked SCINDE IRREGULAR HORSE. (3) Smooth-bore carbine by Garden & Son. Note the similarity of the butt boxes.

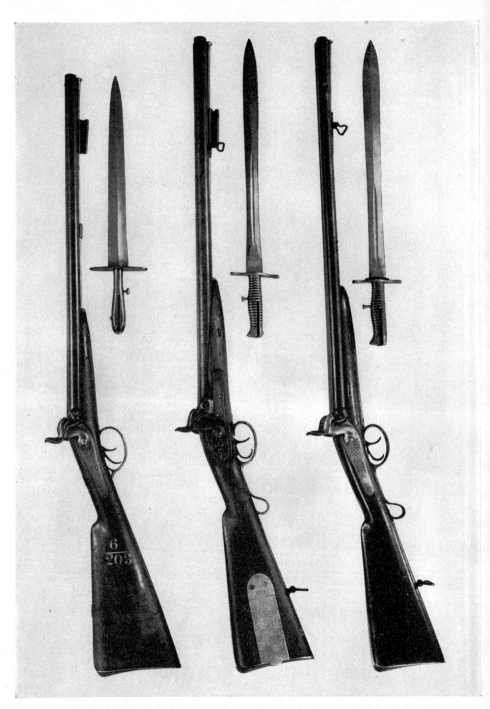

68. Double-barrelled Constabulary carbines. *Left to right:* (1) Wilkinson's carbine of 1836. (2) Musket-bore carbine by Cutler & Son. (3) The standard carbine with the bayonet fitting on the side of the barrel, made by Tipping & Lawden.

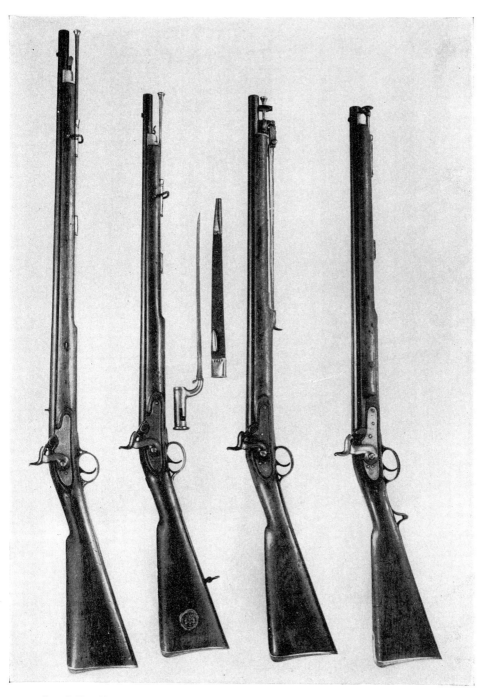

69. Miscellaneous carbines. *Left to right:* (1) Smooth-bore musket for Sergeants of the Line. (2) Sealed pattern constabulary carbine of 1840 with spring catch bayonet. (3) Police carbine with folding bayonet. (4) Victoria carbine with side-action lock.

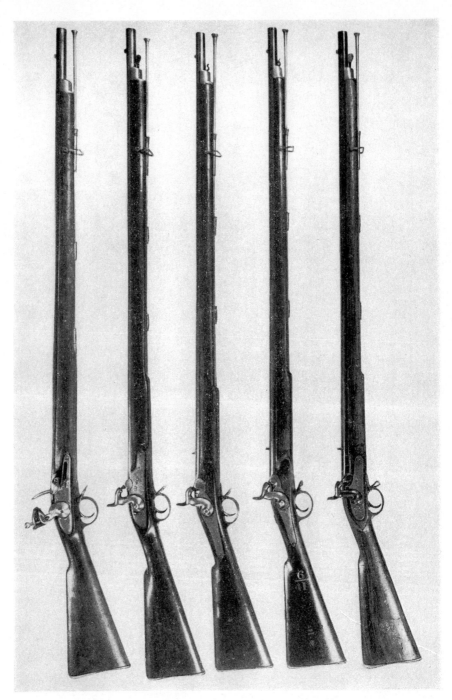

70. The last smooth-bore muskets. *Left to right:* (1) Victorian flintlock. Note the rounded lock-plate. (2) Converted percussion musket, Pattern 1839. (3) Lovell's back-action lock musket, Pattern 1838. (4) The same musket with the small lock. (5) Lovell's musket, Pattern 1842, with the side-action lock. All these muskets have 39 in. barrels.

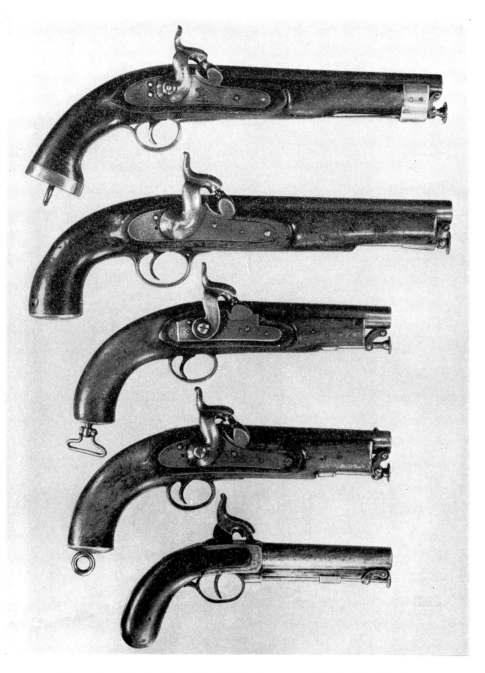

71. Percussion pistols. *Top:* East India Company pistol with 9 in. barrel.
(2) Pattern 1842 pistol with 9 in. barrel, marked 16 L (16th Lancers).
(3 and 4) Naval and Coastguard pistols. (5) Police pocket pistol of 1848.

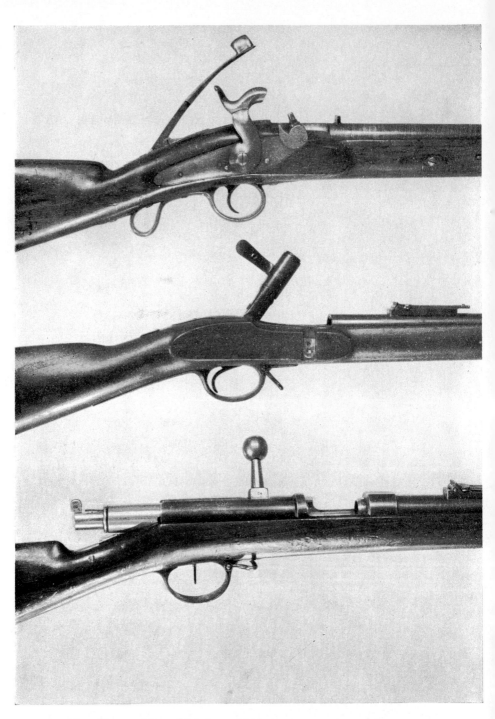

72. Experimental breechloaders. *Top:* Jenks's carbine. *Middle:* Joseph Needham's needle-fire musket marked No. 854 PATENT. *Bottom:* Lovell's copy of the Prussian needle-fire musket marked ENFIELD 1850.

failed. Furthermore, he pointed out that the existing stock of bayonets could not be adapted. Accordingly he submitted a fitting of his own design.

Wellington, obviously baffled by such a sweeping condemnation of his choice and outraged that any decision of his should be questioned, sent back a reply that must have thundered down the corridors of the Ordnance Office in Pall Mall like a cannon shot. He demanded to know who had sanctioned the present spring and declared that, if it was so bad, then there was "a fair cause for Regret that the old simple English Bayonet with which our Armies had so long prevailed and against which no serious complaint had ever been made should have been set aside except upon the first Authority in the Service". The Master General and the Board hastened to assure him that the General Officer Commanding had been consulted at the time and, slightly mollified, he agreed that a Board of Officers should meet Lovell, but

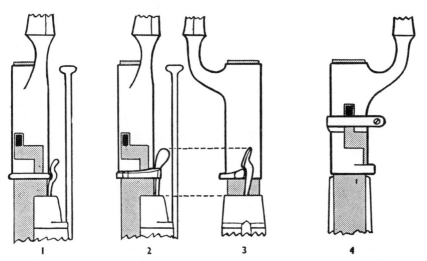

FIG. 28.—Bayonet fittings. (1) Hanoverian spring. (2 and 3) Lovell's spring catch (side and underneath views). (4) Enfield rifle locking-ring.

still grumbling that he was "not disposed to concur in Mr. Lovell's objections". However, the Board soon approved of Lovell's new fitting, a spring fixed under the muzzle which acted sideways on a projection on the socket. A General Order authorizing the alteration was promulgated in September, 1844.

There was another exchange between these two in 1850, when the Commander-in-Chief recommended an improved light cavalry sword made by Reeves & Greaves. Lovell immediately raised several objections and remarked: "Changes always entail expence and should be avoided if not productive of very decided advantages." Wellington's reply on this occasion was straight to the point: "His Grace apprehends

L

that Mr. Lovell must have been misinformed or is speaking without adequate knowledge of the subject."

Tempers, in fact, were growing short. There was a growing realization that the British service firearm, for all Lovell's efforts, had its shortcomings. The basic part of Lovell's musket, the relationship between barrel and ball, was, after all, no different, except in finish, to the first model Brown Bess. The range at which the soldier was expected to give effective fire had steadily increased until the smooth-bore musket could not accomplish its task. This was given publicity in 1846 when a series of experiments with muskets was organized by the Inspector General of Fortifications and the result published under the title *Report of Experimental Musket Firing carried on at the Royal Engineer Establishment Chatham between 8 April & 8 May 1846* (WO 1/447, pp. 463–85).

The intention was to ascertain the range and accuracy of the musket. Percussion muskets were fired from a rest across the River Medway, the range being determined by observing the point of impact on the water with theodolites. At an angle of elevation of 5° the maximum range was about 650 yards, the point blank range being 75 yards. The really shattering results came when the firing was directed against a target 11 ft. 6 in. high by 6 ft. wide. At a range of 250 yards ten shots all missed and at 150 yards only half the shots hit the target. To produce any result, it was necessary to aim 5½ feet above the target at 200 yards and 130 feet at 600 yards. The report reached the not unnatural conclusion that "as a general rule, musketry fire should not be made at a distance exceeding 150 yards and certainly not exceeding 200 yards as at and beyond that range it would be a mere waste of ammunition to do so".

These were results produced under ideal conditions. In actual warfare the efforts of the British soldier against native adversaries in South Africa and New Zealand became ludicrous. The problem which all military authorities now had to face was the design of a gun which would combine a long range with easy loading; the accuracy of a rifle with the speed of a musket. The obvious solution was the breechloader.

In 1841, four carbines with the breech action of William Jenks of Springfield, Mass., U.S.A., were bought from an agent Dr. Alexander Jones, who had had them made in Belgium (Plate 72). In this action a lever pulled a piston out of the breech revealing a loading hole on the top of the barrel. American trials of a rifle with this action showed that it could be fired four times a minute up to thirty shots without cleaning. (*Army & Navy Chronicle*, Washington City, 1838–39.) This speed does not seem to have been attained by the British troops to whom the carbines were issued—the 2nd Regt. North British Dragoons, the 7th Dragoon Guards, the 10th Royal Hussars and the 13th Royal Dragoons. Nor were they particularly impressed. They reported cleaning and loading difficulties and the carbines were discarded (WO 44/539).

The gun which aroused most interest was, of course, the needle-fire breechloader. Invented by M. Dreyse of Sommerda in Thuringen, who was once a workman of Pauly, it utilized a cartridge in which the ball was seated on a wooden base which also had a small recess containing the primer. This was ignited by a needle passing through the powder charge. The action was copied in many countries but the Board of Ordnance in London did not show any interest in it until 1849. In that year a searching inquiry was made into its organization by a Select Committee of the House of Commons, and the British musket came under criticism. (See *Report from the Select Committee on Army and Ordnance Expenditure*, 1849.) In the summer Lovell went to Germany to examine the arms recently introduced there. On his return he was told to prepare a number of muskets or rifles (as he thought fit) on the French and German patterns. The French inventor Montigny was also given facilities to make one of his needle-fire muskets "of the English form and Calibre".

Very little was done, however, until the following April when a Committee of officers was set up to inquire into the subject of Small Arms. The Surveyor General was President, Col. Chalmers, Secretary, and Lovell, as usual, was in attendance as technical adviser. Throughout the summer many types of rifles were compared—including an Afghan*—but not until September was there any indication of process. Two needle-fire muskets of the Prussian pattern were then ordered to be made and tried against two regulation rifles sighted up to 600 yards and two regulation muskets which were to range up to 300 yards. The Committee's doubts about the needle-fire construction were expressed in their instructions to Lovell that the two breechloaders should be made "with such attention in their construction as may obviate the inconvenience of the escape of Gas at the junction of the Barrel". They are both in existence, one in the Tower and the other at Enfield. They have an overall length of 4½ ft. with a 2 ft. 9in. barrel rifled with four grooves. The side of the frame is stamped ENFIELD 1850 (Plate 72).

According to Sir Howard Douglas (*A Treatise on Naval Gunnery*, 4th Edit. 1855, pp. 513–4), who was present at the trials, the needle-fire rifle had the highest rate of fire and was reasonably accurate, but the operation of opening and closing the bolt of the breech required a great deal of strength, particularly when the piece became heated and dirty. It was all very disappointing and Lovell, "looking to the very serious nature of the change that is coming about and the responsibility placed upon him", obtained permission to visit Germany again because, as he admitted: "he does not feel that he is yet sufficiently master of the subject in all its bearings to propose a musquet that shall fulfil all the requisites of the new system". The Board instructed him to bring back one of the latest German breechloaders and also an example of the French Minié rifle.

The European countries were now closely watching each others'

* An Afghan jezail or rifle "stocked and locked at Enfield" is listed in the catalogue of the Rotunda (Class VII, No. 105).

movements. There was an air of expectancy, a feeling that any moment some new all-powerful weapon would be devised. The Prince of Prussia proposed an exchange of information, but the Master General, supported by the Duke of Wellington, refused. The British were more discreet. They arranged for a spy to attend the French experiments, warning him: "The French are not over ready to let us into their secrets so we must be careful." (WO 40/85–6).

The new French weapon which was attracting attention, the Minié rifle, was the result of a series of experiments conducted in France to find a method by which a bullet could be easily rammed down a barrel and then expanded to take the rifling on its exit. At first, the chamber of M. Delvigne was tried, the bullet being expanded on the shoulders of the chamber by blows from the ramrod. Proper expansion was not always obtained and, in 1844, Col. Thouvenin substituted a steel pillar or "tige", which acted as an anvil. A conical bullet with a flat base which made a better contact on the pillar was then introduced.

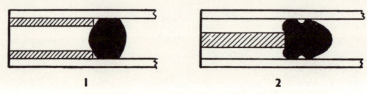

FIG. 29.—Breeches for expanding bullets. (1) Delvigne's chamber breech. (2) Thouvenin's pillar breech.

This method of forcing the shot into the grooves of a rifle was popularized in this country by Charles Lancaster, the gunmaker. His pillar-breech rifle was much used by sportsmen and a military model was the subject of several trials (Plate 73). With a back-action lock, it is not unlike the Brunswick in general appearance. The barrel is 2 ft. 9 in. long and is rifled with four grooves to take a cylindro-conoidal bullet. In the photograph the breech has been taken out to show the pillar. There were several snags with this type of breech: the pillar was liable to be broken or bent, and after several rounds the space round it, which contained the charge, became so fouled that the powder rose above the stem and prevented proper expansion of the bullet when it was struck by the ramrod. The stiking head of the rammer was normally recessed so as to properly seat the bullet and not deform it. The other end was threaded to take a special tool with a circular milling head which fitted over the "tige" to clear the chamber. Although Lancaster could hardly patent this breech, he registered it (No. 1418) under the Designs Act of 1842, and the barrel shown is marked with the date of registration 19th April, 1848.

All these breeches where the bullet had to be hammered by the rammer caused a certain amount of fatigue and an unsteadiness in taking aim. To obviate this Capt. Minié, an instructor at Vincennes, modified a hollow bullet previously suggested by Delvigne. The flat end of the bullet was hollowed out and an iron cup inserted. The force of the charge then drove the cup into the bullet causing its sides to expand into the rifling—at least that was the idea. Sometimes the cup went right through the bullet or the solid part left the barrel, leaving the hollow rear jammed in the rifling. The idea of a plug driven into a bullet to increase its size was first mooted by William Greener in 1836, when he submitted to the Ordnance an oval ball into which fitted a tapered plug. The evidence of a trial by the 60th Rifles suggested that the plug did not always work, and the Select Committee at Woolwich rejected the idea as "useless and chimerical." They were to regret these words, for, after a long campaign for compensation, Greener was awarded £1,000 in 1857.

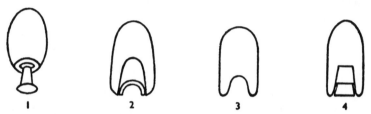

FIG. 30.—Expanding bullets. (1) Greener's with wedge plug. (2) English Minié with iron cup. (3) Pritchett hollow bullet. (4) Enfield with boxwood plug.

When Lovell returned from his European journey—his travelling bill (WO 52/774) traces his route through Calais, Brussels, Liège, Frankfurt, Strasbourg, Carlsruhe, Stuttgart, Ludwigsburg, Augsburg, Munich, Vienna, Dresden, Berlin and back via Hanover, Cologne and Liège—Minié rifles made in France and Belgium were tried against rifles à tige made by Lancaster and by the Ordnance at Enfield.* The results both in accuracy and rate of fire showed the undoubted superiority of the Minié, and the reaction was swift. The breechloading rifles of Montigny, Melville, Callow, Kufhal and Malherbe, which had been under consideration, were rejected. In May, 1851, Lovell was told to prepare dies and tools for making Minié bullets, and the following minute was recorded:

"It being determined that the Belgian Minnie [sic] Musquet be the Arm adopted throughout the British Army, the amount of £76,000 voted in this years' Estimate for the Construction of Small Arms to be appropriated as follows,
Disbursements at Enfield £12,422   3   0.
The remainder of the sum to be exclusively applied (and with the least possible delay) to the construction of Arms upon the newly adopted Principle, applying all the different Articles in Store, what are convertible to the foregoing purpose to effect the object in view."

* Specimens of these Enfield rifles, dated 1850, have barrels of ·702 in. cal. rifled with four grooves. The flat-topped pillar, made integral with the breech-plug, is 1·5 in. long and ·33 in. in diameter.

In the following month, the Duke of Wellington agreed that the Infantry and Marines and other troops using infantry weapons should be issued with "the Minié Rifled Musquet".*

Lovell, at first, made four copies of the Belgian pattern and, not liking the rifling, prepared another two with grooves of "equal depth throughout". His difficulty was the Duke's insistence that the calibre of the bullet should not be reduced. With an elongated shape this meant an increase in its weight. Eventually, on 9th October, Wellington agreed that 50 of the new bullets should not exceed 60 (the standard number) of the old ammunition. Four days later, the Small Arms Committee fixed the principal features of the new rifle:

Weight with Bayonet 10 lbs. 8¾ oz.
Barrel length   3 ft. 3 ins.
Diam. of bore   ·702 ins.
Number of grooves   4 (of equal depth from end to end with a half turn).
Ball with iron cup   680 grains
Powder charge   2½ drams

This was something of a compromise because the new calibre barrel would not take a musket bullet. The British Minié bullet also differed from its French counterpart in having a smooth outer surface without any cannelures.

With the rifle and its bullet decided upon, the bayonet became Lovell's next concern. Although the Minié or Patt. 1851 rifle resembled the 1842 musket, its barrel's exterior diameter was smaller and Lovell was obliged to work out a process whereby he could shrink the sockets of existing bayonets to make them fit. By the end of the year, 1,500 had been altered and the work was proceeding at the rate of 400 a week.

In February, 1852, the first 500 Miniés were ready and twenty regiments and depots in Southern England and the Channel Islands were issued with twenty-five stand each. An officer and two N.C.O.s from each regiment were sent to Woolwich for a week's instruction under Major Brownrigg of the Grenadier Guards. At the same time orders were put in hand for the setting up of another 23,000 by the following gunmakers:

	Total Number	Weekly Rate	Price
Holland & Son	5,000	100	23/5
W. Adams	5,000	100	23/2
Hollis & Sheath	3,250	100	23/6
Swinburn & Son	3,250	100	23/6
Tipping & Lawden	3,250	100	23/6
Thomas Turner	3,250	100	23/6

Strange to relate, these orders caused a dispute between "the operative gunmakers and the Contractors" so that the Lovells, father and son, had to hurry to Birmingham to effect a settlement. As we shall see, they got little thanks for the intervention. But by the end of March manufacture was well under way and the twenty selected regiments

* On 28th April, 1855, *The Times* printed a joint letter from Delvigne and Minié asking that the Minié musket should be called the Delvigne-Minié, but their request seems to have been ignored.

received a further issue, bringing them up to 100 rifles each. Applications were then invited from other units.

The principle of the Minié was now generally accepted and it was applied enthusiastically to many other arms, including the Paget carbine, the Cape double-barrelled carbine and the old smooth-bore muskets of the 1842 and Sea Service patterns. There was even a suggestion that a cannon should be made in the same fashion. Three hundred and fifty of the double-barrelled carbines were ordered in May, 1851, for the 12th Lancers (Plate 66). Originally intended to be smooth-bore, their maker, Charles Lancaster, was ordered to rifle them with four grooves for the Minié bullet in July. This rifling caused great difficulty and consequently the carbines were not ready for the regiment when it embarked for the Cape. They were not delivered until a year later (WO 3/318), and were subsequently handed over to the Cape Mounted Riflemen in 1854, when the Lancers left for Madras (WO 3/322).

The conversion to rifles of the old smooth-bore muskets meant that there were now three types of rifles and two types of ammunition in use:

		Weight of Bullet	Charge
(1) Patt. 1851 (for infantry)	·702 in. cal.	680 gr.	2½ drms.
(2) Altered Patt. 1842 (for Marines)	·758 in. cal.	850 gr.	3 drms.
(3) Altered Sea Service (for Sailors)	·758 in. cal.	850 gr.	3 drms.

The balls for all these rifles were of the same Minié pattern designed to be expanded by an iron cup and were called cup balls. The immense difference in weight caused by the alteration in shape of the round musket ball which weighed 480 grs. will be noticed. To overcome the problem of providing enough ammunition for all these rifles special machinery was erected at the Royal Laboratory, Woolwich and on 31st December, 1852, 100 boys, 11 artificers and 38 labourers were reported employed on this operation.

Nevertheless the weight of the ammunition was still a drawback. With 60 rounds the complete Minié weighed 17 lb. 9 oz. 14 drs., more than the old musket or the Brunswick. As it had been the aim to lighten the infantryman's arm Viscount Hardinge, who had just been appointed Master General, determined to remedy this. The Committee on Small Arms fortunately came to the conclusion that it was not the calibre of the English musket which should be maintained but the weight of the bullet. They suggested that the bore could be reduced "to such a diameter as to receive an elongated Projectile of the weight of the existing spheroid Leaden Ball—viz. 480 grains, with a charge of 2½ drams". Hardinge, who had written: "At no period of our history have we ever been in a state so favourable for a change in the pattern of our Small Arms owing to the low state of stores", now seized the opportunity to invite the leading gunmakers, Purdey, Westley Richards, Lancaster, Wilkinson and Greener to submit patterns of a rifle approaching this specification. This was the first time that such a move had been made and was undoubtedly due to the persistent outcry made by the gun-makers and the sporting public that a better rifle was possible. The plan was to try the gunmakers' rifles against the Minié, the Brunswick and an improved Minié designed by Lovell. The trials continued throughout the summer, with the gunmakers often making changes to the bullet or rifling of their entries. The Committee published its report in August, 1852 (*Report of Experiments with small arms carried on at the Royal Manufactory, Enfield*, 1852). It was later included (minus target diagrams) as an appendix to Lt.-Col. The Hon. A. Gordon's *Remarks on National Defence*, 1853.

Westley Richards's entry did not arrive in time and Greener withdrew his, so that this left a straight fight between the three privately made arms of Lancaster, Purdey and Wilkinson and the three government rifles. Of the latter, the Brunswick was soon abandoned. The regulation Minié's faults were already known, but one result of the trial was the design of a more cylindrical bullet for it. Lovell's improved Minié with a ·635 in. bore was designed to fire a heavy and a light bullet weighing 686 gr. and 562 gr. Only the heavy ball gave good results, but it was difficult to load and its weight was a disadvantage. Wilkinson's musket fired a solid bullet of ·537 in. diameter with two greased grooves and was recommended for trial by a rifle regiment. Purdey's bullet, based on the Minié pattern, was "of a very beautiful shape", and his rifle was admired for its quality. The Committee were most intrigued with Lancaster's rifle, which had an elliptical barrel with an increasing spiral; but like all the rest it had both good and bad points. They decided, therefore, not to choose any of the rifles but to recommend a theoretical rifle embodying the following features:

The Musquet including bayonet to weigh about 9 lb. 3 oz.
The Bore to be ·577 inch.
The Barrel to be in length 3 feet 3 inches.
The Barrel to be in weight 4 lb. 6 oz.
The Barrel to have 3 grooves.
The Barrel to have a constant spiral of one turn in 6 feet 6 inches.
The Barrel to be fastened to the stock by 3 bands.
The Ramrod to have a swell near the head.
The Bayonet to be fixed by means of a locking ring.
The Lock to be made with a swivel.

They also recommended a new bullet, of a modified Minié shape without a cup, designed by the gunmaker Pritchett, who was awarded £1,000 in 1854 for the use of his bullet.

Two of these rifles were made at Enfield, one intended for Line regiments sighted up to 200 yards, and the other with two sights (one a modified Westley Richards) for use by riflemen up to 800 yards. In the meantime all work on the Patt. 1851 rifles was suspended. In December, the new rifle with the Pritchett bullet was successfully tried up to distances of 800 yards and at the end of the month the Committee sent in a report which resulted in the adoption of what was to be known as the Patt. 1853, or Enfield rifle.

One thousand of the new rifles were ordered and also 2,000 with shorter barrels as carbines for the Royal Artillery. The carbines were armed with sword bayonets. Claims were now made on behalf of the Lancaster rifle with the elliptical bore, which was "freed" or widened at the breech and had an increasing spiral. In March, 1855, its inventor was given an order for 2,842 oval-bored carbines for the Royal Sappers and Miners, complete with brass mounted sword bayonet, at £4 2s. each. Apart from the shape of the bore (dimensions are given in Appendix C), this Sappers' carbine is similar to the shorter model of the Enfield later adopted for Sergeants and Rifle Corps. Charles Lancaster was awarded £6,600 for his invention by the Ordnance in December, 1856. However, as far as the main rifle was concerned, the superiority of the Enfield over the Lancaster was finally established at trials conducted at the new Small Arms School at Hythe under Col. Hay. On 5th October, 1853, contracts were placed for the supply of 20,000 Patt. 1853 rifles. The first issues to regiments began in May, 1854 (WO 3/323).

Modifications were soon being made. In the first model Enfield the barrel was held to the stock by three steel bands secured by screws, but in the next model the bands were made of case-hardened iron and were retained by springs inserted in the side of the stock. The breech screw which was at first made flush with the tang had its head raised for easier access. Other improvements were the strengthening of the lock swivel and the cock, and the fitting of a ramrod with a built-in jag. The sight first used was Westley Richards's pattern with a graduated leaf which could be folded down forwards or backwards. This was replaced by a sight combining the principles of Westley Richards, Charles Lancaster and the Ordnance sight of 1851. By pushing the sliding bar up two inclined flanges, the soldier could obtain elevations up to 400 yards without raising the leaf. Following experiments at Hythe, a new bullet with a box-wood plug was introduced, ·55 in. in diameter and 1·09 in. in length (Fig. 30).

However, the full story of the Enfield rifle, its various patterns, the competition with the precision muzzleloaders of Whitworth and Lancaster, and its conversion to a breechloader must be left to others. With the adoption of the rifle as the standard arm of the British Service, this chapter and the main narrative of this book come to an end; but the tragic end of George Lovell must be recorded.

His misfortunes commenced in 1845 with the death of his son Robert, while acting as purchasing agent of gun stocks on the continent. In the following year, after a strike at Enfield, one of his workmen made a murderous attack on him. In 1847, his troubles with the contractors began in earnest. They never forgave him for the strict manner in which he exercised control over the viewers. Even the workmen gunmakers, on whose behalf he had several times intervened, were led to believe that it was on his instructions that they were paid nothing for work rejected at the view. The attempts to blacken Lovell's character were all revealed in the evidence of William Greener before the Parliamentary Committee of 1849. Worse was to come. In 1852 his son Francis George, Assistant Inspector of Small Arms, was found to have falsified the accounts of gunstocks in order to compensate the suppliers for deterioration on the Ordnance wharves. It was apparently an unselfish act, but it cost him his job. His father was admonished and obliged to move his home to Birmingham. It must have been a sad journey for the old man, who had recently lost his wife.

Next came the discovery that many of the Minié rifles had been badly sighted, and how his detractors seized on this mistake! Finally, during the hearing of the 1854 Parliamentary Commission on Small Arms, witness after witness rose to accuse him of discriminating against the gunmakers in favour of the Enfield factory. The Board, who had steadfastly defended Lovell—they tried without success to convince the gunmakers that they had not dismissed his son because of the complaints about the viewing of arms—now felt that they should obtain a statement from him. Lovell, who had retired, lay seriously ill. His last letter to his employers, in the shaky writing of a dying man is a pathetic document. He died soon afterwards broken in health and spirit.

He was a strict but kindly man, devoted to his duty and almost fanatical in his desire to make the British military firearm the finest in the world. If the reader has the opportunity to examine any of the arms described in the last two chapters, he will perhaps agree that in this resolve Lovell did not fail.

CHAPTER XI

REPEATERS AND REVOLVERS

EARLY attempts to increase the rate of fire of firearms resulted in combinations of barrels, but such was their weight that they were usually mounted on some form of carriage and any advantage in the number of shots was offset by the loss of mobility and the time taken to reload. The next development was to supply a single barrel with charges, either from a series of chambers or from a magazine. The chambers were normally contained in a revolving cylinder fastened to the breech. The great difficulty in this was to ensure the correct alignment of chamber and barrel and to minimize the gap between the two which caused a loss of pressure and often a dangerous escape of gas.

The magazine method was even more complicated. The butt was designed to hold two tubular magazines, one for powder and one for shot, these charges being separately transferred to the barrel by some kind of revolving breech or carrier. The vertical revolving types with a long side lever have been named after the Italian gunmaker, Michele Lorenzoni, and those with a horizontally working breech take their name from the gunmaking family of Kalthoff. The advent of the true flintlock enabled all these mechanisms to be simplified and by the end of the seventeenth century there were several London gunmakers experimenting with different forms of repeating mechanisms.

James Gorgo, a Huguenot refugee, made pistols and guns with a most unusual revolving action. Three or four chambers were used, but no attempt was made to align the chamber and barrel, the ball being deflected into the barrel by a funnel-shaped breech. In July, 1698, the Gunmakers' Company seized "a gun with four chambers" from Gorgo's workshop in Soho (GMB). Another experimenter was John Shaw, the King's Gunmaker in Ordinary. He was paid 14s. in 1701 by the Ordnance "for mending 2 Engine Guns". Earlier, John Dafte, a descendant of an Elizabethan family of armourers, produced revolvers with a snaphance lock. The unsigned, all brass, revolver in the Royal United Services Institute* in London is probably an example of his work and, although far too expensive and complicated for the Ordnance, would have appealed to officers as a personal weapon (Plate 76).

The Kalthoff magazine action was developed in Holland and was then taken to most parts of Europe by the widely travelled members

---

* This early revolving pistol was transferred to the Royal Armouries, HM Tower of London (No. XII.1780) in 1963.

of the family. One settled in London under the patronage of that enthusiastic inventor the second Marquis of Worcester. In his *Century of Inventions* the latter describes how, in 1628, he engaged the services of "the unparalleled workman both for trust and skill, Caspar Kalthoff." On premises at Vauxhall the Marquis brought together a number of engineers and workmen in what was called "a College of Artisans" under Kalthoff's direction. Many of the inventions which are described in the *Century* were made there. Although Kalthoff appears to have been employed mainly as an engineer—the "Water Commanding Engine" made him famous—some of his energies were devoted to firearms and he appears on the Charter of the Gunmakers' Company in 1638.

Among Worcester's claims was No. 58—"How to make a Pistol to discharge a dozen times with one loading and without so much as once new Priming requisite; or to change it out of one hand into the other, or stop ones horse." This was probably not an action on the Kalthoff principle. Examples of Kalthoff's guns are at Windsor Castle (No. 226), in the Tøjhusmuseet, Copenhagen (Nos. B 762–4) and in the Kremlin Museum, Moscow (No. 7539). Another one in the Kremlin dated 1665, was probably made by Caspar's son of the same name who was employed by the Czar of Russia for that purpose. A fine carbine on the same principle was made by the Dutchman Harman Barne who worked in London from 1650 until his death in 1661.

Besides describing his inventions in his book, Worcester included many of them in a Patent, No. 131, in 1662. Other Patents followed. Abraham Hill, a Fellow of the Royal Society, took out a Patent in 1665 (No. 143) which covered "Another invencon for gunns and pistols with several devices for the speedier and more effectual discharge". One of these was for "A Gun or pistol for small shott, carrying seven or eight charges of the same in the stocke of the gun". This undoubtedly referred to the Lorenzoni action, and a pistol with this action, signed by the inventor, has been recorded. In the decade 1670–80, several guns of this type were made by the English gunmaker who signed his work JOHN COOKSON. Although he is believed to have worked in the capital, all attempts to trace this man in the London archives have failed and there is no evidence that his guns were considered by the Ordnance. Towards the end of the eighteenth century the system was revived by the London gunmaker H. W. Mortimer, many of whose pistols were bought by officers.

Another gunmaker—a gun bearing his name is also in the Kremlin— had the following advertisement printed in *Mercurius Publicus* of 12th December, 1661:

"At the sign of the Stirrop in Chiswell Street, near the new Artillery ground, there are made and sold by William Martindall, from the pocket Pistol to the whole cannon, all sorts of Guns that are charged with three or four several charges, also swords with pistols of like nature affixed, of stronger force and speedier and more secure service than ordinary."

The vague terms of this notice, like the previously mentioned patents, preclude any identification of the action used, but the specification of Charles Cardiffe's patent, No. 216 of 1682, is more explicit. He informed the King "that he hath, by his long experience, found out an expedient with security to make musketts, carbines, pistolls, or any other small fire-arms to discharge twice, thrice or more severall and distinct shotts in any single barrel and lock with one primeing and with double locks, oftener reserving one or more shotts till occasion offer which hitherto by none but himself hath been invented or known, the mistery or mayne lying in the charge."

In these guns the barrel was loaded with alternate charges of ball and powder and the ignition applied to the foremost charge. As each charge exploded the flame fed back to the charge behind it and so on until all the charges were gone, in the manner of the Roman Candle. If solid balls were used, they had to be a very loose fit to enable the ignition to spread past them. Porta describes the careful loading necessary in these guns in his *Natural Magick*, 1658 (12th Book). They could be fired by simply applying a match to the muzzle if they were loaded to the brim, or a touchhole could be bored (attended by an appropriate lock) at a position on the barrel according to the number of shots required.

The great disadvantage of this action was that once the gun started to fire it could not be stopped. Cardiffe, however, points out that, by using two locks, one or more shots could be reserved. A tight-fitting wad placed behind the front series of charges prevented the chain of fire from reaching the reserve charges, which could be set off by the rear lock when necessary. He was not correct in asserting that he was the inventor. In 1580, "John the Almain" recommended one of his country-men who could make an arquebus "that shall containe ten balls or pellets of lead, all the which shall goe off, one after another, haveinge once given fire" (CSP). It was an old idea and a simple one, but fraught with danger to the unwary.

By the end of the seventeenth century, the Ordnance had tried most of these repeating guns and had accumulated a few specimens, mainly of the multi-barrelled type in their Armouries. Their lack of faith in anything other than the simple musket is illustrated by their action in 1701, when they expressed themselves very willing to part with "an engine in the Tower, with a great many gun barrels fixed in it", which, useless to them, was considered a very suitable present for the Emperor of Morocco (CSP). But there were always inventors ready to bring forward some grandiose scheme and plenty of gunmakers prepared to demonstrate their skill by the construction of some elaborate piece. The Puckle Machine Gun was a good example of this.

James Puckle (1667–1724) was a notary public, a partner in a London practice. In 1696 he published *England's Interest; or, a brief discourse of the Royal Fishery*, to help promote a company formed to protect the fishing industry. He followed this in 1699 with *England's Way to Wealth & Honour*, but like many another business man he found it difficult himself to achieve the last two desirable objects. Despite a highly moral work, *The Club*, first published in 1711, he was to become involved in the dubious finances of the South Sea Bubble episode.

On 15th May, 1718, he patented his "portable gun or machine called a defence, yt discharges so often and so many bullets and can be so quickly loaden as renders it next to impossible to carry any ship by boarding". It was designed on the lines of the modern revolver but with the dimensions of a wall gun or piece of light artillery. The fixed barrel was supported by a folding tripod and this was served by cylinders containing a varying number of chambers. These cylinders were revolved by hand but by means of the handle at the rear they could be screwed up against the barrel, the coned mouth of each chamber forming a fairly gas-tight join with the countersunk breech. A particularly endearing feature of the gun was its ability to fire round bullets against Christians and square ones against the Turks, the chambers being bored accordingly (Plate 77).

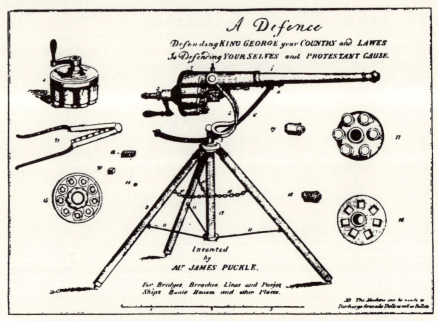

Fig. 31.—Puckle's Machine Gun. The original drawing in the printed Patent.

Puckle had previously brought his invention to the notice of the Ordnance in November, 1717, when they allowed him to stage a demonstration at Woolwich during a proof of artillery. In the following January, Puckle sent a petition to the King and this was referred to Col. Albert Borgard (Chief Firemaster of England and later Assistant

Surveyor of Ordnance) for his report. This must have been unfavourable for no further interest was shown and, in commenting upon the issue of his patent, the Ordnance Minutes describe the guns as having been "tryed at Woolwich & disapproved".

The inventor did not mention this in his advertisements, of course, and he appears to have found no difficulty in forming a company. Investors were exhorted that "Defending King George your Country and Laws is Defending your Selves and the Protestant Cause". During October and November, 1721, the following announcement was inserted in the *Daily Courant*:

"Whereas the Interested in the Patent for the Machine or Gun invented by Mr. Ja. Puckle, have agreed to call in Two Shillings per Share to be paid in the Hands of Peter Hartopp, Esq.; for making a Number of the said Guns for Sale; This is to give Notice That Attendance will be given at Tom's Coffee House in Cornhill on Tuesday and Wednesday in every week till the 30th. November, from Ten in the Morning till Three in the Afternoon; and that such as shall omit to pay in their said call, will be excluded the Profits that shall arise by the Sale of such Guns."

The sceptical were only too ready to pour scorn on Puckle's project and a satirical print called "The Bubbler's Mirrour, or England's Folley" shows bubbles which are labelled "the Royal Fishery" and "Puckle's Machine". The latter bears the legend "Paid in 4 Pound per Share, Sold at 8 Pound per Share". The Machine was described as:

"A rare invention to Destroy the Crowd
Of Fools at Home instead of Foes Abroad
Fear not my Friends, this Terrible Machine
They're only Wounded that have Shares therein,"

However in March, 1722, the *Daily Courant* carried another advertisement:

"Several sizes in Brass and Iron of Mr. Puckle's Machine or Gun, called a Defence, being now perfected, such Persons as are desirous, may have a Sight of the same at Seasonable Hours till Friday next the 30th. Instant, at the Workshop thereof, in White-Cross-Alley, Middle Moorfields; and on Friday the said 30th. Instant and every Wednesday and Friday following. (Holidays excepted) Attendance will be given at Mr. Puckle's Office in Pope's Head Alley, Cornhill against the Royal Exchange, from Three to Five in the Afternoon to treat with such Gentlemen or Merchants as have a Mind to be furnished with any of them."

At the end of the month the *London Journal* reported:

"On Wednesday Sev' night last, in the Artillery Ground, was a Performance of Mr. Puckle's Machine; and tis reported for certain that one Man discharged it 63 times in seven Minutes, though all the while Raining; and that it throws off either one large or sixteen Musquet Bullets at every discharge with very great Force."

However, the Ordnance remained unimpressed, and the only

record of the guns use appears in *A History of the Voyages and Travels of Capt. Nathaniel Uring*, London, 1727. This includes an account of an expedition, under the command of Capt. Uring, sent to the Islands of St. Lucia and St. Vincent by the Duke of Montagu for the purpose of forming a British settlement. The armament carried by the seven ships concerned included 56 cannon, 1,163 muskets and "2 Machine Guns of Puckles". The presence of the new weapons made little difference and no mention is made of them in the narrative. Uring and his men were driven off by the French and eventually all the artillery was landed at St. Christopher.

Three examples of Puckle's guns are recorded, two in the Tower of London and one in the Tøjhusmuseet, Copenhagen, and their dimensions are given below.* The advertisements make it clear that the guns were not made in any standard size and that both iron and brass were used for their construction. The iron gun in the Tower is, however, a very crudely made piece and may have been an experimental gun.

	Tower Iron	Tower Brass	Tøjhusmuseet Brass
Barrel Length	35 in.	32·7 in.	28·7 in.
Bore	1·6 in.	1·2 in.	1·3 in.
No. of Chambers	11	9	9
Type of Chamber	Square	Square	Round
Ignition	Match	Flintlock	Match

One of the reasons for the lack of success of the early repeaters and revolvers was that the common musket, over a sustained period, could be fired nearly as fast without the need for careful loading or the risk of premature explosion. Even so, several attempts were made to improve the musket's rate of fire. One idea was to speed up the process of loading. In the normal drill of loading, the paper cartridge was bitten open, part of the powder tipped into the priming pan and the rest poured down the barrel. The ball with the paper acting as a wad was then rammed home. One of these motions could be cut out by enlarging the touchhole and relying on the act of ramming to force enough powder through it into the pan. The drill could be speeded up still further, especially when the barrel was clean, by dispensing with the ramrod, dropping the ball without paper into the barrel and banging the butt on the ground to force the ball and powder home. By this means the rate of fire could be increased from two or three rounds per minute to four or five, but the proportion of misfires rose and accuracy declined.

This practice was never officially encouraged in the British Army, but soldiers often used it and there was always the odd inventor to bring it up. On 7th March, 1777, William Tupmann advised the Ordnance that "Musquet Cartridges made to a Carbine Calibre will run down the Barrel without ramming in Consequence of which they may be fired 3 times faster if allowed a Double Ball which will help to press the Cartridge down with the assistance of a small thump against the

---

* A fourth example was seen by W.W. Greener at St Petersburg and illustrated in his book *The Gun and its Development* (1885). It was included in the 1961 *Catalogue of the Artillery Museum*, Leningrad, but has since disappeared.

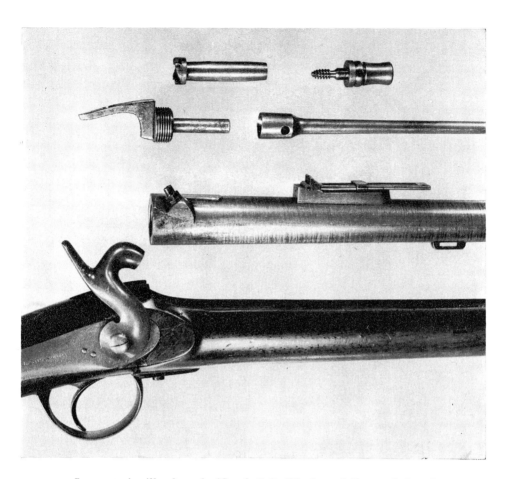

73. Lancaster's pillar-breech rifle of 1848. The barrel dismantled to show the breech-plug with its pillar facing the conical end of the rammer. Above are the special cleaning tools.

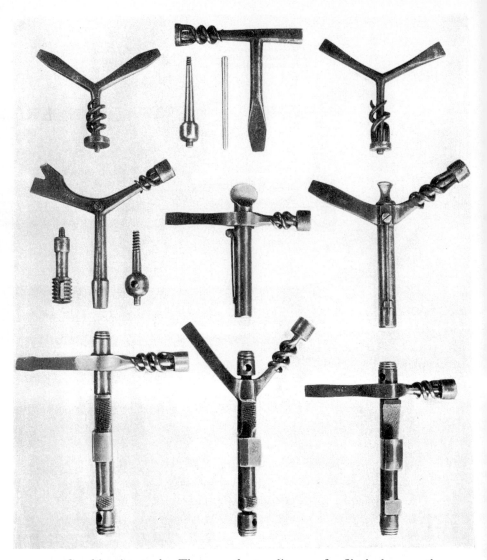

74. Combination tools. Those on the top line are for flintlock arms, the two small upright ones being issued with the Baker rifle. The left-hand tool in the middle line was issued with Lovell's percussion arms, the two small jags on either side of it being for the Brunswick rifle. The rest are tools for the Enfield rifle, those on the lower line being fitted with mainspring clamps. The middle one of these is marked JAS ASTON INVENTOR (Aston was Armourer at the Small Arms School, Hythe).

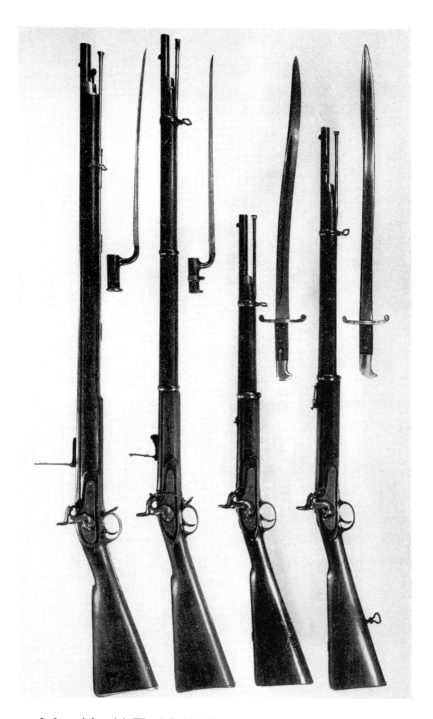

75. *Left to right:* (1) The Minié rifle, Patt. 1851. (2) The Enfield rifle,
Patt. 1853. (3) Patt. 1853 Artillery rifle. (4) Lancaster's oval-bore rifle.

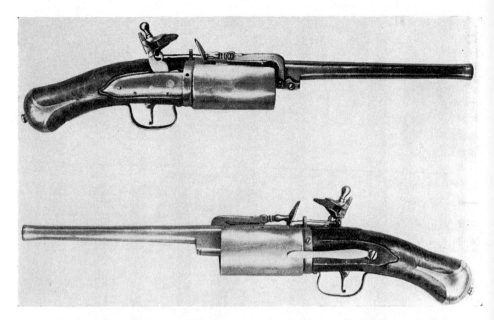

76. Seventeenth-century flintlock revolver. The cylinder is protected by a brass shield so that the pans with their sliding covers are hidden.

77. The brass model of Puckle's gun in the Tower of London. The spare set of chambers rests on the ground underneath the gun. Note the square ends.

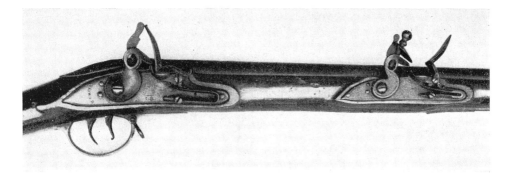

78. The two locks of the Chambers gun made for the Ordnance in 1815.

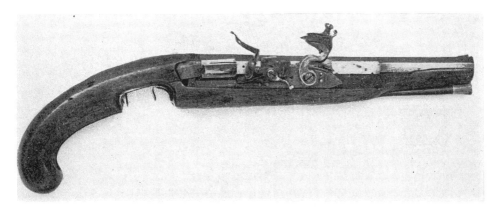

79. Pistol with sliding lock marked BELTON. *Pitt Rivers Museum, University of Oxford.*

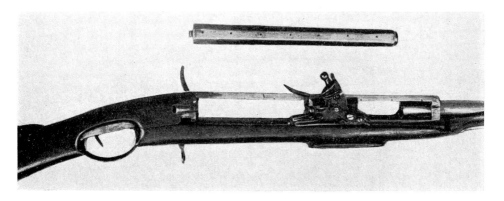

80. The mechanism of a repeating gun made for the East India Company by Jover & Belton. The detachable breech with its seven touch-holes is shown above. *Royal United Service Museum.*

Page 245

81. Two examples of the Collier revolver. The top one marked
14 PATENT and the lower PATENT No. 23.

Ground with the Butt end of the Musquet which would answer very near as well as ramming and go equally far." The self-priming principle was tried on several occasions. In 1791, Col. Thomas Blomefield, the Inspector of Artillery, conducting some experiments on gun barrels at Woolwich, recorded the relative sizes of the touchholes in use— Common $\frac{1}{10}$ in., Self-priming $\frac{15}{100}$ in.

The main disadvantage of loading with a loose ball was that, with no wad to take up the excessive windage, the accuracy of the shooting was effected. With fire being directed at such close quarters, this was not too serious a matter. There was no guarantee, however, that the loose ball would stay in position, and the possibility of it moving away from the powder or even falling out of the barrel was of some concern. To obviate this, several devices were tried. In 1796, Maj. V. Gardner suggested that a nail should be inserted into the musket barrel at the breech end so that a ball dropped down would be caught on it and retained in the right position. The idea of a nail protruding in a barrel was not very practical and, when the matter was put in the hands of Henry Nock, he substituted a ring which formed, in effect, a chamber. The French engineer Deschamps produced several chambered breeches in 1718 (See *Machine et Inventions Approuvées par l'Académie Royale des Sciences*, Paris, 1735), and Marshal Saxe in his *Rêveries* (*see* Plate XV of the Amsterdam edition of 1757) recommended a similar device for his "Fusils à Dé": "Ces fusils auroient un dez au fond ou secret pour qu'ils ne fussent pas dans la necessité de bourer leur charge."

Nothing seems to have been done with the muskets altered by Nock and, in 1807, Ezekiel Baker performed a similar modification at the instigation of Col. French who now claimed the principle. Again no trial seems to have been made, although on each occasion the Select Committee at Woolwich recommended one. In 1810, the Board were at last moved to hold an inquiry and it appeared that Gardner, whose prior claims were now recognized, had been involved in a dispute with Nock as to how far in front of the powder the ring should be placed. Nock had suggested a gap of $\frac{1}{10}$ in. between powder and ball, but Gardner, who had originally thought in terms of $\frac{1}{2}$ in., now insisted that the gap should be increased to the diameter of the ball. Benjamin Robins, in his *New Principles of Gunnery*, 1742, p. 57, had stated that "no bullet should at any time be placed at any considerable distance before the Charge", and the Inspector of Small Arms, James Miller, also feared that with a large gap there was a risk that the powder in the pan would shake into the barrel through the touchhole and leave the gun without the means of ignition. But Gardner was adamant and finally, when a trial was ordered the Committee's first task was to decide the size of the gap.

Five muskets were constructed with rings set to various gaps. These were fired without ramming at a target sixty feet away, consisting of a frame in which $\frac{1}{2}$ in. Elm boards saturated with water were set at $\frac{3}{4}$ in. intervals. Standard balls of $14\frac{1}{2}$ to the lb. were carefully chosen and a charge of 6 drams measured for each shot. The method of loading

M

was described: "After priming with a blank cartridge containing the service charge, the remainder of the powder is poured into the barrel and the paper thrown on the ground. A naked ball is then dropped into the muzzle and by its gravity is wedged in the ring or contracted part of the barrel so firmly as to be extracted with difficulty." In this fashion the rate of fire was increased by 50 per cent, and in order to ensure that this could be maintained one of the muskets was fired continuously for 30 rounds until it became too hot to handle. After cooling, it again functioned perfectly without cleaning.

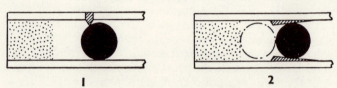

FIG. 32.—(1) Gardner's original nail-breech of 1796. (2) Nock's modification; the ring-breech set for a one-ball-diameter gap.

The effect of the gaps was gauged by the number of boards penetrated:

(1) Gardner's barrel loaded with gap of one ball diameter ... $9\frac{3}{4}$
(2)   ,,   ,,   ,,   ,,   ,,   ,, half an inch ... $9\frac{3}{10}$
(3)   ,,   ,,   ,,   ,,   ,,   ,, one tenth of an inch ... $9\frac{1}{4}$
(4)   ,,   ,,   ,,   ,,   the ball in contact with powder ... $8\frac{9}{10}$
(5)   ,,   ,,   ,,   ,,   a proof ball *$\frac{1}{2}$ in. from powder ... $10\frac{4}{5}$
(6) Common musket barrel loaded and rammed in usual way ... $10\frac{1}{2}$

On these excellent results 100 India Pattern muskets were converted to Gardner's Pattern with the rings set to a gap of one ball diameter and issued to three regiments of Foot Guards for field trials. As so often happened after a successful trial, the troops discovered all kinds of faults. There were misfires and hangfires, an increased recoil, and, finally, wet cleaning rags became jammed in the chambers. Adverse reports were received from all three regiments and the idea was finally rejected in 1813 (WO 44/626). In the next year James Thomson included an identical breech in his Patent No. 3784.

Any invention which could be reasonably applied to the service musket stood a better chance of consideration by the Ordnance than a more complicated weapon. It was inevitable, therefore, that the use of superimposed charges should be revived. At first an improvement of the Roman Candle idea was suggested. In 1780, John Aitken, a Fellow of the Royal College of Surgeons, took out Patent No. 1270 for "A New Method of Loading Tubes, Callibers, or Bores". In this method each charge of ball and powder in the barrel was sealed from its neighbour by "intermedia or colfings", i.e. wads of leather or other suitable sub-

* A ball of $11\frac{1}{2}$ to the lb.

stances, and was supplied with its own touchhole. The touchholes were ignited in turn by a sliding lock. It was an improvement on the Roman Candle method in that the fire could be controlled, but to ensure that each touchhole was fired in correct sequence a complicated mechanism was required.

A repeating gun of this nature was first submitted to the U.S. Congress in 1777 by Joseph Belton. He came to London in 1784 and persuaded the Master General, the Duke of Richmond, to give his gun a trial. The following Board's Order was made:

> "28th. July 1784 Ordered that Joseph Belton proceed to Woolwich with the Gun of his Invention and that he do instruct the Comptroller of the Laboratory, the Inspector of Artillery and the several Field Officers who have examined the said Gun in the use of it and in every particular relating to the manner of Loading and Firing it. And when the Officers are in full possession of all the particulars relating thereto that they do cause the same to be deposited in the Royal Military Repository at Woolwich and that they do give him a Certificate that they do understand the use of his Gun when he will be paid the sum of £15. 15. 0 as a Reward for his Invention together with the sum of £6. 6. 0 for the piece."

This gun was described in the *Official Catalogue of the Museum of Artillery in the Rotunda, Woolwich* (Class IX, No. 22), as a breechloader with a chamber 11 in. long holding seven charges, and a nineteenth-century illustration (source not known) suggests that this chamber was detachable. The remains of the gun, somewhat battered and minus its chamber, are now in the Tower. It was operated by two triggers, the first being used to pull the backward-facing lock into position and the second to release the sear.

Failing to interest the Ordnance in any large purchase of his gun, Belton went into partnership with the London gunmaker William Jover of Oxford Street. In 1785, Jover approached the East India Company with a pistol and carbine. A favourable report on each was made by their representative Archibald Campbell, who wrote of the carbine: "As the Company's Cavalry in India may expect to be outnumbered the quantity of fire from Troopers armed with Jovers carabines will in some degree compensate for the want of numbers." He does not describe the action but there is little doubt that it was Belton's sliding lock and a musket with this action signed Jover and Belton, very similar to the Tower example, is in the Royal United Services Institute (Cat. No. 2519).† It is engraved with the East India Company's mark, the serial number 124 and the date 1786* (Plate 80). On the virtues of the pistol Campbell opined: "The advantages of having so much fire in reserve by a pistol of his construction would certainly be attended with essential consequences in Action" (EIC Home Misc. 84). The pistol illustrated (Plate 79) was not made for the Company but must have been similar to the one examined by Campbell.

At the end of the Napoleonic Wars, a similar turn of events occurred,

---

* In 1786, the East India Company paid Jover and Belton £2,292 8s. 0d., presumably for these guns (EIC Cash Journal).

† The RUSI musket was subsequently transferred to the Royal Armouries, HM Tower of London (No. XII.2442).

the principle of superimposed charges being first adopted by the United States and then given a trial in this country. In 1813, Joseph G. Chambers of Pennsylvania was granted a patent for a system of "repeating gunnery". In the following year, the U.S. Navy placed contracts for repeating muskets, pistols and swivels made on the Chambers principle. The muskets were designed to fire 12 shots and the swivels, meant for use in the tops of ships, were composed of 7 barrels suitably mounted and capable of firing 224 shots. Chambers appears to have started using sliding locks and then reverted to the Roman Candle method.

In 1815, John Bland, a "Black and White Smith" of Philadelphia, who had helped to make the guns in America, came to England to sell the idea to the Ordnance. He brought with him a pistol to fire 5 or 6 shots and Capt. Dundas, the Assistant Inspector of Small Arms, who examined it noted:

> "the Balls are made so full by being covered with a linen patch as to leave no windage in the Gun and require much force to be carried down .... There is a hole made in the Ball which is filled with powder and this hole is the vent by means of which the after discharges are successfully made."

A swivel gun and a musket were then submitted to the Woolwich Committee. The swivel was specially examined by Naval officers, who felt that its unrestrained fusillade of bullets would be more of a danger than an asset on board ship. The musket was designed to hold one shot in reserve, a normal lock being provided as well, and once the eleven specially loaded charges had been fired by the foremost lock the musket could be used in the normal way. For the purposes of the trial an India Pattern musket was converted by letting a pistol lock into the stock with its touchhole $10\frac{1}{2}$ in. in front of the normal one. This was connected by a stiff wire running through a slot under the stock to the front trigger (Plate 78).

Ignoring Bland's pleas that such a gun would be invaluable in leading and repelling charges, and that in any case it could always be used as an ordinary musket, the Committee decided that the time and care necessary to load the barrel was too much of a liability (WO 44/621). An unsuccessful attempt was made to interest the Ordnance in a similar musket in 1821. Another patent for firing superimposed charges with a sliding lock was granted to Jacob Mould in 1825 (No. 5099), the illustration to the specification showing both flint and percussion locks.

The introduction of the percussion system with its simpler lock removed some of the difficulties attendant on the application of the flintlock to multi-shot guns. However, a very successful flintlock revolver was produced just before the percussion cap came into general use. It was brought to England by the American engineer Elisha H. Collier and was patented here in 1818 (No. 4315). Apparently based on the designs of another American, Capt. Artemus Wheeler, the revolver was also patented in France by a compatriot, Cornelius Coolidge.

The original revolver as patented had several ingenious features. The cylinder was rotated automatically on its spindle by a spiral spring (it had first to be wound up) and another spring gave it a backward and forward motion. As each chamber came into line with the barrel, therefore, it was thrust forward, a cone end making a gas-tight joint with the breech, as in the Puckle Gun. When the cock fell, a small bolt was projected into the rear of the cylinder, locking it against the recoil. A priming magazine was combined with the steel, so that the revolver could be made ready to fire by simply pulling back the cock and closing the pan.

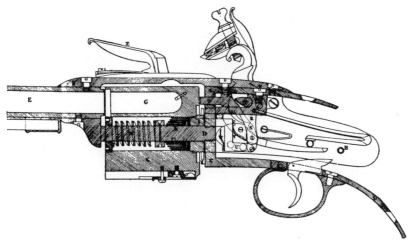

Fig. 33.—The complicated mechanism of Collier's revolver. One of the drawings in the printed Patent specification. The two coil springs operating the chambers can be seen.

Collier demonstrated his revolver before the Select Committee at Woolwich in November, 1819, and, although they appreciated its ingenuity, they could not help but reject it as too complicated and expensive (WO 44/623). To effect some simplification, Collier then omitted the automatic rotator from his later models so that the cylinder had to be revolved by hand. In 1824 he obtained another trial at Woolwich and on this occasion he produced a revolving rifle fitted with a percussion lock. According to a broadsheet issued by him, he fired 100 rounds in 29 minutes, putting 71 shots into the Target at 100 yards—little better than the performance of a musket.

Faced with another refusal by the Ordnance, Collier turned his attention to the sporting market. Another broadsheet, curiously headed "COLLIER'S PATENT FEU-DE-JOIE", recommends the revolver to Officers of the Navy and large merchant ships, and the rifle for "Gentlemen who are in the habit of shooting Deer in their own Parks". The

London rate books show that Collier occupied premises at 54, Strand, in 1824, and 3, North Side, Royal Exchange, from 1825–27. These addresses were retail shops only and the manufacture was apparently done by Evans of 114, Wardour Street, Soho*. In evidence during the famous law suit of 1851, Samuel Colt v. The Massachusetts Arms Company, Collier asserted that he sold over £10,000 worth of rifles, shotguns and pistols mainly to the Indian market through the agency of Bazett, Farquhar, Crawford & Co. In 1836, he patented a steam boiler, (see *On the Superior Advantages of the Patent Improved Steam-Boilers invented by Elisha Haydon Collier, Civil Engineer*, London, 1836) and from then on his interests lay in various engineering projects. None of his succeeding patents had any connection with firearms.

From the date of Collier's last trial until the middle of the century, no repeating gun made any impression on the Ordnance, although the Select Committee at Woolwich faced a veritable barrage of weird guns and projectiles. The repeating devices amongst them are of but passing interest but the more important of them were in chronological order of test, as follows:

1837	J. Lillycrap	Breechloading musket with revolving magazine
1839	John Gurds	3 barrel gun with revolving striker
1842	S. Lilley	Machine with 39 barrels
1843	Thos. Halliday	Musket with 6 chambers to the barrel
1844	Sinier	6 barrel gun
„	C. R. Carlsund	Musket with 4 shot horizontal revolving breech
1845	Caleb Wise	Revolving pistol
1845–53	Thos. T. Beningfield	Electric machine gun

Another suggestion from Mr. Lillycrap in 1842 added a little light relief. He was quite convinced that a soldier could advance into battle wearing a waist-belt bristling with 15 pistol barrels and carrying in each hand a six-barrel pistol. "A touch on a waistcoat button", said the inventor, "and bang goes five of the barrels." "And flat on his back goes the soldier", replied the Committee. The last gun, the electric machine gun, was described in a leaflet as "SIVA or THE DESTROY-ING POWER". It caused considerable interest—even the Duke of Wellington was impressed—but it had to be rejected by the Ordnance because the inventor refused to reveal the secrets of its mechanism. All the oddities were, however, overshadowed in popularity by the simple revolving pistol. A considerable number of them were in use mainly by Army and Navy officers, ranging from early pepper boxes with their groups of revolving barrels to different types of transitional revolvers with single barrels and a number of revolving chambers. Nevertheless many of these actions were defective, some were dangerous, and, up to 1851, the revolver was viewed with distrust, particularly by the Ordnance. In that year a mass-produced but effective revolver was introduced to England in sudden and dramatic fashion.

* See Deane's *Manual of Firearms* pp. 193–4. According to the *Mechanic's Magazine* 1 Nov 1851 John Evans & Sons made 200 muskets and pistols for Collier between Feb and Sept 1822.

Samuel Colt, who needs no introduction, patented his first revolver in London and Paris in 1835 and followed this with an improved model in 1849. In his own country, by dint of a mixture of engineering genius and showmanship, he had built up his business so that a large factory at Hartford, Connecticut, U.S.A., had become necessary to handle the orders for his revolvers. But elsewhere he found it difficult to penetrate the many custom and trade barriers and achieve any large volume of sales. The Great Exhibition held in Hyde Park, London, in 1851, however, gave him the chance to establish a foothold in Europe. Unlike his European rivals, who exhibited a few magnificent guns enriched with precious metals, Colt decorated his stand with hundreds of plain pistols arranged in panoplies of arms that impressed by sheer weight of numbers.

There were, of course some handsomely engraved revolvers on the stand and in typical fashion Colt arranged for these to be distributed among influential people, including the Master General of the Ordnance and George Lovell. It is interesting to note that Lovell visited the Exhibition and obtained the Board's permission to buy some of the exhibits—specimens of steel for sword blades, Lefaucheux's breech-loader and the oval bored rifle of N. S. Jessen of Copenhagen. On Colt's revolvers he made no comment. But Colt did not lack customers. Many of his revolvers were bought by officers embarking for the colonies in India, Africa and Australia, and a batch of twenty-five was purchased for the officers of the 12th Lancers under orders for South Africa (*The Times*, 27.6.1851). Their inventor, impressed by this potential market, decided to set up a factory in London. In the same year he gave a lecture to the Institution of Civil Engineers (see *Minutes of Proceedings*, Vol. XI) who awarded him the Telford Medal, and he demonstrated his revolver before the Select Committee at Woolwich. On each occasion, however, he was confronted with a rival revolver, that of Robert Adams, the London gunmaker, patented in February, 1851.

The two revolvers differed in nearly every aspect, although each had its enthusiastic exponents. Adams's was the better made and was self-cocking, i.e. the action of the trigger revolved the cylinder and cocked the hammer. The Colt had an open frame and a single-action mechanism, the hammer having to be thumbed back to cock it. According to a leaflet published by Deane, Adams & Deane entitled *Experiments with Fire Arms*, Woolwich, 10th September, 1851, the Colt revolver used at the trial was the heavy Dragoon model weighing over four pounds, with six chambers. Their own revolver was a lighter model of 2 lb. 14 oz., the cylinder holding five bullets of 32 bore.

Although Adams claimed in this leaflet that his revolver had beaten Colt's at the Woolwich trial, there was little to choose in accuracy between the two; but the Adams was undoubtedly faster, a consideration for officers fighting native hordes. At first then, Colt received little encouragement. But there was one point on which he had a decided advantage—his method of manufacture. Up to this date, very little use had been made of machinery in the manufacture of firearms in England. Colt's revolvers were, however, produced almost entirely by machines under the control of comparatively unskilled labour. All the parts were interchangeable and repairs were simple and cheap.

Colt's first move was to rent an office and showroom at No. 1, Spring Gardens, and appoint Charles Frederick Dennett, an American living in London, as his manager. With the help of Charles Manby, the Secretary of the Institution of Civil Engineers, he leased part of the workshops that had been erected on the Thames Bank near Vauxhall Bridge during the building of the Houses of Parliament. These premises he converted into a factory, the main building and entrance being in Bessborough Place. During 1852, he was occupied with the recruiting and training of staff—none of whom were gunmakers—and the installation of machinery. On 1st January, 1853, the factory started work. With a 30 h.p. steam engine, five steam hammers, a drop forge, five rifling machines and a battery of turning, boring and milling lathes, a production of 1,000 revolvers a week was possible. Many distinguished visitors were taken round the factory, including Charles Dickens who wrote a flattering description of it in *Household Words* (27.5.1854). All Colt had to do now was to obtain orders. But this was not easy.

In 1853, the Ordnance, busy with the Enfield Rifle, showed little interest in Colt's work, but correspondence in *The Times*, said to have been started by one of Colt's agents, drew attention to the fact that the Russian Navy was being issued with revolvers. At the beginning of 1854, the Admiralty decided that the British Navy should be similarly armed and insisted that it should be done quickly. This was Colt's opportunity. In a very short while, on 8th March, he had secured a contract for 4,000 revolvers of his Navy Model at £2 10s. each. The contract included percussion caps from Eley Bros. of London, and powder flasks from H. Van Wart & Co. of Birmingham. The revolvers were given a trial by Col. Chambers (also a recipient of a pair of Colt's presentation pistols!) but it was a mere formality. No one doubted the effectiveness of the Colt. It had the simplest of mechanisms—only four working parts—and above all it could be turned out in vast quantities quickly.

Further orders totalling 5,500 followed in January and August for the Baltic and Black Sea Fleets. The work was being conducted at such pressure that the Ordnance sent three viewers to the factory so that the revolvers could be dispatched direct to Portsmouth.

Next came a small issue of revolvers to the Mounted Staff Corps and some units of the Police Force. Letters in *The Times*, probably inspired by Colt who had a great respect for that paper, successfully demanded that the revolver should be issued to the Army. At the beginning of 1855, the Ordnance ordered 5,000 Colt revolvers for the Army in the Crimea, and a further 9,000 were ordered in August. Unfortunately for Colt, Viscount Hardinge would not agree to a general issue of revolvers to cavalry—only the 12th and 17th Lancers were officially armed with them—and the pistols were destined mainly for Company Officers and Sergeant Majors of the infantry (WO 3/325 & 3/118). They also found their way into the hands of some strange units like the Crimean Railway Expedition and Count Zamoyski's Cossacks of the Sultan (WO 1/378 & 6/74).

The sudden rise of the revolver in popularity is graphically illustrated by the returns of the London Proof House (taken from the Gunmakers' Company Minute Books):

	Pistols		Revolvers
1850	4,588		425
1851	5,744		954
1852	6,045		6,121
1853	3,586		13,916
1854		36,863 }	13,916
1855		75,509 }	No separate account taken.
1856	2,036½		12,604
1857	468		9,211

How far these figures relate to government revolvers is difficult to judge. Some Colt revolvers are stamped with the WD and Broad Arrow mark and bear two official proof marks; a VR and Crown, and a P with crossed flags. Others, even if bearing a government mark on the frame have the Gunmakers' Company proof marks on the cylinder. This was partly due to the fact that the Company accepted proof of cylinders without barrels—a cased pistol often carried a spare cylinder—and that in 1855, while alteration were being made to the Tower Proof House, the Gunmakers' Company took over the proof of Government arms made by the London trade. A War Office return of percussion revolvers in store dated 31st January, 1859, shows 17,344 at home and 713 abroad (WO 33/4).

But the tide of success was beginning to turn for Colt. In February, 1855, Frederick Beaumont patented his double-action revolver and in the following month the Ordnance ordered one hundred for trial. Robert Adams managed to secure the rights of this improvement in July, and thus enabled his self-cocking revolver to be thumb-cocked as well. Towards the end of the year he opened negotiations with the Ordnance for the supply of 2,000 revolvers, and, in 1856, formed a new company, the London Armoury Company, to take over contract work for the Ordnance. The revolvers, known to collectors as the Beaumont-Adams, were made in 54 and 38 bore (see Appendix C for dimensions). Some were apparently made in 1855, being marked DEANE, ADAMS & DEANE, LONDON. These were fitted with the rammer patented by John Rigby in September, 1854, but the later models have the rammer patented by James Kerr in July, 1855. Engraved on the frame with the WD and Broad Arrow mark, they bear the words LONDON ARMOURY on the top strap (JAAS, Vol. II, pp. 45–58).

With the end of the Crimean War in sight and his rival bidding successfully for orders, it became apparent to Colt that there would not be sufficient orders to keep his large factory in full production. The final blow was the refusal of the East India Company to give him any orders. In December, 1856, Colt began to dismantle his machinery, and he handed the premises back to the Office of Works in the following year. In 1858, the buildings were re-opened as a Government Small Arm Repair Establishment and a training school for Armourer Sergeants.

Colt's venture in London only lasted four years but how great was the effect of his factory's success during that short period will be shown in the next chapter. The story of the revolver within the period covered by this book would not be complete without mention of the Treeby Chain Gun of 1855. In that year Thomas Wright Gardener Treeby, a London engineer, took out his first Patent No. 1552 for a revolving gun. The main difference from the conventional revolver and the reason for the gun's name was that the chambers were made separately instead of being bored out of one solid cylinder, and were linked together in an endless chain which moved through the breech something like the belt of a modern machine gun.

In both the Collier and the Puckle revolvers it will be remembered that the chambers could move forward and lock on to the barrel. Treeby adopted the reverse process by making the barrel move backwards to achieve the same result. It was connected to the frame by the tapered steel sleeve with a convenient handle, which, when rotated, produced the necessary movement. The action of this sleeve was at first designed to cock the action as well, but this idea was abandoned, the hammer being used for this purpose. A second patent was taken out in 1858 and this introduced several modifications. A rubber ring on the mouth of each chamber acting as a gas seal was replaced by a cone and taper arrangement, and the free-moving chain was given an extra pair of pulleys as an additional support (Plate 82).

On 14th June, 1859, the London *Standard* reported a trial of Treeby's chain gun and a breechloading rifle which he also patented. The chain gun was demonstrated at the Small Arms School at Hythe and, according to a booklet issued by Treeby, a belt of 30 chambers was discharged in 1 min. 20 sec. No official orders for the guns transpired and it is doubtful whether many were made. The number in existence does not exceed a dozen. Varying slightly in detail, the following dimensions have been noted as generally applicable:

Overall length	3 ft. 3 ins.
Overall weight	$10\frac{1}{2}$ lb.
Barrel length	20 in.
Calibre	·50
No. of grooves	5
No. of Chambers	14

CHAPTER XII

MANUFACTURE AND PROOF

THE British military firearm can, to some extent, be identified by the marks which appear on its lock, stock and barrel. To try and explain the meaning of these marks and the history behind them is the purpose of this chapter.

By the end of the seventeenth century, the gunmaking industry of London had congregated in the vicinity of the Tower of London. The premises of the Ordnance were somewhat scattered. There were workshops in the Minories, storehouses in Goodman's Fields, and various buildings within the Tower, on the Tower Wharf and at the old Artillery Ground at Spitalfields. This was the headquarters of the Honourable Artillery Company before it moved to its present position in Moorfields. It also contained the residence of the Master Gunner, an artillery range and the Government Proof House. In a report on the ground by Ordnance officers in December, 1658, the Proof House was described as "all that Shedd built upon ye East wall of ye Gunn range for proofe of hand gunns. And that other Small structures of Bricke att ye East end of ye Armoury wch hath beene & daily is used for ye loadeing, search, bloweing [?] and viewinge of Hand gunns before & after proofe."

Exactly when the Ordnance began proving firearms is not known. The first reference to any control by the Government department over the manufacture of firearms appears in 1572, when a Bill for the True Making, Proving and Marking of Callyvers, etc. was passed through the House of Commons. It dealt only with the view of guns and powder flasks and did not become law. Here are the "chief and principal poyntes" noted in a manuscript in the Public Record Office (SP 15/21):

"That the search [?] as well of the flaske as of the peece maie for the better Service of hir Matie and the realme be surveyed and viewed, by such as shalbe appoynted by the Mr. of the Ordynance.

That everye pson that hensforth shall sett upp the trade & Misterye of Gonnemaking maie first for the better tryall of his workemanshipp be appoynted to make his prouf peece in the house or shopp of some one that is alreadye a Mr. or known to be a workeman and so to be admytted accordinglye or els not.

That for the better service of hir Matie and the realme It maie be ordred That every Gonnemaker that now useth the arte of Gonnemaking or hereafter shall use the same within this realme shall fetch and have at the handes of the Mr. of Th'ordynance or where els hee shall appoynt. One Bullet of Steele to be unto them a true and pfcte patron [pattern] for the better and more juste proceeding in the height and bignes of the pece generallye throughe the hole realme according to the tenor of this acte."

Before 1600 the proof of arms appears to have been the prerogative of two City Companies, the Blacksmiths and the Armourers, who exercised the right according to their interpretation of their charters. In both companies the gunmaking members were in a minority and the facilities extended to them for the proper control of their craft by viewing and proving were barely adequate. It was for this reason that they eventually formed their own Company. Nevertheless each Company had its own Proofmaster and its own mark.

The Blacksmiths adopted their emblem, the hammer and crown, for their mark. As stamped on gun barrels, the hammer is not very distinct and can be taken for the capital letter T. A proper proof house and garden with "a frame of Tymber for triall of peics" was built by the Company in 1602, and sixpence paid "for a moulde, a measure and a hard bullett" (BAB). In 1627, however, they petitioned the Lord Mayor for the use of the Artillery Ground (BMB). Most of their influential gunmaking members transferred their allegiance to the Gunmakers' Company and the hammer mark is found only on military matchlock and snaphance muskets of poor quality The musket shown on Plate I bears this mark and also a gunmaker's mark containing the initials JW, almost certainly those of John Watson, a freeman of the Blacksmiths in 1625, who became Master of the Gunmakers from 1639 to 1644.

As already mentioned in connection with the 1631 Commission, the mark of the Armourers' Company was a crowned A. It was a rich and powerful company and as early as 1570 gunmakers are recorded among its members. Towards the end of the sixteenth century, alien gunmakers were encouraged to become "brothers" of the Company and, in 1600, they were sufficiently organized to arrange for a proper view and proof to be conducted on search days, when the Master and Wardens of the Company went forth to examine newly made arms and armour. A standard "mould, hight and charge" in musket and caliver sizes were provided, and it was decreed that "the charge of the same proffe shalbe att the coste and charge of this company (Except trayning powder, bulletts and wadd to be att the charge of the maker) And that ymedyatly after [the] same proffe every pece proved and good and suffycient shalbe then marked with the letter A and Crowne" (AMB).

These rules were amended on 10th October, 1620, when the P and Crown mark was introduced:

"Item this day Henry Rowland gonnemaker did delyver unto this Court vi Charges of brasse, beinge ij for muskette, ij for bastard muskette,

& ij for Calyvers allso iij heights, one for a muskett, one for the bastard muskett & one for the Calyver, allso one payre of mowlds for bulletts of the three severall sises allso iiij markes or stampes, ij with P & Crowne for proofe & ij with A & Crowne for Armorers, wch foresaid Charges, heights, Mowlds & markes are to serve for the proofe of peeces of all sorts in our Company hereafter." (AMB)

In 1621 Henry Rowland was made "proofeman" and continued until his death, when his place was taken by William Burton, who was ordered to find a house with a "convenient backside to it". This suggests that the proof of firearms, unlike armour, was not conducted at the Company's Hall. During the Commonwealth, the Crown in the Armourer's mark was a source of embarrassment to them and finally, on 19th February, 1650, it was recorded that "the Officers of the Tower . . . taking Excepcons at the Companies old Marke being the A and Crowne, This Court doth think fitt to appoint a new Marke to Marke armes with by this Company til further order which this Court have Agreed to be the A and Helmet". I have never seen this mark on a gun—although it is well known on armour—and presumably the A crowned was reinstated at the Restoration.

When the Gunmakers' Company received its charter in 1638, their two marks—a view mark, a crown over V; and the proof mark, a crown over GP—were apparently put into immediate use, although they are not actually described in the first rules for the Proofmaster. It seems likely that at first the Proofmaster's house was used as a proof house (the Company had no Hall), but, in 1657, a proper proof place was erected on "wast ground lying next the Bullwark under the Citty Wall". It is still there, although considerably larger than the original size of "16 foot square litle more or lesse". By the eighteenth century, of the three City companies, only the Gunmakers' continued with their proof. There were, however, gunmakers who by patrimony or choice were members of other companies. To distinguish their barrels it was ordered on 1st April, 1736 "that upon all Barrels which shall be proved for the future for persons not free of this Company the Proof Master strike only the Mark of G.P. Crown'd once on the same part of the Barrell where the sd Mark has been Customarily Struck" (GMB). In practice, the mark used seems to have been a G and Crown (see Appendix D).

These non-member gunmakers were known as "foreigners"—what we now would call foreigners were described as aliens—and on 25th June, 1741, when it was considered that the existing arrangement was likely to cause confusion, an order was made "That for the future the Proof Master stricke on all Barrells proved as forreign two marks (Vizt) G.P. Crowned and V crowned as the barrels of Free members of this Company And a mark with F crowned struck between them" (GMB). This F-crowned mark appears on many firearms of the eighteenth century and has caused much confusion in the past by being wrongly attributed to a fictitious barrel maker called Foad. Another Gunmakers' mark which is described in their Minute Books but which has not yet been identified on any gun was the O and Crown struck "on ye square next above the touchhole" of Guinea and Barbary guns. Introduced in 1670, it was a view mark—the guns were not apparently proved—applied by a specially appointed Viewmaster.

The foregoing Company marks have been mentioned because some are found on military firearms not only of the sixteenth but of the seventeenth centuries. Their presence on a gun barrel of the eighteenth century normally indicates, however, that the arm is not a Government one. Before the Civil War, members of the City companies exercised the post of Proofmaster for the Ordnance without detriment to their private businesses. In 1607, the gunmaker William Hamond appears in the accounts of Sir Roger Dalyson, Lieutenant General of the Ordnance, both for payment for muskets and calivers and as a recipient of wages as one of the two Proofmasters (SP 14/39). The Proofmaster was mainly responsible for the proving of Ordnance and gunpowder, and how far his authority extended over small arms is not clear. The actual proof appears to have been under the direction of the Master Gunmaker.

In 1630 Henry Rowland, a member of the Armourers' Company and "his Mats. Maker of smale Gonnes", was paid £7 5s. by the Ordnance "for his extraordinarie paines & charges being imploied at five severall tymes in proving, viewing & searching of sondrie Dutch Musketts". The five shillings was for "paper for wadding of ye Musketts at the tymes of their proffe". Other gunmakers, however, engaged in repairing arms, were also allowed to prove barrels if necessary (PRO 30/37). It is not clear whether the guns were proved at the Armourers' or Blacksmiths' houses and received their appropriate proof mark, or whether the Government proof house was in operation and a government mark in the form of a CR and Crown applied.*

In March, 1645, the Army Committee ruled that the Office of Ordnance should "receive in to their charge & make proofe of all Armes etc. that shall bee contracted for and shall give Certificates to ye Partyes for what they shall receive". The Parliamentarians, however, adopted the same principle of appointing a gun contractor to supervise the proof of small arms. From 1646–52 William Watson, one of the Commissioners of 1631 and a Master of the Gunmakers' from 1645–48, held the appointment, at the same time acting as a supplier and repairer of arms On his death he was succeeded by his brother John, the office being described as "Master Gunmaker to ye Commonwealth to view, prove and make all Sorte of Handguns for ye Service of ye State", and carried a salary of 16d. a day. It was a system open to abuse and, in 1655, the precaution was taken of appointing assistants and ensuring that at least two of them were present when a certificate of proof was given. A similar measure was adopted by the Gunmakers' Company, who continued to elect Assistants in View and Proof throughout the seventeenth and eighteenth centuries.

Firearms of the Commonwealth period can be distinguished by two

* A proclamation of 1628 decreed that Land Service muskets should be marked CR, and Sea Service patterns with CR and an anchor. In 1630, however, these marks were apparently altered to the rose, crown and CR (for Land Service) or the rose, crown and anchor (Sea Service).

special proof marks. One is a shield containing the Cross of St. George representing England, and the other a shield with the Harp of Ireland. These two shields represent the Arms of the Commonwealth laid down by Act of Parliament in 1649. Previous to this on 10th May, 1643, *A Declaration or Ordinance of the Lords and Commons assembled in Parliament etc.* had been published in pamphlet form, decreeing that

"no person or persons whatsoever, doe at any time from henceforth buy, sell or take to pawn or exchange any Horse, Horses, Muskets, Carabines, Pistols, Pikes, Corslets or any other Armes, marked with the markes above specified, that no Smith, Gun-smith whatsoever, either alter or deface the marke above specified, being either on Horse or Armes".

The mark which is illustrated in the pamphlet (*see* JAHR Vol. XI, pp. 254–5) and is also entered in the *Journals of the House of Lords* (23rd March, 1643), consists of the combined initials L and C surmounted by a five-pronged coronet. No example of this mark has, however, been traced.*

With the Restoration, the proof was returned to the King's Hand-gunmaker, George Fisher the Elder, and, in November, 1664, petitioning for payment of his services, he reported that he had viewed 38,189 Muskets, 2,676 Carbines and 6,946 pairs of pistols. In 1663, the holder of the office of Proofmaster seems to have asserted his authority. This official, Major Mathew Baylie, by dubious means had obtained the Letters Patent of Keeper of Small Guns and Keeper of Saltpetre, and these, with his position of Proofmaster, would have given him complete control of small arms. The Ordnance, realizing the danger, managed to suspend the patents, although allowing him to continue with the proof.

The absence of a Keeper of Small Guns soon made itself felt. Gunmakers complained that guns sent into the Tower under contract "remaine now in the Small Gun Office unviewed and become rusty and spoile". In the next year, Richard Batchelor was appointed Keeper, Baylie remained in charge of proof, and George Fisher, Junior, replaced his father as Furbisher of the Small Guns. This was to become the pattern of responsibility for some years: A Keeper of Small Guns acting as Storekeeper; one or two Proofmasters "very well skill'd & knowing in the Manufacture of Great Ordnance, small guns, Powder, etc." to certify the initial condition of the weapons; and a Furbisher to maintain them (HARL 1286).

Gradually the Ordnance began to improve its administration and centralize its accommodation. The old storehouses outside the Tower had either become derelict or had been taken over by other tenants. In 1663, the building began of a Grand Storehouse on an empty piece of ground in the Tower known as the Wardrobe Garden. Built mainly for the storage of arms, it contained a Viewing room—in 1710 a special

---

* Some Civil War muskets have now been found with the mark stamped on the stocks, and two muskets at Littlecote, Berks., have it stamped on the barrels.

octagonal view bench was made—and several workshops for the furbishers. These were later extended to two old towers behind the Storehouse for men employed on stocking and lock finishing. A new Proof House was built on the Tower Wharf in 1682, "between the Kingstairs and middle crane". The wharf in those days did not, of course, present its modern tidy appearance. It served as a dock for loading men-of-war; cannon were temporarily stored there, and towards the eastern end there were a group of workshops, a horse pond and stables for blacksmiths, farriers and carpenters. Amongst these were built the Proof House and its garden. In what seems to have been dangerous proximity there was a powder house (at first made of wood!) and a "Plummery" for the casting of shot.

With the return of the Stuarts, the royal proof marks were reinstated. They are described in a minute of 12th April, 1683 as:

"Stamps wth X & a crown over them for ye locks.*
   „   wth ye rose & crown for view marks.
   „   wth a crown & C2R for Proof Marks."

The last description does not agree with recorded proof marks which do not include a numeral in the Royal Cypher. These marks were confirmed by a notice which appeared in the *London Gazette* for February, 1699, drawing attention to an Act of Parliament against the embezzlement of stores: "the Marks on His Majestys Arms . . . which are, The Kings Cypher in whose Reign they were made and the Rose and Crown on the Barrels, and sometimes the Broad Arrow, also the Kings Cypher on the Locks, and the Tower on the Lock sides of the Stocks of all His Majesty's Musquets, Carbines, Pistols."

The Broad Arrow mark now making its appearance on Ordnance stores was a Government mark which can be traced back to the fourteenth century, when, in 1386, a certain Thomas Stokes was condemned to the pillory for pretending to be a King's Officer and marking some barrels of ale with the "arewehede" mark (*Calendar of Letter Books of the City of London*, Letter Book H, p.295). Although the Broad Arrow mark is mentioned in the 1699 notice it does not seem to have been generally introduced until the reign of Queen Anne. Throughout the reigns of Charles II, James II and William III, the two government marks stamped on gun barrels were the Rose and Crown mark and the Royal Cypher. On the locks the Royal Cypher was engraved in the middle, with the name of the maker across the tail.

The extension of the gunmaking contracts to the Birmingham area and the purchase of arms abroad meant an increase in the Proofmaster's work. Others shared his duties. The Clerk to the Surveyor General, Nathan Gregory, began making regular journeys to Birmingham, taking with him the necessary powder and shot; and Major Wybault journeyed to Holland faced with the proof of 10,000 muskets ordered there. Even in these early days, the proof of arms was no haphazard business, as witness the articles supplied by Henry Crips, the Master Furbisher, in 1703:

* The 'X' is actually an addorsed C mark. This royal mark has also been noted on armour—e.g., the breastplate No. III.1190 in the Royal Armouries.

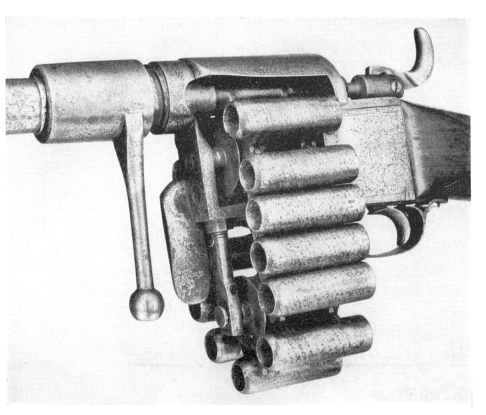

82. Close-up of the Treeby Chain Gun.

83. *Top:* The Adams patent revolver of 1851, Serial No. 198. (2) Deane, Adams & Deane revolver 38 ga., with Robert Adams 1854 patent rammer, Serial No. 16,457 R. (3) Colt's London Navy model revolver, .36 cal., Serial No. 7549. (4) London Armoury Company revolver, 54 ga., with Kerr rammer, Serial No. 24136 R. The last three revolvers bear the WD and Broad Arrow mark. *Collection of J. B. Bell, Esq.*

	s.	d.
"2 Muskett gages for proof & Service @ 4/-	8	0
2 Ditto for carbines at 3/- each	6	0
2 Do. for Pistols at 2/6 each	5	0
1 steel gage Plate of all sizes	18	0
1 Iron rammer to try if ye Barrell are gone off	2	0
4 Turn vices to take guns a pieces att viewing	2	0
1 punche & 1 drift pin	1	0
1 Steel Stamp with half Moon for Cocks return'd	2	6

(WO 51/66, p. 11) "

Up to 1755 when George Markby, a viewer, was permanently stationed there, the Ordnance continued to send its representatives to Birmingham to view and gauge the arms being made, their expenses being deducted from the contractors' debentures. In 1727, the Proofmaster, Jonathan Dawson, and the Master Furbisher, Richard Wooldridge, made the journey to inspect the arms of two regiments, but on more routine occasions an ordinary viewer was sent. In 1742, however, it was William Dawson, a clerk to the Clerk of the Ordnance. This association with Birmingham brings us to the subject of the Ordnance marks and, in particular, to a mark which has caused much confusion in the past to firearm collectors and historians.

During the reign of Queen Anne, the Rose and Crown mark was replaced by the Crown and Crossed Sceptres mark, and the Royal Cypher had a broad arrow added underneath. To start with, the last was literally a broad arrow, but it gradually became narrower and longer. The Crossed Sceptre mark—without the Crown—was an old mark used by Anthony Harris, a cutler member of the Armourers' Company until 1620, when the Cutler's Company complained that it was too much like their mark of the Crossed Keys (AMB). In 1697, Nicholas Allcock, Master Carver to the Ordnance, was paid for decorating the Small Arms Room of the Grand Storehouse with "8 Circular peices of Ornamt at ye bottom of ye Pyramids, Carved wth Crowns & Sceptres." It was not long after this that the Ordnance adopted these two royal symbols as their proof mark. A later bill refers to "Punches With Crown and Sceptres for marking Barrels after proof" (WO 51/250 p. 251).

On all government barrels, from the reign of Queen Anne onwards, two marks were struck, the Crown and Crossed Sceptre mark as a proof mark, and the Royal Cypher and broad arrow mark as a view mark and the sign of government ownership.* The latter was often called the King's mark. The locks continued to be engraved with the Royal Cypher. The maker's name on the tail was sometimes replaced by the word Tower. From the reign of Queen Anne, until 1764 (see Chapter 3), the date is also inserted below the maker's name, at first consisting of the last two figures only and then in full. The Ordnance proof house did not, however, confine its custom to government weapons. From the middle of the eighteenth century, any gunmaker,

* In 1706, James Smith was paid £6 15s. 0d. "for Engraving Cyphers, Broad Arrows, Crownes and Sceptres on several markes" (WO 47/24).

N

merchant or individual could have barrels proved at the Tower for a small fee. But on these barrels the King's mark could obviously not be applied and the Ordnance mark of the Crown and Crossed Sceptres was struck twice.

The majority of barrels came from Birmingham makers and when, in 1813, their own proof house was authorized by Act of Parliament, they used the familiar mark of the crossed sceptres as the basis of their two marks, adding the letters BCP for the proof mark and V for the view mark. This, and the fact that the crossed sceptre mark appears on so many private arms before that date, have given rise to the belief that it was the mark of some private proof house at Birmingham. While these did exist, their marks consisted of various combinations of the letters V and P—not GP—sometimes with a Crown and sometimes without. They are often seen on guns marked LONDON, and the Gunmakers' Company in that city regarded them as counterfeits of their own marks and did not hesitate to seize such guns.

However, they did not extend this drastic treatment to guns which had undergone the Tower proof. Nevertheless, they did not take kindly to the idea of private arms being proved by government officials. It was a loss of both prestige and income. In September, 1751, they complained bitterly to the Surveyor General about the violation of their Company's charter. On the other hand, several gunmakers, not freemen of the Company, appealed to the Ordnance to continue the privilege, pointing out that they would have to pay an "extravagant price" for the Company's proof. As these gunmakers included several contractors like John Hirst, who had given faithful service to the department for many years, the Ordnance resolved that "the Proof may be continued at the Wharf and any Person indulged who asks it".

The Gunmakers' Proof House had another rival in London during the first quarter of the nineteenth century—the private establishment of Ezekiel Baker. Baker took over premises at 24, Whitechapel Road, in 1805. At one side was Size Yard and, at the rear, was a large warehouse which he converted into a small gun factory with its own proof house. The feature of Baker's proof was that it was not confined to a gunpowder test. As he proudly announced on his trade card, his barrels were subjected to "the Fire, Water and Target Proof". His method, described in a printed leaflet issued in 1813, was "first to load the Barrel with Powder, equal to the weight of the Ball that fits the Bore, and after this a second proof, by forcing water in the Barrel; as that will shew the smallest defects which the eye cannot discern on the first proof . . . by the water oozing from the defective parts". Barrels proved in this fashion were stamped with special marks; a GPR (George Prince Regent?) and SP (Special Proof?) both surmounted by the crest of the Prince of Wales's Feathers (see Appendix D). Nevertheless, it was perforce a supplementary proof only (Baker was still subject to the Laws of Proof) and these marks are normally found on his arms in conjunction with those of the Gunmakers' Company.

The greatest blow to the Gunmakers' Company came in October, 1766. They had always proved the firearms of the East India Company which had a warehouse next door to their proof house, but on that date the merchant company decided to transfer the process to the Tower. The Gunmakers', with their finances threatened, introduced several reforms and reduced their prices, but it was not until 1778 that they won back the East India Company's custom. Arms of the Company with the Crown and Crossed Sceptre mark on the barrels can be dated to this period.

The extra work of private proof given to the officials of the Proof House on Tower Wharf was not entirely unwelcome. There were various perquisites attached to the job. In the early days a proof of small arms was an occasion attended by the Proofmaster, Clerks, Furbishers and labourers to whom provisions were supplied, paid for by a charge of 1d. per barrel. As time went on and the Proof Dinner became less of a celebration and more of a well deserved repast, the proceedings came more under the direction of the Master Furbisher, and the Proofmaster appears to have had little more than nominal control. In November, 1784, the private proof was taken over by the Master Furbisher and out of the 3d. charged for each barrel he was allowed 1d. for himself and his men. The payment for the proof of the King's barrels was, however, abolished in 1793, the Master Furbisher being paid a small pension as compensation. Another source of income was the sale of lead and iron sifted from the sand of the Proof Butt.

It was, nevertheless, hard work. Long hours were worked and only four holidays a year were allowed—the King and Queen's birthdays, the Restoration and Gunpowder Treason. Safety precautions were elementary and there were constant reports of accidents. Men were crushed by cannon or blown up at the Proof House, the shot-casters suffered with lead poisoning, and plagues and epidemics often decimated the staff.

When cholera raged throughout the district, the Proof House garden was turned into a cemetery for "those of the humbler class". But medical treatment was provided and a surgeon's bill*of 1683 reveals the unfortunate predicament of John Carter, a labourer who, was treated:

"for a bruise on his privy member which was in great Danger of Mortificacon, for Fomentacons, Cataplasmes, Oyles, Oyntmts, Plaisters and other Medecines both externall and internall used in ye said bruises."
(WO 51/27)

However, the life of this small community had its brighter moments and there was an inn at one end of the wharf. In their spare time the soldiers and men played trapball on the Broad Walk, with dire results to the windows of the Grand Storehouse. At night the lead roofs of the buildings were a target for local thieves and on one occasion the roof of the Proof House was lifted right under the nose of the sentry. Many human incidents are recorded in the Ordnance Minute Books. Here is the account of the death of Edward Vaughan, an armourer, in 1750:

* In 1789, Thomas Guy, the Surgeon attached to the Royal Laboratory, Woolwich, was allowed a bill for inoculating seven recruits at a guinea each (WO52/29).

"Edward Vaughan dying insolvent there was Mony raised by Contributions among his fellow Workmen for burying him and the mony which was immediately raised given to her [the widow] who kept the Money and had him buried by the Parish so that the Men who set their Names in the List (having no Money) being enraged instead of giving her their Quota, spent it on strong Beer."

During the War of American Independence came the first signs that the Ordnance system could not handle the great increase in the number of arms necessary for the British forces. In 1755, the first viewers had been stationed permanently at Birmingham and the arrangement had been for them to gauge and view the barrels and send those passed to the Tower for proof—a nine-day journey by road and canal. Returns in 1764 show that roughly one in ten were rejected at view and a further percentage was then thrown out at proof. The contractor had thus to suffer the loss of the rejected barrels and the cost of their transport from Birmingham to London and back. In 1777, a general warehouse was established at Birmingham to accommodate the viewers but, as they became more discriminating, the percentage of failures increased, the contractors became incensed at what they regarded as unnecessary vigilance and gave other orders priority, and the whole chain of production tended to slow down.

In 1796, the Board decided to reduce some of the waste of time and materials by building a Proof House at Birmingham. An agreement was reached in October with Galton Junr., Ketland & Walker, Whately, Grice and Blair for their barrels to be proved at their own Proof houses by the Ordnance Viewers while building was in progress. By the July of the following year, the Ordnance Proof House was fully operative. Not to be confused with the Gunmakers' Proof House established in 1813, the official establishment was built on the Ordnance premises which lay along the Birmingham and Fazeley Canal between Lancaster Street and Staniforth Street, the main entrance being in Bagot Street. Within a few years, however, the volume of work at Birmingham was to increase beyond its capacity.

One reason for this was the Union of Great Britain and Ireland in 1801, following the Irish Rebellion of 1798. The Board of Ordnance in Ireland, which had been a separate establishment with its own finances and system of manufacture, was abolished. It appears to have been a minor edition of the Board in London, and its officers had little influence over the design of arms. They did, however, arrange the manufacture of arms for their own purposes, buying barrels and locks from Birmingham and having them set up in Dublin. This activity was centred on the Castle, the furbishers' department being in the Pigeon House. These Irish arms are stamped or engraved DUBLIN CASTLE on the locks. Although a certain amount of manufacture continued after the Union, the local gunmakers' prices were higher and much of the work was transferred to England.

In August, 1803, with materials for India Pattern muskets piling up, it was decided to extend the assembly of complete arms to Birmingham. Contracts dated 25th March, 1804, were signed with eleven Birmingham gunmakers to rough stock and set up muskets, and Brownlow Bate, an old viewer, was promoted Superintendent of Tradesmen. An organization very similar to that at the Tower was then established on the Ordnance premises under the Inspector of Small Arms, James Miller. A new proof house "at a greater distance from the View Rooms" with a loading house and protecting wall was built for £1,010 in 1808. Three years later, a new View Room was erected, "the timber of the Roof to be of foreign Fir and the Joists and sleepers of English Oak" at a cost of £220.

The various stages of manufacture and proof at London and Birmingham were the same and an exact description of them was given by John Marshall, Clerk and Paymaster of the Ordnance in Birmingham, during a Court of Enquiry in 1824. Coming from such an official source it is worth setting down here in full:

"The Barrels were viewed before proof to see that they appeared good in every respect and correct as to dimensions, in order that, should any be evidently defective, the time, and also the expence of the powder etc expended in proving them might be saved—The examination they underwent was as follows; the breech pin was screwed out, and an iron plug, which was attached to the end of an iron rod and of the calibre of the musquet, forced down from one end of the bore to the other—the loops were gauged and together with the sight, tried with a hammer to see whether they were brased on properly—the bayonet socket gauge was put on the muzzle—if they appeared good, they were marked and sent to the proof house for proof—they were then proved and afterwards allowed to lie for forty eight hours, in which time any flaws in the metal would be visible—if found correct in every particular, they had the proof mark affixed to them, and also the viewers mark—The next inspection of barrel was by the finished viewer; to whom they were brought by themselves in a burnished state; but, if the barrel was to be browned it was only in a smooth'd state—if the barrel was found perfect in every respect it was marked by the finished viewer on the breech pin [another report says tail pin]

The Bayonets were first gauged—the viewer then took the socket in one hand and laid the point of the bayonet on an anvil keeping the bayonet in an horizontal position: he laid the other hand on the middle part of the blade and forcibly pressed down upon it—it was then turned and pressed on the other side—if it was bent in this proof it was rejected—but, if it stood the proof, the viewer with one hand took hold of the blade, at about one third of the length of it from the point and struck the neck of it forcibly once, upon an anvil—if the bayonet resisted this proof, it was marked by the viewer on the blade, a little above the neck, & received into store.

The Ramrods were proved by putting the end on the ground and taking the head in the hand and pressing upon it, and bending it in various directions; if after this proof it continued straight, it was taken hold of in the middle by one hand and held vertically the head downwards, at a considerable distance above an anvil and allowed to fall upon its head, in order to make it ring, and to ascertain whether it was sound, if it resisted these proofs, it was marked under the head and received into store.

The Locks were brought in a soft state, were gauged and examined in all their particular parts, the springs were ascertained to be of a proper strength, and the face of the hammer was tried with a file to see whether it was steeled—if the lock was proper and serviceable, the viewer affixed his mark on the inside of it, and the broad arrow on the outside.—It was then received into store and afterwards given out to the contractors for setting up, who engraved and case-hardened it—this applies to the India Pattern lock which was not taken to pieces, but only the tumbler pin taken out— the Land Service pattern locks were all taken to pieces when the musquet was brought to the finishing viewer he inspected the Lock.

Setting Up. The next process was that called setting up; which was working up the wood for the stock, and fitting the barrel, the lock, and the ramrod to it—fixing the brass work and screwing all together— smoothing the socket of the bayonet inside, so as to fit the top of the barrel and bringing the musquet into a finished state so that it could be put into the hands of the soldier—the different stages of this process were as follows—

There were delivered from the Ordnance stores to the contractor for setting up, a Barrel, a Lock, a Ramrod and a Bayonet—The contractors gave these to the Rough Stockers, and in addition a piece of Walnut tree roughly shaped for a stock, the Guard, the pipes for the Ramrod, the heelplate, the nose cap, the side piece, the swivels, the trigger and trigger-plate, the pins, wood screws wire and a flint.—The stocks for the India service pattern were to be heart and sap together, but the stocks for the land service pattern were to be heart only.

1st Examination—called the Rough Stock State.
The first operation of the Rough Stocker was that of letting the barrel and lock properly into the wood, and bringing the stock into the shape it ought to have when finished, the surface of it being rough and unpolished—in this state it was brought to the view room, when it underwent the first inspection of the rough stock viewer, whose duty it was to see, that, the stock was sound in every respect and free from cracks and flaws and not cross grained: that the barrel and lock were properly let into the stock and fitted well—the proper gauges were applied to all the parts, the barrel was knocked out and for this purpose the heel of the stock was struck on a bench —lastly the viewer allowed it to fall on the ground (as in the motion of ordering arms) to see if it sounded properly—if he approved of the work, he put his mark on it in the groove for the ramrod under the swivel loop.

2nd Examination—called the Screwing together state.
It was then taken to the finisher, who fitted the brasswork and swivels to it; bored the holes for the pins and prepared the stock for screwing together— the stock by itself was brought a second time to the view rooms, and underwent a second inspection by the rough stock viewer who examined it to see that in letting in the brass work and fitting it and in boring holes for the pins etc.—no part of the wood had been cracked or split; if he approved of the state of it, he made a second mark in the groove where the ramrod lies, under the first mark.

3rd Examination or the making off & cleansed & oiled & coloured state. The stock was then taken away and all the brass work etc. polished, and the stock made off or smoothed and cleansed and oiled and coloured— after which it was brought to the rough stock viewer a third time, who if every thing was properly done, made a third mark, in the groove where the ramrod lies, under the two former marks.

4th Examination or of the finishing viewer. It has been said that the barrel separately and without the stock had been inspected by the finishing viewer in its polished state, and marked on the breech pin.—The Musquet was now brought to him completely put together—the pins were viewed and the lock examined inside—if these were correct, he affixed his mark on the stock at the lower end of the guard. —He then examined the musquet all over and if everything was properly executed, he put a second mark at the end of the guard under the first mark he had made. The above applies to the India Pattern Musquet—in the Land Service Pattern, in addition to the above examination the barrels were taken out of the stock to discover whether the loops were properly on and the locks perfect—and if the barrels were browned, whether they were properly done." (WO 44/519)

Another interesting point which transpired from the 1824 evidence —it came from Jonathan Bellis—was the use of the Storekeeper's mark. Bellis commented that the mark then in use bore the date 1800 and only served to show that the arm was marked that year or subsequent to it. These marks are normally stamped on the butt. Early Georgian ones have the Crown and Royal Cypher only, but later examples have the date underneath as well. One exception was the mark for 1806, a Crown and a broad arrow with that date.

With all the progress made in the production of arms, the Board of Ordnance were, however, still at the mercy of the contractor with his erratic deliveries, his quarrels with his workmen and his manipulation of prices. On 25th July, 1794, the Secretary wrote:

"The Board are however perfectly convinced that the only method that can be taken to prevent in future the present complaint is to have a Manufactory of Small Arms upon the Establishment of the Ordnance which besides producing a supply of Arms in Case of Emergency, would become a Checque upon the proceedings of the Gunmakers and prevent Combinations among them against Government." (WO 46/24)

No immediate steps towards achieving this object were taken but, in 1805, a plan was evolved. The Tower was to take on its own staff of rough stockers, setters-up and makers of small materials, with John Noble, an experienced viewer, as Superintendent.

The locks and barrels were to be provided by the Armoury Mills, Lewisham. These mills were the plate mills which had supplied rough plate for the Royal Armouries at Greenwich in the sixteenth and seventeenth centuries. The London armourers maintained them as late as 1685, but with the disuse of armour, they had fallen into the hands of various tenants. In 1729, they are recorded making tools for the building of roads in Scotland. Twenty years later, Thomas Hollier, a sword contractor, took them over but, by 1754, they had lapsed into a ruinous condition. The next tenant was Richard Hornbuckle, undertaking similar work on bladed and hafted weapons. Then came Jonathan Hennem, whose name has been mentioned in connection with his lock. All these tenants seemed to run into difficulties with the maintenance of the mill and in 1805 Hennem, faced with considerable repairs, was only too glad to give up his lease to the Ordnance.

The services of Thomas Fullerd, the famous Clerkenwell barrel-maker, were obtained and he was made Superintendent of the intended Lock and Barrel Department at a salary of £150 per annum in 1806. While the Armoury Mills were being prepared for occupation, Fullerd's own factory in Allen Street, powered by a steam engine, was hired in order to get production under way. In January, 1808, Capt. Mulcaster of the Royal Engineers, who, with John Rennie the civil engineer, had been responsible for the project, reported that the Lewisham factory was ready. Fullerd did not take charge of the new factory, however, the Superintendent appointed being John Colgate. Originally designed for an annual production of 50,000 barrels* and an equal number of locks, rammers and bayonets, the mills depended mainly on water power from the River Ravensbourne. This was to prove an unreliable source, but at first all went well. Additional power was provided by a steam engine purchased from Lloyd and Ostell for £2,400. Lathes, grinders and other machinery were installed. Cottages were provided for the workmen and bonuses paid for good results. There was even a resident doctor. As the production of barrels rose, a proof house was built on the other side of the stream, and Samuel Allen appointed proofmaster. Pleased with all the progress, the Board decided to move the factory at the Tower to Lewisham.

But with the end of the war the demand for arms dropped drastically. The Birmingham branch was the first to suffer. In 1814 the staff was halved and in the following year Miller, the Inspector of Small Arms, returned to London. Finally, in 1818, the premises at Birmingham were closed. In the meantime, the Board was considering the erection of another factory, on the same lines as Lewisham, at Enfield Lock. Plans were drafted by Rennie and Major John By, who was later responsible for the Rideau Canal in Canada. In the first place, the plan was to move the barrel-forgers and lock-makers to Enfield, leaving the stockers, who had moved from the Tower, at Lewisham; and in 1817 the proof house at Lewisham was dismantled and re-erected at Enfield. But the water at Lewisham was a constant source of trouble and, in October, 1818, the Board decided to consolidate both factories on the new site, "as at Enfield the power of Water is such as may be carried to any Extent required in which respect Lewisham is deficient". The land, the buildings and the unwanted machinery at Lewisham were then sold by auction.

The new factory was situated on an island formed by the River Lea

* For actual production figures see *15th Report of the Commissioners of Military Enquiry,* House of Commons, 23.7.1811.

and an adjacent canal, where it has been maintained to the present day. In April, 1816, George Lovell was appointed its Storekeeper, but there was a division of labour between the two Superintendents, Noble and Colgate, who each retained control over his old staff. It was an unsatisfactory arrangement, jealousy being shown between the two departments, and it was not until their retirement and the appointment of a single Superintendent, James Gunner, in 1824 that harmony was established.

Although I have not traced any special marks relating to the manufactory at Lewisham, arms made at Enfield are well marked and dated. The word ENFIELD and the date are stamped on the lock and sometimes on the barrel. The cyphers of both William IV and Victoria, in conjunction with the crossed sceptre mark, were used as proof marks. The Small Gun Office at the Tower was, however, still functioning, and arms brought into store there by the London gunmakers were still engraved on the lock with the Royal cypher and the word TOWER. A new set of proof marks appears after 1840, a TP and broad arrow under a Crown (presumably standing for Tower Proof), and a Crown and broad arrow. The Enfield Storekeeper's mark consisted of two circles, one within the other. Between the two circles were the words R.M. ENFIELD and in the middle of the inner circle the date was inserted.

It cannot be said that the new factory was an immediate success. Although it was capable of making most of the parts required for small arms, it could not turn out a large order, and Lovell frequently had to suspend the production of one type of arm in order to concentrate his resources on another. In the space of a few years he was trying to rival the production of the Birmingham combines with two hundred years of experience behind them, and it could not be done. It is possible, also, that he set too high a standard for his men, who were now working to a thousandth of an inch. In 1833 he reported the following variations in the sizes of the standard musket bore gauges in use (these were solid cylinders or plugs of case-hardened steel accurately ground and fitted into a steel plate):

R. M. Enfield Set (from Lewisham) date 1807	·753 in.
S. G. Office Set, Tower, dated 1832	·756 in.
According to the tables of Ezekiel Baker 1825	·752 in.
„ „ „ „ of Birmingham Gun Comp. 1829	·760 in.

New sets of gauges standardized on the measurements of the Enfield set were made by Evans of Wardour Street.

In 1837 Lovell produced the following Rules and Tables of Proof for his new percussion weapons:

"All Barrels submitted for proof are to be in the filed state and fine bored with the Breech Pins or Nutts screwed up home, and notched, and must have passed the first view.

In the first proof the Nutts are to be taken out (being previously marked) and replaced by proving Nutts, having a Percussion Nipple attached and a communication through the Centre, the Barrels to be loaded with 16 Drams of loose Powder a wad of the usual substance settled down by one moderate blow of the loading Rod; a Ball of the same diameter as the Bore and another Wad rammed down by two smart blows of the Rod. The Barrels are then to be fitted with Bands into proving stocks which are to be laid to recoil against a Bank of moist Sand beaten firm; the charge being ignited by a Percussion Cap under the spring hammer.

The second or verifying proof taking place after the Barrel has been false breeched and percussioned and with its proper Nutt and Nipple in their Places.

The Proof is to consist of 11 drams of Powder for the Musket and 10 drams for the Carbine and Rifle Barrels, with a Musket Service Ball made up into a Cartridge with the usual number of folds of Paper, the Barrels to be fitted with proving Stocks as before the charge to be fired also by means of a Percussion Cap, under a spring Hammer and the Stock to recoil against the Bank of Sand as before.

The Barrels for Percussion Arms are in all other respects to be subject to the same process of examination and view as is applied to those for Flint Locks and which are fired by a Train.

TABLES OF MEASUREMENT FOR PROOF

Description of Barrels	Length	Weight		Thickness of Iron at		Calibres of Barrels & diam. of 1st Proof Ball	Diam. of Ball for Verifying Proof	Depth of groove in rifle Barrel	Quantity of Powder	
		In the filed State for first proof	When percussioned for verifying proof	Breech End	Muzzle				1st Proof	Verifying Proof
	ft. in.	lb. oz.	lb. oz.	in.	in.	in.	in.	in.	drm.	drm.
Muskets	3 3	5 1½	4 12¼	0·168	0·078	0·753	0·683	—	16	11
Carbines	2 2	3 3½	3 1½	0·158	0·078	0·733	0·683	—	15	10
Rifles	2 6	4 6½	3 15½	0·173	0·107	0·700	0·683	0·032	15	10*

The re-arming of the British forces with percussion arms forced the Board to consider a means of manufacture either "by advertising for a contract according to one pattern, subject to a severe examination on delivery; or by establishing a Manufactory of our own". The last part of the statement is a curious reflection on the standing of the existing factory. The first course was decided on and, in 1839, Lovell and Gunner went to Birmingham to re-open the Ordnance premises. The whole place was refurbished and partly rebuilt by Thomas Pashley. By 1841 the old system had been re-established, the materials being made in Birmingham and then issued to the setters-up there and in London. Enfield, while able to produce most parts and assemble them, had only a small output in comparison. In theory it was not a bad system. The two groups of gunmakers could be set against each other to obtain competitive prices for setting-up, and the working conditions at Enfield

* The Bore of the Rifle Barrel when finished and subjected to the verifying proof is 0·704 in.

used as a check on rates of pay and costs of materials in the supply of parts. But when the railways connected the two towns, the gunmakers soon got together. Every failure on their part to keep to contract was blamed on the "vexatious view", and all attempts on Lovell's part to maintain a planned production were frustrated.

So much so in fact that, in July, 1848, the Board commented bitterly "either that the manufacturing powers at the command of this Department with regard to small arms are much less than they were supposed to be or that there is a great want of energy in calling them forth". Lovell at first took punitive action against the gunmakers. If they did not comply with the terms of their contract, he struck them off the list of contractors. The gunmakers were, however, now well organized and had powerful friends and, while they showed a marked lack of anxiety to complete their orders, they expressed considerable annoyance at losing them. Lovell was reprimanded for his arbitrary action and, in February, 1849, the Board endeavoured to introduce a new system whereby contracts were advertised for competitive tender, without any restriction or interference with the prices paid by masters to their workmen. In a very short while, however, this proved no better and the Board were forced to take the very action for which they had reproved Lovell.

In 1849, the Select Committee of the House of Commons conducted an inquiry on Army and Ordnance expenditure. During the hearing of evidence the Ordnance system came under severe criticism, but mainly on the grounds of its strict standards of view and the fact that it did not give contracts for complete weapons. It is obvious that at this stage neither the Ordnance nor the gunmakers considered the wholesale use of machinery as a solution to their difficulties.

In Birmingham, countless small one-room workshops with families working laboriously by hand still produced the parts of a gun exactly as they had done in the seventeenth century. In the streets women and children carrying bundles of barrels or parcels of locks and other parts from workshop to warehouse were a familiar sight. At Enfield, under Lovell's guidance, machinery had been slowly introduced for certain processes; a lock plate driller in 1842; percussioning machines (worked by boys) in 1845; a Nasmyth's steam hammer in 1851; and a rifling machine of his own invention together with a planing machine of Whitworth's construction in 1852. But for some reason machines for making stocks had always failed to impress. Those used at the U.S. factory at Springfield were offered and rejected as early as 1841. Nothing in the nature of a proper production line had been visualized and the final assembly depended on the skill of craftsmen.

When next the searching gaze of Parliament fell on the industry, however, the outlook of the Ordnance at least had completely changed. In 1854 a Parliamentary Committee was created to consider "the Cheapest most expeditious, and most Efficient Mode of providing Small Arms for Her Majesty's Service". The Ordnance now came forward with proposals that would make the supply of Small Arms independent of contractors. These centred on a large Government factory to be built at Woolwich, where arms were to be made entirely by machinery. This sudden reversal of their previously held opinion was due to the example set by Colonel Colt's London factory.

In their evidence before the Committee, the three main Ordnance witnesses, Capt. Sir Thomas Hastings, a member of the Board and the Principal Storekeeper, John Anderson, Chief Engineer of the Royal Arsenal, Woolwich, and Lt.-Col. Tulloch, Inspector of the Royal Carriage Department, spoke in glowing terms of Colt's factory and how they had been converted to the opinion "that it would be both cheap and useful and efficient to put up a Government factory". No suggestion by the gunmakers' representatives on the Committee that machine-made guns were poorly finished, would not interchange, and would cause immense wastage, could dissuade them from this view. Col. Colt himself gave evidence, heaping scorn on the puny hand-made efforts of the English gunmakers and talking of muskets in terms of millions.

But the Ordnance could bring forward first-hand evidence only of a factory making revolvers, and whether this method could be applied successfully to the manufacture of long guns was open to question. The effect on employment in the gun trade by a sudden loss of Government orders had also to be considered. The plan of Anderson's proposed factory, with all its machinery arranged in tidy parallel rows, and bordered by neat railway lines was very much a theoretical effort. Perhaps wisely, the Committee came to the conclusion that "the advantage of an increased use of machinery and the expediency of making all muskets in a Government factory are not therefore in any way necessarily connected". They recommended, first, that the contract system should be continued, and secondly, that a Government factory should be tried to a limited extent on the existing premises at Enfield (see *Report from the Select Committee on Small Arms*, The House of Commons, 1854).

A commission composed of Col. Burn, Capt. Warlow and John Anderson went to the U.S.A., where they inspected the national armouries at Springfield and Harper's Ferry. They bought a set of machinery for shaping stocks and the manufacture of locks and other parts and persuaded James Burton, formerly the Master Armourer at Harper's Ferry, to come to England to take charge of production. He arrived in England in October, 1855, just after the factory had started the production of locks and bayonets. The two water wheels of 20 h.p. were supplanted by a new steam engine and the factory went into full production in 1856. In the proud words of John Anderson: "a manufactory which was formerly rude, antiquated and extremely limited in its powers of production has now become worthy of the country" (WO 33/4). It was not the end of all difficulties by any means, but it was the beginning of modern firearm manufacture in England.

APPENDIX A

BRITISH MILITARY FLINTLOCK ARMS FROM 1740

	Length				Weight			
	Barrel	Arm	Bayonet Blade	Arm Compl. With Bayonet	Arm	Bayonet	Grooves	Calibre
	ft. ins.	ft. ins.	ft. ins.	ft. ins.	lb. oz.	lb. oz.	No.	Inches
MUSKETS								
Long Land	3 10	5 2	1 5	6 8	10 12	1 1	—	·75
Short Land	3 6	4 10	1 5	6 4	10 8	1 1	—	,,
Duke of Richmond's	3 6	4 10	1 5	6 4	10 4	1 1	—	,,
India Pattern	3 3	4 7	1 5	6 1	9 11	1 0	—	,,
Sea Service, Long	3 1	4 5	1 5	5 11	9 10	1 0	—	,,
,, ,, , Short	2 2	3 6	1 5	5 0	8 7	1 0	—	,,
New Land	3 6	4 10	1 5	6 4	10 6	1 0	—	,,
N.L. Light Infantry	3 3	4 7	1 5	6 1	10 1	1 0	—	,,
RIFLES								
Baker's(Sword Bayt)	2 6	3 10	1 11	5 10½	9 2	2 0	7	·70
,, ,, ,,	2 6	3 9½	1 11	5 10	8 14	2 0	7	·62
,, (Socket Bayt.)	2 6	3 9½	1 5	5 3½	8 12	12	7	·62
,, (Hand Bayt.)	2 6	3 9½	1 5	5 4	8 8	1 0	7	·62
Cavalry	1 8	2 11	—	2 11	6 0	—	7	·62
CARBINES								
Heavy Dragoon	3 6	4 9	1 5	6 2½	8 14	1 0	—	·65
Light ,,	3 0	4 3½	1 5	5 9	7 10	1 0	—	·65
Dragoon, Patt. 1796	2 2	3 5½	1 3	4 9	8 0	13	—	·75
Elliotts	2 4	3 7½	1 1	4 9	7 2	.12	—	·65
Manton's, Patt. 1833	1 8	3 0	—	3 0	7 2	—	—	·65
Paget's	1 4	2 7	—	2 7	5 0	—	—	·65
Light Infantry	3 6	4 9	1 5	6 2½	7 12	1 0	—	·65
Artillery	3 1	4 4	1 1	5 5½	7 12	12	—	·65
Sergeants'	3 3	4 7	1 5	6 0½	8 0	12	—	·65
,, India Patt.	3 1	4 4½	1 1	5 6	7 12	12	—	·65
,, New Land	2 9	4 1	1 5	5 6	9 5	1 0	—	·75
Cadets' ,, ,,	2 10	4 1	8	4 9	6 7	8	—	·65
Cape, D.B.	2 2	3 6	—	3 6	11 2	—	—	·73
PISTOLS								
Heavy Dragoon	1 0	1 7	—	1 7	3 2	—	—	·65
,, ,,	1 0	1 7	—	1 7	3 0	—	—	·56
Life Guards	10	1 5	—	1 5	2 10	—	—	·65
Blues	10	1 4½	—	1 4½	2 8	—	—	·56
Dragoon,Patt.1796	9	1 3	—	1 3	2 9	—	—	·75
Light Dragoon	9	1 3	—	1 3	2 6	—	—	·65
Sea Service, Long	1 0	1 6	—	1 6	3 7	—	—	·56
,, ,, Short	9	1 3	—	1 3	3 0	—	—	·56
SEVEN BARREL GUNS	1 8	3 1	—	3 1	12 0	—	—	·46
WALL PIECES	4 6	6 1	—	6 1	37 0	—	—	·98

Note: Weights of flintlock arms of the same model vary considerably. Wherever possible several specimens have been weighed and an average figure given. Measurements are also subject to a small variance.

	Barrels	Locks	Rough Stocking	Making off Stocks	Filing Barrels	Setting up	Rammers	Flints (per 1000)
	£ s. d.	s. d.	s. d.	s. d.	s. d.	s. d.		
MUSKETS								
Long Land	7 6	6 0	4 0	9	5	6 3	} Steel 1/3 } each	
Short Land*	7 6	6 6	4 0	9	5	6 5		
Sea Service*	5 10	5 0	2 10	6	5	5 0	Wood 11/- p. 100	} 14/-
MUSKETOONS								
Sea	7 0	5 0	2 10	6	4	4 0		
Burgoyne's	7 0	5 0	2 10	6	4	9 0		
CARBINES								
Sergeant's	6 6	6 2	3 4	8	4	6 0		
Artillery	6 6	6 2	3 4	8	4	6 0		
Elliott's	6 6	6 2	3 4	8	4	6 0	Steel 1/- each	} 10/-
Cadets'	6 6	6 2	5 6	8	4	6 0		
Blues	6 6	8 0	4 4	8	4	7 0		
Light Dragoon	6 6	8 0	5 0	8	4	9 0		
PISTOLS (per pair)								
Land (pistol bore)	5 6	7 6	3 9	1 0	6	7 0	Wood 4/6 p. 100	} 10/-
„ (carb. bore)	5 8	7 6	3 9	1 0	6	7 0		
Sea Service	5 6	7 6	3 6	8	6	5 0		
WALL PIECES	1 12 0	14 0	12 6	1 6	—	14 6	} Steel 2/6	20/-

Brass Work: for all Land pattern arms, including such items as heel or butt plates, side-pieces, handles or trigger guards, thumb pieces or escutcheons, tail pipes and trigger plates, was purchased by weight at 1s. 8d. per lb. The average weight of this for a Land musket was 1 lb. 12½ oz. and for a Sea musket 1 lb. 4 oz. The charge for the latter was 1s. 2d. per lb. Certain items were priced separately: long fore pipes 6d.; short pipes 1½d.; nosecaps 2d.

Iron Work: for pistols, carbines and muskets included; swivels 2¼d. per pair; tail springs 2d.; triggers 7s. per 100; sights 8s. per 1,000; woodscrews 4s. per 100; breech and side nails 1s. 6d. per 100; carbine ribs 1s. 2d.; rings 1½d.; rib nails 1d.; bolts 3s. per 100; belt hooks 9d. Higher charges were made for parts of wall pieces; swivels 3s. 6d.; swivel loops 14s. per 1,000; triggers 2d.; screws 1d.

Prices for other accessories were: bayonets 1s. 7d.–2s. 10d.; scabbards 8¼d.; musket slings 1s. 4d.; carbine slings 1s. 3d.; triangle turnscrews 4d.; brushes and wires 2d.

   * Details of the estimated cost of a single musket in January, 1785, are given in WO 55/13 p. 51. They include such charges as 3d. for proving the barrels and 1d. for fitting the bayonet, and a mount to £1 13s. 3½d. (Short Land Pattern) and £1 4s. 8d. (Sea Service Pattern).

APPENDIX C
BRITISH MILITARY PERCUSSION ARMS UP TO 1855

	Length				Weight			
	Barrel	Arm	Bayonet Blade	Arm Complete with Bayonet	Arm	Bayonet	Grooves	Calibre
	ft. ins.	ft. ins.	ft. ins.	ft. ins.	lb. oz.	lb. oz.	No.	Inches
MUSKETS								
Patt. 1838 (Large Lock)	3 3	4 7	1 5	6 0½	9 14	1 1	—	·753
(Small Lock)	3 3	4 7	1 5	6 0½	9 10	1 1	—	·753
Patt. 1839	3 3	4 7	1 5	6 0½	10 0	1 1	—	·753
Patt. 1842	3 3	4 7	1 5	6 0½	10 0	1 1	—	·753
Sgts.', Line Regts.	2 9	4 1	1 4½	5 6	8 6	14	—	·733
Sea Service	2 6	3 10	1 5	5 3½	9 4	1 1	—	·753
RIFLES								
Patt. 1851 or Minié	3 3	4 7	1 5	6 0½	9 8§	15½	4	·702
Patt. 1842	3 3	4 7	1 5	6 0½	10 0	1 1	3 or 4	·758
Sea Service	2 6	3 10	1 5	5 3½	9 4	1 1	3 or 4	·758
Patt. 1853 or Enfield	3 3	4 7*	1 5	6 0½	8 8‡	11‡	3	·577
„ Artillery	2 0	3 4	1 11	5 3½	6 8	1 12	3	·577
Brunswick								
(back-action)	2 6	3 10	1 10	5 7¼	9 2	2 0	2	·704
(side-action)	2 6	3 10	1 10	5 7¼	9 6	2 0	2	·704
Sgts.', Foot Guards	2 9	4 1	1 5	5 6½	9 2	14	2	·704
Navy, Heavy Model	2 9	4 1	—	4 1	11 10	—	2	·796
Jacob's	2 0	3 4½	2 6	5 10½	10 6	2 8	4	·526
Cape, D.B.	2 2	3 6	—	3 6	9 10§	—	4	·733
Paget's	1 4	2 7½	—	2 7½	5 6	—	3	·686
CARBINES								
Victoria	2 2	3 6	—	3 6	7 9	—	—	·733
Sappers & Miners	2 6	3 10	2 1	6 0½	8 8	1 12†	—	·733
S&M, Lancaster's	2 8	3 11½	2 0	5 11½	7 6	1 9	oval	·577¶
Artillery	2 6	3 10	1 5	5 3½	8 8	1 1	—	·733
Constabulary	2 2	3 6½	1 1	4 8	6 15	11	—	·653
Constabulary, D.B.	2 2	3 6	1 5	5 0	7 8	1 3	—	·653
Cape, D.B.	2 2	3 7	—	3 7	9 10	—	—	·733
Cadets'	2 3	3 6½	9	4 3	6 4	9	—	·653
Yeomanry	1 8	3 0	—	3 0	6 8	—	—	·653
PISTOLS								
Patt. 1842, Lancers'	9	1 3½	—	1 3½	3 4	—	—	·753
Sea Service	6	11½	—	11½	2 3§	—	—	·567
Constabulary (Pkt.)	4½	9½	—	9½	1 4	—	—	·653
East India	9	1 3	—	1 3	3 0	—	—	·653
REVOLVERS						No. of Chambers		
Deane & Adams 54g.	5¾	11¾	—	11¾	2 6½	5	3	·434
Colt's Navy	7½	1 1¾	—	1 1¾	2 9½	6	7	·358
Deane & Adams 38g.	7½	1 1½	—	1 1½	2 15½	5	3	·490

* Shortened to 4 ft. 6 in. in 1859. § Considerable variance in weights noted.
‡ Later model weighed 8 lb. 14½ oz., bayonet 13½ oz.
† Original sword bayonet weighed 2 lb. 3 oz.
¶ At muzzle—·577 in. minor-axis, ·593 in. major-axis.
At breech—·580 in. minor-axis, ·598 in. major-axis.

APPENDIX D

BARREL AND LOCK MARKS

1,2	View and proof marks of the Armourers' Company.
3,4	Ditto. 1650–60.
5–8	Hammer and Crown marks of the Blacksmith's Company.
9,10	View and proof marks of the Gunmakers' Company c. 1640.
11,12	Ditto. c. 1690.
13,14	Ditto. c. 1740.
15,16	Ditto. c. 1850.
17,18	Foreigner's mark of the Gunmakers' Company. 1741 onwards.
19–21	Ditto (?). An earlier mark, which has been noted on guns dating back to 1721.
22	A reconstruction of the O and Crown mark of the Gunmakers' Company for African guns.
23,24	Private view and proof marks of Ezekiel Baker.
25–30	View and proof marks of private Birmingham proof houses.
31,32	View and proof marks of the Birmingham Gunmakers' Proof House. After 1813.
33–36	Ordnance view and proof marks. During the Commonwealth.
37–40	Ditto. Reign of Charles II.
41–44	Ditto. Reign of James II.
45–48	Ditto. Reign of William III.
49–52	Ditto. Reign of Queen Anne.
53,54	Ditto. From a musket dated 1722.
55,56	Ditto. From a musket dated 1739.
57–60	Tower view and proof marks for private arms.
61,62	Ordnance view and proof marks c. 1790.
63,64	Ditto. c. 1830.
65,66	Ditto. c. 1835.
67,68	Ditto. c. 1841.
69–71	Enfield view and proof marks c. 1840.
72,73	Ordnance view and proof marks. Reign of Queen Victoria.
74	Barrel viewer's mark 1835.
75,76	Ditto. Eighteenth century.
77	Ditto. c. 1810.
78	Ditto. 1855.
79	Lock viewer's mark 1710.
80	Ditto. 1762.
81	Ditto. c. 1810.

Note: With the exception of No. 22, all the above marks have been copied from firearms examined by the author. Wherever possible good examples have been chosen, but inevitably some are worn and appear incomplete.

1   2   3   4   5   6   7   8

9   10   11   12   13   14   15   16

17   18   19   20   21   22   23   24

25   26   27   28   29   30   31   32

33   34   35   36   37   38   39   40

41   42   43   44   45   46   47   48

49   50   51   52   53   54   55   56

57   58   59   60   61   62   63   64

65   66   67   68   69   70   71   72

74   75   76   77   78   79   80   81

APPENDIX E

LOCK MARKS

82,83   Royal Cyphers engraved on lock plates. James II.
84,85   Ditto. William III.
86,87   Ditto. Queen Anne.
88   Ditto. George I. Musket dated 1715.
89   Ditto. Dutch made musket c. 1720.
90   Ditto. George III. Musket c. 1805.
91   Ditto. Musket c. 1810.
92   Cypher of William IV. Carbine dated 1835.
93   Cypher of Queen Victoria. Musket dated 1846.
94   Badge of Irish regiment. Dutch made musket c. 1720.
95   Badge of Royal Welsh Fusiliers. Musket made by James Freeman c. 1725.
96   Mark of East India Company. Musket dated 1793.
97   Ditto. Carbine c. 1810.

STOCK MARKS

98   Ordnance Storekeeper's mark. From 1770, normally has a date underneath. See page 271 for further information.
99   Storekeeper's mark of East India Company. No. 96 also used.
100   Enfield Storekeeper's mark 1837.
101   Board of Ordnance ownership mark, superseded in 1855 by WD mark.
102   Obsolete, condemned or sale mark.

Notes on Stock Marks not illustrated

The letters CR often appear on percussion arms preceded by the Roman numerals I, II or III. These indicate that the arm was at one time relegated to the First, Second or Third Class Reserve.

Regimental marks are often stamped on the butt-tangs of guns. Many of these are straightforward abbreviations easy to identify, e.g. 2. D.G.—2nd Dragoon Guards, 16. L.—16th Lancers. Others have been found to refer to obscure Volunteer regiments raised during the Napoleonic Wars. The vast numbers of these (the reader is referred to the printed Volunteer Lists) and the fact that many have the same initials have made it impossible to prepare a list of abbreviations which would be of any real value: From 1860 onwards, official lists of regimental marks are given in *Armourers Instructions, Ordnance Regulations* and *Volunteer Regulations*. They consist of regimental abbreviations, e.g. 1. R.A.—1st Battery Royal Artillery; and county abbreviations together with a letter placed above or after denoting the type of regiment; V—Volunteer, Y—Yeomanry Cavalry, M—Militia. Thus MxY—Middlesex Yeomanry Cavalry. Some of these lists are, however, contradictory and only a few of these late marks will be found on guns described in this book.

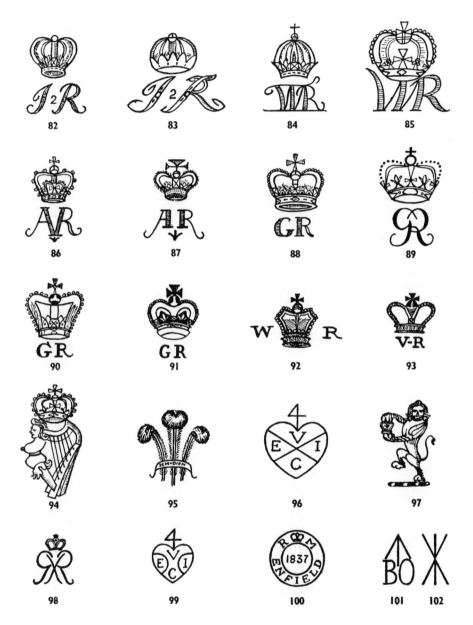

82

83

84

85

86

87

88

89

90

91

92

93

94

95

96

97

98

99

100

101   102

SELECT BIBLIOGRAPHY

AERTS, W.: 'British Firearms at the Time of Waterloo', *Journal of the Society for Army Historical Research*, XXV (1947), pp. 67–9.

AKERMAN, John Y.: 'Notes on the Origin and History of the Bayonet', *Archaeologia*, XXXVIII, pp. 423–30.

ANON.: *Textbook for Officers at Schools of Musketry*, revised edition, London, 1877.
— *Report from the Select Committee on Small Arms*, House of Commons, 1854.

BAKER, Ezekiel: *Remarks on Rifle Guns*, eleventh edition, London, 1835.

BAILEY, D.W.: 'Joseph Egg, Joseph Manton and the Percussion Trials of 1820', *Journal of the Arms & Armour Society*, VII, no. 3 (September 1971), pp. 60–72.
— *British Military Longarms, 1715–1815*, London, 1971.
— *British Military Longarms, 1815–1865*, London, 1972.
— *British Military Longarms, 1715–1865*. A reprint of the above two books in a single volume, London, 1987.
— 'Royal Naval Longarms, 1700–1870', *Guns Review*. Part one, May 1980, pp. 354–8; part two, June 1980, pp. 429–32; part three, September 1980, pp. 684–7; part four, October 1980, pp. 756–9.

BEAUFOY, Mark (pseudonym: 'A Corporal of Riflemen'): *Scloppetaria*, London, 1808. Reprinted, Richmond, 1971.

BLACKMORE, David: 'Some Notes on the British Military Flintlock in Service', *Journal of the Arms & Armour Society*, XI, no. 2 (December 1983), pp. 90–2.
— *Arms & Armour of the English Civil War*, Royal Armouries, London, 1990.

BLACKMORE, Howard L.: "Gillmore's Musket 1816", *The Gun Collector*, January 1953, pp. 796–800.
— 'The Douglas Flintlock 1817', *The Gun Collector*, April 1953, pp. 818–20.
— "Gardner's Musket 1811", *Journal of the Arms & Armour Society*, I, no. 3 (September 1953), pp. 25–33.
— 'The Seven-Barrel Guns', *Journal of the Arms & Armour Society*, I, no. 10 (June 1955), pp. 165–82.
— 'An Eighteenth Century Musket Trial in Ireland', *The Irish Sword* (The Journal of the Military History Society of Ireland), II, no. 7 (Winter 1955), pp. 172–6.
— 'The Experimental Firearms of Henry Nock', *Journal of the Arms & Armour Society*, II, no. 4 (December 1956), pp. 69–109.
— 'Chambers Repeating Flintlock', *The American Rifleman*, September 1958, pp. 21–3.
— 'Address Col. Colt, London', *Gun Digest*, 1958, pp. 79–84 and

309–12. Reprinted as "Colt's London Armory" in S.B. Saul (ed.), *Technological Change: The United States and Britain in the Nineteenth Century*, London, 1970, pp. 171–95.

— 'British Military Firearms in Colonial America', *The Bulletin of the American Society of Arms Collectors*, no. 25 (1972), pp. 13–23.

— 'William Caslon, Gun Engraver', *Journal of the Arms & Armour Society*, X, no. 3 (June 1981).

— 'Military Gun Manufacture in London and the Adoption of Interchangeability', *Arms Collecting*, vol. 29, no. 4 (November 1991), pp. 111–22.

— 'Tales of a Touchhole', *Journal of the Arms & Armour Society*, XIV, no. 1 (March 1992), pp. 1–4.

BLAIR, Claude (ed.): *Pollard's History of Firearms*, Feltham, Middlesex, 1983.

BROOKER, R.E., Jr.: *British Military Pistols, 1603–1888*, Dallas, Texas. 1978.

BROWN, H.R.S.: 'The Rifle in the British Service', *The Rifleman*, seven parts, April–November 1935.

BUSK, Hans: *The Rifleman's Manual*, London, 1858. Reprinted, Richmond, 1971.

— *Hand-Book for Hythe*, London, 1860.

CHAMBERLAIN, William H.J., and TAYLERSON, Anthony W.F.: *Adams' Revolvers*, London, 1976.

CHESNEY, F.R.: *Observations on the Past and Present State of Firearms*, London, 1852.

COOPER, J.S.: *For Commonwealth and Crown*, Gillingham, 1993.

COTTESLOE, Lord: 'Notes on the History of the Royal Small Arms Factory, Enfield Lock', *Journal of the Society for Army Historical Research*, XII, pp. 197–212.

— *The Englishman and the Rifle*, London, 1945.

DARLING, Anthony D.: *Red Coat and Brown Bess*, Ottawa, 1970.

— 'The Liege-Made British Short Land Pattern Musket circa 1775', *Army Cavalcade*, Sydney, 1988, pp. 2–12.

— 'Two British Land Service Muskets of the War for American Independence Period (1775–1783) with Scottish Regimental Association', *Dispatch* (Journal of the Scottish Military Collectors' Society), no. 115, pp. 13–20.

— 'A 18th Century English Military Rifle', *The Canadian Journal of Arms Collecting*, vol. 10, no. 2, pp. 53–63.

DEANE, John; *Deane's Manual of the History and Science of Fire-arms*, London, 1858.

DOUGLAS, Sir Howard: *A Treatise on Naval Gunnery*, London, 1855. This contains a valuable appendix 'On Rifle Muskets'.

EAVES, I.D.D.: 'Some Notes on the Pistol in Early 17th Century England', *Journal of the Arms & Armour Society*, VI, no. 11 (September 1970), pp. 277–344.
— 'Further Notes on the Pistol in Early 17th Century England', *Journal of the Arms & Armour Society*, VIII, no. 5 (June 1976), pp. 269–329.

FERGUSON, J.: *Two Scottish Soldiers*, Aberdeen, 1888.

FFOULKES, Charles J.: *Arms & Armament*, London, 1915.
— *The Gun-Founders of England*, Cambridge, 1937.

FIRTH, C.H.: *Cromwell's Army*, London, 1902.

FORTESCUE, J.W.: *A History of the British Army*, London, 1899–1930.

FREMANTLE, T.F.: *The Book of the Rifle*, London, 1901.

GEORGE, John N.: *English Pistols and Revolvers*, Onslow County, USA, 1938.
— *English Guns and Rifles*, Plantersville, South Carolina, USA, 1947.

GILKERSON, W.: *Boarders Away, II, With Fire*, Rhode Island, USA, 1993.

GREENER, William: *The Gun*, London, 1855.
— *The Science of Gunnery*, London, 1841.

GREENER, William W.: *The Gun and its Development*, ninth edition, London, 1910.

GROSE, Francis: *Military Antiquities respecting a History of the English Army*, London 1786, with an addendum of 1789. Reprinted, Glendale, New York, 1970.

HARRIS, C. (ed.): *The History of the Birmingham Gun-barrel Proof House*, Birmingham, 1946.

HAW, S.B.: 'The Revolver (1819)', *The Marksman*, I, pp. 41–4 and 62–5.
— 'The Treeby Chain Gun', *Army Ordnance*, XIX, pp. 289–90.

HAWES, A.B.: *Rifle Ammunition*, London, 1859.

HAWKER, Peter: *Instructions to Young Sportsmen, etc.*, ninth edition, London, 1844.

HODGETTS, E.A.B. (ed.): *The Rise and Progress of the British Explosives Industry*, London, 1909.

HUTTON, Alfred: *Fixed Bayonets*, London, 1890. Contains a useful bibliography of the bayonet.

JACOB, John: *Rifle Practice*, fourth edition, London, 1858.

JERVIS, J.W.: *The Rifle-Musket*, London, 1854.

LOTBINIÈRE, Seymour de: 'The Story of the English Gunflint; Some Theories and Queries', *Journal of the Arms & Armour Society*, IX, no. 1 (June 1977), pp. 18–53.

LOVELL, George: *Suggestions for the Cleaning and Management of Percussion Arms*, London, 1842.

MACKAY SCOBIE, I.H.: 'The Regimental Highland Pistol', *Journal of the Society for Army Historical Research*, VII, pp. 52–7.

MOLLER, G.D.: *American Military Shoulder Arms* ('Vol. 1, Colonial and Revolutionary War Arms'), Colorado, 1993.

NEAL, W. Keith, and BACK, D.H.L.: *Forsyth & Co.: Patent Gunmakers*, London, 1969.
— *Great British Gunmakers, 1540–1740*, Norwich, 1984.

NEUMANN, George C.: *The History of Weapons of the American Revolution*, New York, 1967.

OMAN, Charles W.C.: *Wellington's Army 1809–1814*, London, 1913.

PETERSON, Harold L.: 'The British Infantry Musket, 1702–1783', *Military Collector & Historian* (Journal of the Company of Military Collectors and Historians), III, pp. 77–80.
— *Arms and Armor in Colonial America 1526–1783*, Harrisburg, USA, 1956.

POLLARD, Hugh B.C.: *A History of Firearms*, London, 1926. See also 'Blair, C.', above.

REID, Sir A.J.F.: *The Reverend Alexander John Forsyth and His Invention of the Percussion Lock*, Aberdeen, 1909. Reprinted, 1955 and 1957.

REID, William: 'Pauly, Gun Designer', *Journal of the Arms & Armour Society*, II, no. 9 (March 1958), pp. 181–210.
— 'Pauly, a Postscript', *Journal of the Arms & Armour Society*, II, no. 11 (September 1958).
— 'The Fire-arms of Baron Heurteloup', *Journal of the Arms & Armour Society*, III, no. 3 (September 1959), pp. 59–81.

ROADS, Christopher H.: 'The Introduction of the Brunswick Rifle 1830 to 1836', *Journal of the Arms & Armour Society*, III, no. 4 (December 1959), pp. 85–105.
— *The British Soldier's Firearm, 1850–1864*, London, 1964.

ROSA, Joseph G.: *Colonel Colt, London*, London, 1976.

SCOTT, Sir Sibbald D.: 'On the History of the Bayonet', *Journal of the Royal United Service Institution*, VI, pp. 333–48.
— *The British Army; its Origin, Progress and Equipment*, London, 1868–87.

SCURFIELD, R.: 'British Military Smoothbore Firearms', *Journal of the Society for Army Historical Research*, XXXIII, pp. 63–79, 110–13 and 147–61; XXXV, pp. 86–9; and XXXVIII, p. 445.
— 'Early British Regulation Revolvers', *Journal of the Society for Army Historical Research*, XXXV, pp. 109–20 and 152–64.
— "The Weapons of Wellington's Army", *Journal of the Society for Army Historical Research*, XXXVI, pp. 144–51.
— 'Two British Percussion Pistols', *Journal of the Society for Army Historical Research*, XXXVII, pp. 57–63.

SKENNERTON, Ian D.: *Australian Service Longarms*, Margate, Australia, 1975.
— *Australian Service Bayonets*, Margate, Australia, 1976.

— and RICHARDSON, Robert: *British & Commonwealth Bayonets*. Margate, Australia, 1986.

STERN, Walter M.: 'Gunmaking in Seventeenth-Century London', *Journal of the Arms & Armour Society*, I, no. 5 (March 1954), pp. 55–100.

TAYLERSON, Anthony W.F.: 'The London Armoury', *Journal of the Arms & Armour Society*, II, no. 3 (September 1956), pp. 45–58.

— ANDREWS, R.A.N, and FRITH, J.: *The Revolver, 1818–1865*, London, 1968.

TOMLINSON, H.C.: *Guns and Government. The Ordnance Office under the later Stuarts*, Royal Historical Society, 1979.

TYLDEN, G.: 'Some Problems of the Early Breech-loaders', *Journal of the Society for Army Historical Research*, XVIII, pp. 41–3.

— 'On the Use of Firearms by Cavalry', *Journal of the Society for Army Historical Research*, XIX, pp. 9–15.

— 'On the Carrying of Arms', *Journal of the Society for Army Historical Research*, XX, pp. 154–9.

WALTON, T.: *History of the British Standing Army, 1660–1700*. London, 1894.

WATTS, John, and WHITE, Peter: *The Bayonet Book*. Privately printed, 1975.

WILKINSON, Henry: *Engines of War*, London, 1841. Reprinted, Richmond, 1973.

WINANT, Lewis: *Early Percussion Firearms*, New York, 1959.

WOODEND, Herbert J.: *British Rifles. A Catalogue of the Enfield Pattern Room*, London, 1981.